True Stories?

CULTURAL POLITICS

Further titles in preparation

True Stories?

Documentary drama on radio,
screen and stage

Derek Paget

MANCHESTER UNIVERSITY PRESS
MANCHESTER and NEW YORK

distributed exclusively in the USA and Canada by ST. MARTIN'S PRESS

Copyright © Derek Paget 1990

Published by Manchester University Press
Oxford Road, Manchester M13 9PL, UK
and Room 400, 175 Fifth Avenue,
New York, NY 10010, USA

Distributed exclusively in the USA and Canada
by St. Martin's Press, Inc.
175 Fifth Avenue, New York, NY 10010, USA

British Library cataloguing in publication data
Paget, Derek
   True stories? documentary drama on radio, screen and
stage.– (Cultural politics).
   1. Documentary films
   I. Title II. Series
   791..43'53

Library of Congress cataloging in publication data
Paget, Derek, 1946–
      True stories? : documentary drama on radio, screen, and stage /
   Derek Paget.
      p. cm.
   Includes bibliographical references.
   ISBN 0-7190-2962-7. — ISBN 0-7190-2963-5 (Pbk.)
   1. Documentary mass media. I. Title
   P96.D62P34   1990
   070.1—dc20   89-12892

ISBN 0 7190 2962 7 hardback
       0 7190 2963 5 paperback

Photoset in Linotron Joanna
by Northern Phototypesetting Company, Bolton

Printed in Great Britain
by Bell & Bain Limited, Glasgow

Contents

Acknowledgements

I should like to record my grateful thanks to a number of people who have contributed directly to the writing of this book. Ph.D. research on *Oh what a lovely war*, crucial to the book's argument, was helped tremendously by Penelope and Charles Chilton. Both thesis and book have also been materially assisted by Professor Edward Braun, Peter Cheeseman, Jerry Dawson, Chris Honer, Brian Murphy, Rony Robinson, Chrys Salt, George Sewell, Alwyne Taylor, David Thacker and Gary Yershon. In all cases I am grateful for encouragement and hospitality, as well as help and information.

The debts I owe to David Edgar (whose articles on documentary and drama started the whole project off) and to Clive Barker (of the universities of Stratford East and Warwick) are similarly great; my ideas have been both informed and shaped through several stimulating discussions with them. Tony Jackson of Manchester University, too, was always the most helpful, thorough and inspiring of thesis supervisors, and John Banks of Manchester University Press has sustained my efforts through his energy and his commitment to this book.

I must also thank all past 'Documentary Drama' students at Worcester College of Higher Education for many hours of enjoyable theoretical discussion and practical exploration. Finally, my thanks to Jessica Paget for all her help, which has gone well beyond an interest in True Stories.

The promise of fact

Modern man worships 'facts' – that is, he accepts 'facts' as the ultimate reality . . .
He believes that facts in themselves provide evidence and proof, and he willingly
subordinates values to them . . . (Jacques Ellul)[1]

'True Stories' reach the modern consumer of dramatic entertainment in
stage plays, films, radio and TV programmes; some are 'based on fact',
others claim an extra, 'documentary', element. Anyone growing up in a
first-world culture in the late twentieth century will consume a large
number of True Stories by the time they reach adulthood. They are a
staple of television drama production, and television in modern society
is 'accepted as being as natural as gas, water or electricity', as Stuart Hood
has put it.[2] True Stories are equally popular in those other users of drama,
the cinema and the theatre. (The distinction between 'drama' and
'theatre' will be used to distinguish between acted performance
designed for a theatre *building* or *space* – 'theatre', and that very much
wider range of practice which includes *all* media utilising acted performance – 'drama'.)

The great variety of True Stories available can be easily illustrated. At
virtually any time it is possible to look up theatre, cinema or TV schedules
and find pertinent examples. When I began this book, for instance, the
films *Cry freedom* and *The last emperor* were on general release in the UK, and
the film *A world apart* (sub-title: 'Based on a true story') had just opened; in
London's West End a doomed and expensive musical celebrated the life
of *Ziegfeld*, and on the 'Alternative' London theatre circuit, The Place
offered the play *Picasso*. In addition, BBC TV had just completed showing
the 1986 Australian TV mini-series *Vietnam*, while Channel 4 had been
showing the tele-biography (in several episodes) of *Hemingway*.

These examples encompass: two 'serious' attempts to portray South
African racist politics; the charting of the end of Chinese imperial rule; a
frivolous musical about a famous showman aimed at the 'good night out'
brigade of tourists and coach parties ('A Musical Extravaganza with Cast
of 50' proclaimed the show's advertisement); an experimental play about
a famous artist (capitalising on a spate of Picasso books); a re-appraisal in
semi-soap style of Australia's part in the USA's ghastly South-East Asian

adventure (inflected with that valuable 1980s selling point revaluation of the Swinging Sixties, and studded with newsreel footage); and, finally, a 'star' actor (Stacy Keach) impersonating an American writer deemed fascinating even to a non-literary public, because habitually presented as a kind of intellectual Action Man.[3]

Labels for what I am calling True Stories are many, especially for TV productions. As broadcast television has taken that hold on a mass audience hitherto the preserve of the cinema, television programme makers have often tried to assert something definitive about certain dramatic products' relationship to 'facts'. Thus it is possible to find in television scheduling not only 'documentary drama', but also 'drama-documentary', 'docudrama', 'dramadoc', 'dramatised documentary', and 'faction'. All these formulations have been coined to try to fix the precise nature of the meeting of two apparent opposites; all refer to differing rhetorical strategies, differing contexts of development within the broadcasting institution, and traceable past histories. Such formulations have tried, Canute-like, to hold back a tide of unease about the boundary between the 'factual' and the 'fictional' which has occasionally erupted into open controversy. Confusion of modes extends beyond the 'simple' drama: 'authentic' news footage is quite routinely embedded within both 'fictional' and 'factional' scripts, and parts of programmes otherwise unproblematically 'factual' (such as 'current affairs' programmes) are sometimes sub-titled 'reconstruction', and utilise drama as a further means of communicating their 'truthful' messages. BBC TV's *Crimewatch UK* is one series regularly employing actors and actresses to 'reconstruct' real events.[4]

It is rarely acknowledged that what is at stake is the means by which *reality itself is mediated*. This book will not attempt to fine tune definitions (in the misguided belief that it is possible to chart an unerring definitional path through this conceptual jungle). Instead, my starting point is the observation that the manifest need to find labels for these practices *at all* is of more significance than any definition could possibly be. The book's guiding principle is that, whatever the label, the documentary mode in television drama is 'not so much a programme category, it is a debate', and that this debate extends into the True Stories of other media.[5] My wish is further to open up this debate in order to theorise the many and various offerings of modern culture passing themselves off in some way as 'true stories'.

A greater problem than that of definition is to navigate between the Scylla of an ultimately meaningless proliferation of examples on the one hand, and the Charybidis of a tediously exhaustive discussion of a few 'key' works on the other. My assumption has been that certain features of the True Story, like its basic evocation of The Fact, will be readily enough recognisable, and that the reader will be able to cross-check theoretical claims against his/her own experience of this common mode of cultural production. Examples used are intended to illustrate either important points of genre development, or the way True Stories frequently address issues society finds difficult to manage.

The most fundamental point to make is that whenever television programme makers, film-makers, or screen/tele/stage playwrights tell True Stories, they try to persuade us to consume their product with a very particular promise – the Promise of Fact. Prior assurance of 'truth', prior 'authentication' provides a cultural passport to credibility in the True Story. 'This really happened,' the makers of such films and plays tell us, 'it is completely factual,' (or 'based on fact'). With such assurances they 'buy' our attention, believing that audiences will suspend disbelief more easily in the acted performance which follows. Or so they hope.

This promise illustrates how 'the facts' have become a fetish in the twentieth century, and not only in the world of entertainment; it is usually thought that whenever they are produced, they will virtually compel belief. The power of the Fact has been, as it were, leased out to the drama, and the use to which it has been put is the concern of this book. The True Story will be seen partly as the last stop on realism's magical suspension-of-disbelief mystery tour, the last artistic gasp of a project which now extends well beyond staged 'naturalism' into the apparently unproblematical 'realism' of the TV documentary, or the cinéma vérité film. The moment-by-moment surveillance of closed-circuit television and the instantly-constructed past of home video have seemingly shifted the boundaries even further. (Significantly, both the CCTV and home video camera are now routinely used as 'eye witnesses' in news broadcasts and courts of law.)

But facts, too, are constructed as somehow dull. Millions of listeners to the BBC Radio One DJ Steve Wright, for example, hear a mini-feature called 'Another True Story' every afternoon (in amongst a veritable galaxy of 'characters', gobbets of news, information about the weather and other things, jingles, self-advertisements, and pop records). The feature, introduced and closed by the sung phrase 'It's Another True Story' in irritating jingle form, sums up certain representative attitudes to the True Story. Wright's True Stories are pieces of information devoid of supporting context, relayed in a deadpan and ineffably dull-sounding

way (sometimes by one of his 'boring' characters), which are meant to be
funny. The information given is so random that it is connected to nothing
other than the general looniness of the programme (the other day the
history of shortbread was solemnly rehearsed, for example). The hilarity of
all this is accentuated by the over-acted *seriousness* with which Wright's
spoof 'studio audience' receive the information ('How amazing!', 'Oh,
that's *really* interesting!', 'Well, I never!', etc.). True Stories, it would seem
are so solemn, so boring, so redolent of that awful place the classroom,
that they are only fit to be sent up.

Straight facts – 'documentariness'

If the makers of plays and films go beyond a 'based on fact' rubric and say,
'We can prove what we're saying too! Look at this!' (showing us authenticating documentation), then the process has been taken one step
further, direct authentication penetrating into the performance text
itself. The entertainment has become 'documentary'. Amongst the True
Stories I shall discuss, those bearing the designation 'documentary' will
be of particular importance. 'Documentary drama' is my principal term
of reference, not because I believe that other formulations are without
use, but on the grounds of documentary drama's longer history of usage.
The phrase subsumes all others (although I recognise that there are
dangers in this – were this a book about broadcast TV alone, there might
be time and space to discuss other formulations in detail).

Documentary drama has the potential to exploit an especially problematical gap between overtly 'factual' cultural products, like news
broadcasts, current affairs programmes and the 'straight' documentary,
and 'fictional' works using the rhetoric of drama (whether these works
are related to the 'single play' or to the 'documentary proper'). 'Facts', it
is sometimes held, are transparent and easy to deal with – in the well-
known phrase, they 'cannot lie'; 'fiction', by contrast, is more devious.
The mixing of these two modes is always potentially subversive, even
though that potential is rarely realised in practice.

Because the fact in a documentary drama has a higher profile than it
does in the generality of True Story (projected into the performance,
embedded in text rather than sub-text), work which results often ex-
hibits a 'discourse of factuality'. The function of this discourse is to verify
(or *appear* to verify) what we are seeing. The verifying discourse is almost
always imported from non-dramatic modes of signification – like the
news broadcast, the current affairs programme, and the documentary

proper. It normally comprises such rhetorical strategies as voice-over, captions, charts and statistics, and direct ('talking head') address of the camera/audience. All these things have been so naturalised in our culture that they are perceived as the mediation of 'straight facts'. This process will be traced in the very provenance of the term 'documentary'.

The discourse of fictional drama (realistic characterisation, use of 'tension' and dramatic irony, theme and counter-theme, plot and sub-plot) sugars with entertainment the pill of fact (which, as even Steve Wright knows, is difficult to swallow). Further confirmation and corro-boration may be provided by 'accurate' costume, props and setting, all of which will help acted performances seem more 'realistic'. The resultant 'documentary' and 'dramatic' mixture is collapsed into a concept of 'truthfulness to life-past', which in turn is collapsed into a universalised concept of 'truthfulness to life'.

Some methods by which documentary material has been used in the past will seem to be at odds with the kind of mediation most common at the moment, but the connecting link is factual ratification – the 'docu-mentariness' existing within a text to be received otherwise as a 'created' work of drama. The term 'documentary drama' describes a wide, but particular, signifying practice in modern cultural production which exists in media both old (theatre), new (radio and film), and very new (televison). The specific practices of the form have been inflected by all the media listed above, via interdependent past histories which will be examined. The period between the two World Wars was especially important in opening up new (and variously committed) ways of re-pre-senting reality in the theatre, on radio, and on film.

Theatre provides a crucial reference point from which correctives to impressions generated by (and from within) the photographic media can be offered. The theatre is still, after all, a major training ground for the specific practices constituting 'drama'. It goes on equipping men and women to work throughout the drama-using media. Few performers arrive before the cameras without some kind of theatrical apprentice-ship. Although cinema and television provide greater economic oppor-tunity for individual 'drama workers', those workers are likely to have even less collective control over production there than they do in the theatre. Finally, theatre has a longer tradition of being *theorised*, and as a result has been a leader in practices alternative to mainstream naturalism. In 'alternative' theatre a control is still possible over the means of production undreamt of in commercial cinema, with its institutionalised financial structures. *True Stories?* will examine a broad spectrum of cultural production, from the mainstream and the margins, in which certain modes claim our attention and interest because of their basis in demonstrable fact.

The True Story and its place in ideology

The True Story is an important form to analyse from a cultural materialist perspective because, while the insulation of 'English' or 'cultural study' from 'real life' is often taken as read, here is a form which claims (even pro-claims) a direct linkage to that very 'reality'. This has occasioned profound critical uncertainty. Are True Stories merely dramatised journalism? Because event-specific, are they therefore 'not-art' (to be regarded as in some way 'disposable' and lacking the much-prized 'permanence' of 'art')? Do they, or should they, have a moral or ethical relationship to facts which tempers their 'art-fulness', and therefore reduces it? If watertight definitional categories are not at stake, is any level of 'creative' use of fact (invention? distortion?) permissible? In pursuit of such questions, many critics have preferred to pound the documentary drama between the hammer of 'fact' ('this claims to be factual, but it lacks objectivity, it's biased/propagandist, therefore not true') and the anvil of 'entertainment' ('it may be factually accurate, and true in that sense, but it's unaesthetic/inartistic, not entertaining/boring').

The desire to replicate and re-possess a long-past, or just-past, reality in cultural production (especially a national trauma like Vietnam, or the Holocaust, or the End-of-Empire) often reveals the effort to show 'what actually happened' at its most ideological. Instead of opening up debate about, say, Apartheid South Africa, the reverse effect may occur, subjects being aired for appearance's sake and political realities left untouched. To critique such films/plays is to begin to resist that effacement (and displacement) of important issues upon which the status quo depends. 'Factuality' and 'documentariness' is often accepted at the level of a commonsense not 'natural' at all, but profoundly ideological. Raymond Williams has said that most TV documentary drama 'relies on what is taken as an intrinsic element of television: its capacity to enter a situation and show what is actually happening in it', but this capacity (as Williams well knew) is much over-estimated, and not at all what it seems.[6]

John McGrath has remarked that UK society is still a class society, and that 'the class which owns, controls or manages private capital and state capital is a coherent social entity with immense power; the British state and its institutions are organized in the interests of that ruling class'.[7] This is part of what McGrath calls a 'minimal statement' of his own political position; without such a statement he believes discussion of the mediation of reality is impossible. The belief that 'the interests of the ruling class' are also served by the reality mediated in many True Stories is the frame through which the argument of this book will proceed.

The twentieth century myth of facts

Man can no longer grasp what he can achieve, and he therefore accepts the facts as he is told them, rather as, in former times, he would have made an Act of Faith with regard to an ecclesiastical dogma. (Robert David MacDonald)[1]

Preconceptions – a Falklands illustration

Why has a 'documentary' inflection to a 'dramatic' work become evident in the second half of the twentieth century? Why should the information-based documentary proper, formerly the province of the film, latterly present in television production, be a popular mode at all, providing a 'window' on reality? This chapter will chart the provenance of the term, in which are inscribed the reasons for some of the dominant cultural preconceptions about documentary, preconceptions which derive from a modern faith in facts.

Our understanding of the film and television documentary proper shapes our expectations of the documentary True Story. We expect to gain information, to acquire access to hitherto unrevealed (or narrowly distributed) 'facts' when we consume anything 'documentary'. From initial ignorance (total or partial), we anticipate that we shall be put 'in the know'. The information base is at one and the same time interesting (persuading us that the piece of cultural production in question is worth consuming), and authenticating. It is also, of course, challengeable by anyone believing that they are more 'in the know', having better access to, or understanding of, the 'factuality' in question. For this reason the documentary drama has often been particularly controversial during its short existence. One such recent controversy in the UK involved Charles Wood's 1988 tele-play *Tumbledown*.

Intended for transmission on BBC-TV in late 1987, this play was caught up in a dispute between the BBC and another writer, Ian Curteis. who had also written a play about the 1982 Falklands War. Commissioned in the immediate aftermath of that war, this play ran into difficulties at the very point of its production in 1986–7. The BBC's sensitivities about the whole Falklands issue need to be seen in the context of the uncertainties which had been rumbling on since the end of the war in 1982, and which boiled up as the UK approached an election in 1987. The removal of *The Falklands play* from the schedules was extended to *Tumbledown* apparently on the basis of a curious 'one out, all out' logic, which was constructed for publicity purposes as one more example of that lack of bias on which the BBC so prides itself.[2]

What was really at issue was the way the war as public *event* was to be re-presented. The existence of controversy indicated the lack of easy consensus about what the Falklands War stood for, as well as how it had been conducted by the Conservative Government. Both plays were part of a wider dispute about public access to information in time of war which had run alongside the conflict itself. Reithian claims of even-handedness habitually made by British broadcasters were under challenge from a conviction politics Government whose leader imagined she was re-fighting the Second World War. Thus, all news coverage during the conflict had to be 'positive' in the Government's terms (mistakes had to be ignored, holes in the military strategy elided – in short, the conduct of the war could not be *criticised* at all). Post-Falklands War the Thatcher Government saw all 'non-positive' accounts of the war as indications of a left-wing conspiracy in the media. It became quite paranoid about this.

The aftermath of the Falklands War had seen no diminution in the ferocity of the debate about what level of information was possible and impossible, what was likely to 'assist an enemy' and what the public in a democratic state had a 'right to know'. The Labour MP Tam Dalyell chipped away at Government orthodoxies about the sinking of the *General Belgrano*, revealing (by implication, if nothing else) their mendacity. The Tory Government stuck grimly to its version not only of the infamous sinking, but also of the 'heroic British' status of the whole conflict (erasing at a stroke the history of their own pre-invasion incompetence). The pressure felt at the BBC may be read from the decision not to transmit two very different plays about the Falklands which happened to activate the establishment's unease with documentary drama. Ironically, Curteis's tele-play was revealed, when published in 1987, to be an arrant piece of right-wing hagiography.

With a Conservative Government safely re-elected, and Ian Curteis apparently gone to ground, *Tumbledown* was transmitted in 1988. Its depiction of a Guards officer wounded in the Falklands War and subsequently ill-treated by officialdom, still occasioned cries of 'Bias!' from the right-wing press before and after transmission. But any discussion of the Falklands War was easily displaced, because it became obvious that this documentary drama was merely a variant on the 'Wounded Hero' movie. The 'media event' of the *Tumbledown* controversy having neatly displaced any debate about the real event of the Falklands War, the debate now shifted to what should and should not be done with and for Wounded Heroes.

The Wounded Hero – an example to us all

In the 'Wounded Hero' film genre, the unfortunate recipient of what appear to be totally crippling injuries triumphs against adversity and outperforms the able-bodied. A classic example of the factually-based British 'Wounded Hero' film is the Second World War story of Douglas Bader. Bader recovered from the pre-war amputation of both legs to become a wartime fighter pilot. Shot down over enemy-occupied France, he even contrived to make several escape attempts, ending up in Colditz Castle. This was a prison camp for escape specialists, which contained only high escape-achievers. On release Bader rejoined the aerial fray, and became a post-war celebrity in the UK, a living symbol of that Achievement-Against-The-Odds which was somehow typical of the Spirit Which Won The War. After such a subject has lived his or her (mostly his) exploits, the story is of course ripe for iconisation as a True Story. In Bader's case Lewis Gilbert's 1956 film (based on Paul Brickhill's 1954 book) *Reach for the sky* typified this process.

True Stories of this kind are incorporated into ruling-class ideology precisely because they efface the real difficulties disabled people might encounter as they try to rebuild lives visibly re-structured by 'serving their country'. Such difficulties are collapsed into rhetorics of nationalism, representative heroism and/or achievement-against-the-odds. These constructs are thought to be profoundly comforting to those not Examples themselves, but in need of examples (the bulk of the population). Inspiring Examples are necessary to ensure the population carries on with the mundane tasks which serve a ruling-class project more directly. 'Entertainment' serves the hegemony by eliding 'difficult' subject matter into readily-comprehensible structures. This is not necessarily a kind of *conscious* conspiracy on the part of the Rulers. Such sagas are naturalised to the extent that they seem quite unproblematically to bear out the hegemony's most-treasured concept – that the freely-choosing individual is the real and true centre of the universe. *Tumbledown* is a distinctly post-Imperial variant on the same theme, shifting the Wounded Hero myth a tiny oppositional step or two.

It is also very parochial; *Tumbledown* was in fact rejected by the film company Goldcrest, because they could not see the Falklands being of interest to American audiences. The USA (as the Goldcrest reader percipiently noted) already had Hal Ashby's 1978 Vietnam-Vet film *Coming home*, in which the Jon Voight character begins as a distinctly unpleasant crippled veteran, and is eventually humanised by the almost inevitable love-of-a-good-woman (Jane Fonda). The cultural marker for Voight's character's outperformance of the able-bodied was inscribed, not in feats of 1940s derring-do, but in quintessentially 1980s American feature film terms of heterosexual success.

Both films know that the post-modern hero cannot be too heroic, and that victory over disability has to be constructed differently in the present historical conjuncture. The orgasm which Fonda experiences with Voight (and which she significantly cannot achieve with her 'able-bodied' husband) inscribes the film with the kind of values of heterosexist self-discovery which dominate recent films about Vietnam. *Tumbledown* was no more disruptive of orthodoxies concerning the rightness of a particular war than the Voight/Fonda star-vehicle. Both films allow some criticism of their respective ruling classes, but only just enough to provide a titillating basis for a personalised True Story. In the American example, the film represented a cultural admission that the traumatic subject of Vietnam needed to be aired. It is part of that process of revaluation of a national failure which ultimately led to the unveiling of the nation's belated monument to the war dead of Vietnam, and which finally allowed the Vietnam Vet to 'come home'.

The films are better seen as a kind of cultural reference point, symptomatic of a society's need occasionally to permit its 'entertainers' to pose a problem (in order partly to defuse it). The actual wars become adjuncts to the story of the individual in both films. Watching *Tumbledown*, it was difficult to understand why any fuss had been made at all at the level of 'information about the Falklands War'. Any specificity was elided into the kind of anti-warism to which a large majority of people could give fairly easy assent. Yet *Tumbledown* was seen as a 'dangerous document' to the extent that two London newspapers, the *Evening standard* and the *Daily mail* carried Blimp-ish statements about it.

The main worry on the Right was the film's threat to a sanitised ruling-class version of the Falklands conflict. That threat could only partly be circumvented by the delaying tactics which held up the

tele-play's transmission. In addition, ruling-class sensitivities were
exercised by the inference that the British Nation was incapable of looking
after its Wounded Heroes. Such a story (which might have been told after
any of Britain's previous colonial wars throughout history) was unaccept-
able, perhaps because it was being told through the verbatim testimony of
a person himself a member of the ruling class. The Myth of the Wounded
Hero was being attacked by the Hero himself; Robert Lawrence wasn't
noble in his suffering, he was irascible, awkward, ungrateful – he *opposed*
that Establishment to which he rightly belonged. It was as if a school
prefect at Prize Day had shamed the school by throwing his prize at the
guest speaker. Such a document as *Tumbledown* was allowable, but had to
be issued with a Government Health Warning and a little haggling over
'the facts' (just sufficient to discredit them a little).

Basic similarities between these two films extend to their *dramatic*
methods, and to their use of known events as a kind of 'background'
supporting a resolutely personalised 'foreground'. Both appear to
release a certain amount of information about a traumatic historical
background, but this information is carefully 'marketed' through the
formal properties of the individualised foreground activity. But *Coming
home* and *Tumbledown* diverge interestingly in their mix of fact and fiction,
the fact in *Tumbledown* being that much closer to the surface of the fiction
(which exacerbated the controversy). Until we reach some theoretical
understanding of cultural production which negotiates such mixes, we
are powerless before the manipulation not only of 'feeling' and
'emotion' but also of information (collapsed into the 'personal', even
when 'documentary'). Theoretical understanding must begin with an
interrogation of the very notion of 'documentary'.

The provenance of 'documentary'
– 'creative interpretation of actuality'

'*Documentary*: 4> Factual, realistic; applied esp. to a film or literary work,
etc., based on real events or circs., and intended primarily for instruction
or record purposes. Also ellipt. as subj.' (1972 Supplement to the *Oxford
English Dictionary*). 'Documentary' appears to function in a similar way to
'historical' when used before the word 'drama' – simply as a descriptive
term. Herbert Lindenberger has noted that, in 'historical drama', the first
word is 'qualifying the fictiveness of the second'.[3] But with 'documentary', matters are complicated by a 'crossing-over' of the word from a
descriptive into a nominative usage. 'Documentary' as a noun is by now

very familiar (as in 'television documentary', for example). That this is a very recent addition to the available meanings of the word is confirmed by the Oxford English Dictionary. In its 1961 edition, three meanings are given, all adjectival. The fourth meaning given above, added ten years later, acknowledges that noun-use of 'documentary' which is now a demonstrably common one. Of a number of references given in support of this fourth meaning, the earliest is significantly taken from Paul Rotha's Film till now (1930). Rotha was not only a film historian and theoretician, he was also a documentary film director.

The photographic media have a vital place in the story of the term documentary. The documentary film of the 1930s (in particular the John Grierson-inspired GPO and Crown Film Unit work, and the parallel work of Robert Flaherty and Joris Ivens in the USA) 'loaded' the word with its truth-telling significance. The mention of 'literary work' indicates the unproblematical similarities perceived by Grierson, Rotha et al between cinematic and literary modes. Nothing could better illustrate the symbiotic relationship existing between old and new media in the twentieth century. The new medium, film, took as its model what Colin MacCabe has called 'the classic realist text', the realist novel of the nineteenth century.[4] An apparently new discourse based on images was given the narrative motor of an earlier word-based culture of the European and American bourgeoisie.

This 'realist text' has become gradually mortgaged to an essentially conservative politics. Grierson's project was essentially one of political containment for, and on behalf of, a UK establishment whose liberal wing backed him financially. Grierson's colleague Basil Wright once described the UK documentary film movement as 'a method of approach to public information'.[5] Profoundly influenced by the American Walter Lippman's ideas of social extension through education, Grierson believed passionately in the power of information as social cement. In the USA, the documentary film similarly served the ideology of the New Deal. The 'new' discourse was policed by residual elements of previous cultures; texts in a 'new' medium were inflected with the ideological armoury of the literate Victorian gentlemen.

Grierson, his group, and their American allies charged the word 'documentary' with its peculiar resonance – that a cultural product so described would both observe reality and explain something about that observed reality to its audience. In 1932, Grierson made the very first principle of his 'First Principles of Documentary' that it 'would photograph the living scene and the living story'. His oft-quoted 1933

formulation was that the documentary should be 'the creative interpretation of actuality'.[6] 'Actuality' itself has an interesting semantic history, but
suffice it to note that the same 1972 *Supplement* offers a quotation from a
1941 BBC publication which gives 'documentary' as a synonym for
'actuality'. More recently published dictionaries have moved even
further towards both the noun use of 'documentary', and towards
equivocation concerning its claims as a presentation of 'actuality' or
'reality'. It is no wonder that people are quite genuinely confused about
the meanings of such words; usage alone demonstrates them to be at a
problematical borderline between concepts of 'fact' and 'fiction'.

Night mail (1936) is a classic and celebrated example of the Griersonian
documentary: ostensibly about the mundane details of the London to
Scotland mail train, the working routines of the railmen and Post Office
sorters are transformed into 'art' through a potent mix of 'dramatic'
camera-angles and cutting (for example, in a memorable sequence in
which post-bags are swung out from the speeding train and caught in the
net of a mechanical grab). Spoken poetry and atmospheric music
(W.H.Auden and Benjamin Britten, no less), and a very 1930s intellectual's reverence for the heroic figure of the Worker construct an epic
celebration of mundanity. In a climactic sequence, poetry and music
combine with visual images to give an heroic construction to the train's
final laborious climb over the hills of the Border, and its dash into
Lowlands Scotland. 'This is the night mail crossing the border,' runs
Auden's famous verse, imitating the powerful rhythm of the steam
locomotive as it climbs, 'bringing the cheque and the postal order'. The
'downhill run' towards Glasgow is accompanied by rapidly-cut images of
train and landscape, and a breathless rush of twenty lines of verse in
which internal rhymes double the pace:

> Letters with holiday snaps to enlarge in,
> Letters with faces scrawled in the margin.
> Letters from uncles, cousins and aunts,
> Letters to Scotland from the South of France,
> Letters of condolence to Highlands and Lowlands,
> Notes from overseas to the Hebrides.[7]

Here, indeed, is 'actuality' mediated 'creatively'; the quotidian routines
of working men tricked out by bourgeois intellectual invention. 'The
hand of little employment,' as that well-known middle-class intellectual
Hamlet once remarked, 'hath the daintier sense.'

The problematical semantic relationship of 'documentary' and 'drama' is well illustrated by Night mail. Non-fictive 'documentary' is made 'dramatic' by a self-consciously poetic overlay (the poetry inhering in image and music as well as in words). Many difficulties have ensued from the Griersonian approach, notably an uncertainty about what balance, if any, to strike between the competing claims of aesthetics and morality. In 1939, Grierson wrote that the 'documentary idea demands no more than that the affairs of our time shall be brought to the screen in any fashion which strikes the imagination and makes observation a little richer than it was. At one level, the vision may be journalistic; at another level it may rise to poetry and drama' (Hardy, pp.18–19). Inscribed within this statement are many of the uncertainties of the documentary movement as to its claims to be 'art'.

The dilemma has also bedevilled theatre criticism; the 'Theatre of Fact' of the 1970s was described at the time as 'a theatre whose complex form and concentrated function raise ethical questions that cannot easily be separated from the claims of the aesthetic'.[8] Partly because of the way the term 'documentary' has been developed, then, its use in the phrase 'documentary drama' has only a superficial resemblance to Lindenberger's earlier explanation of 'historical drama'. Because unproblematically assumed to be somehow closer to 'actuality', or 'reality', 'documentary' has its own peculiar force. Its promise is not just the Promise of Fact mentioned earlier; it offers instruction or information on some matter, and it offers to instruct and inform in the best possible 'artistic' taste. No 'qualification' of drama is involved; two words of equal status have been yoked together by cultural practice.

An undisclosed force stems from the way in which 'documents' are used at all within a drama; this causes the ethical/aesthetical problem. By using documents at all, the dramatist problematises (calls into doubt or question) both the fictional nature of drama and the factual nature of information. S/he implicitly transgresses the boundaries of a discourse usually held to be antithetical to the dramatic. If documents have been foregrounded (or, given priority in the drama), they will have been problematised at least to some extent for an audience. Encountering the document in a theatrical setting defamiliarises the document – it becomes necessary for the audience to adopt an attitude to the documentary material itself in order to 'read' the drama.

Documentary mater-reality

This 'documentary materiality' is important to an understanding of the entry of Faith in Facts into dramatic practices. American historian Hayden White makes a distinction between the novel and 'historical works', which 'unlike literary fictions . . . are made up of *events that exist outside the consciousness of the writer*'.[9] True Stories also have sources existing 'outside the consciousness of the writer' and these sources can even be collected and presented. The 'source material' of documentary drama is often tangible; it is frequently to be found in the possession of the writer(s). In 1987 there was a controversy in the UK over Jim Allen's Holocaust play *Perdition*, which alleged that Zionist European Jewry colluded with Hitler and his henchmen in the Final Solution, their culpability made more manifest by the subsequent excesses of Zionist Israel. Such a provocative political line mobilised powerful vested interests intent upon defending their versions of events. With the play withdrawn from production by the Royal Court Theatre, debate about Allen's play was displaced from the drama itself to the sources; such was their materiality, and such the effect of that materiality. The published text of *Perdition* has 71 pages of play to 81 pages of record/discussion of the controversy and account of the sources.[10] 'Versions of events', it would seem, are always more important than mere plays.

Sources may be categorised in the following way: they can be single (and therefore apparently 'simple'), or multiple (and therefore, again apparently, 'complex'). The simpler they are, of course, the easier they are to defend at the level of facts alone. The trial transcript is a good example of the 'single source'. Examples are legion, but Eric Bentley's 1972 *Are you now or have you ever been* and Blair/Fenton's 1983 *The Biko inquest* are good ones. In the former, hours and hours of McCarthy Trial transcripts were reduced by Bentley to two hours stage time. In the latter, the transcript of the 1977 South African inquest into Steve Biko's death in detention was edited down by two journalists. The single source covered three weeks of inquest and several thousand pages of transcript; the final performed product lasted for just over two hours of stage time. By contrast, in *Cry freedom* (a 'multiple source' piece) this same True Story material became a five-minute scene (the source being the 128-page summary of the inquest in the Donald Woods book *Biko*).

Theatre Workshop's 1963 *Oh what a lovely war* typifies the multiple source stage play. The published edition has a two page Appendix detailing the play's sources. These comprise books, newspapers, military despatches, regimental histories and 'many other publications of which no note has been kept'. Such source documents (often *primary* sources) assume a much higher profile than is the case in a historical drama (where *secondary* sources are more often the norm). It is not unusual to find the primary sources packaged in the Introduction to (or in some part of the editorial apparatus of) the documentary play. In Rolf Hochhuth's 1965 Auschwitz play *The representative*, sources are quoted extensively in the published edition (even invading the very text itself in the form of dense stage directions which are in essence extended footnotes).

The range of usable material is large. In 1968, dramatist Peter Weiss listed the following possibilities: 'Records, documents, letters, statistics, market-reports, statements by banks and companies, government statements, speeches, interviews, statements by well-known personalities, newspaper and broadcast reports, photos, documentary films and other contemporary documents are the basis of the performance'.[11] To these could be added film, photographs, audio and video tape. These recorders of history add their visual and aural inflections to that construction of the past which is 'history'. By appropriating these documents, drama continues both to transgress its boundaries as 'art', and the document's claim to record.

Inside the temple of facts

Modern man needs a relation to facts, a self-justification to convince himself that by acting in a certain way he is obeying reason and proved experience. (Ellul, p.85)

The 'documentariness' of a cultural product, then, resides in a particular orientation towards documents, which has been defined by usage. This orientation relates to shifts in the twentieth century in what Raymond Williams has called 'structures of feeling'.[12] Documentary modes participate in, indeed are a symptom of, two distinct, but interlinked, structures of feeling: one is expressive of a faith in facts, grounded upon positivist scientific rationality; the other is expressive of a profound political scepticism which disputes the notion that 'facts = truth'.

The scientific rationality of the nineteenth and early twentieth centuries expressed humanity's growing confidence in its ability to exercise control over the environment by explaining natural phenomena. In literature, this growing tendency to wish to be rational rather than fanciful found its expression in the movement known as 'Naturalism', defined by John Willett as a 'form of literary Positivism ... basically post-Darwinian and inclined towards an environmentalist and often evolutionary explanation of life; it often takes the form of close reportage and documentation'.[13] The Naturalists' desire to 'show things as they really are' has inflected many areas of artistic expression in this century, but the new photographic media have held out particular hopes of achieving a replication of a reality conceived as essentially *visual* in nature. As John Ellis puts it, the photo image is 'firmly within the paradoxical regime of presence-yet-absence'; as such it can so seductively appear as if it is *really* present.[14]

Various areas of study and thought have typified the 'faith in facts' as a means of making sense of the nature of existence. E.H.Carr (in his book *What is history?*) observed that the 'nineteenth century fetishism of facts was completed and justified by a fetishism of documents'. Documents, in his eloquent phrase, became 'the Ark of the Covenant in the temple of facts' (p.16). As the political situation in Europe has changed during the present century, and as the hold exerted by established religion has faded, facts have acquired a quasi-religious status. Through the mass media and the information agency, facts and information have begun to supply religion's place as a provider of certainties. Thus 'showing things, describing things, as they are' has become an act of faith for scientific rationality; it has also become important to the arts.

The shift in orientation towards the pre-eminence of the fact is marked by the rise of the documentary movements in film and radio from the late 1920s, and in television from the early 1950s. The documentary mode has become one to which we are accustomed, and to which we give fairly easy assent. When we read or hear the programme designation 'documentary', we have the particular expectation that naturalism's original promise (of being more 'real' and thus more 'true') will be extended further. This has had repercussions for the photographic media; we are conditioned into regarding them as 'objective', simple 'records' of external reality. It has taken film and television criticism some time to emerge from an unproblematic view of the way in which their images link to form a narrative. Until quite recently there seemed to be a belief amounting almost to certainty that no viewpoint was necessarily inscribed into film and television documentaries; the label alone was a guarantee that a programme could be considered value-free. In film, this certainty began to be disturbed in the late 1950s by the New Wave (and its journal *Cahiers du cinéma*); in television, the work of the British Film Institute journal *Screen* during the 1970s was crucial in disturbing the belief that 'the camera cannot lie'. From this work, perspectives on the camera's very plausible ideological lying have gradually emerged.

Objectivity

The expectation of 'value-freeness' is most clearly evident in the widely-held notion that a documentary should have an Olympian 'objectivity'. C.P.Scott, editor of the *Manchester Guardian* in the 1920s, typified this attitude in his *bon mot* 'Comment is free, facts are sacred'. As Raymond Williams has said, crises of technique in modern literature are linked 'with a sense of crisis in the relationship of art to society, or in the very purposes of art which had previously been agreed or even taken for granted'.[15] The documentary has always had such an apparently obvious 'purpose' that audiences have been persuaded to take its objectivity 'for granted'. This culturally naturalised assumption betrays a distinctive orientation towards facts acquired through exposure to shifts in 'structures of feeling'.

But as Brecht observed in 1948, 'for art to be unpolitical means only to ally itself with the ruling group'.[16] All art must be seen as political, and one must be especially suspicious of 'non-political' art. The open proclamation of political tendency, so far from being undesirable could be seen as more truly democratic than the 'unbiased' cultural product. The Marxist view of the utility of proclaimed tendency was well put by the East German theatre director Hanns-Anselm Perten in 1968, when he noted that an 'excessive offer of information' had the effect of 'putting the critical conscience to sleep . . . and of making the masses believe that they are receiving objective information'.[17] Perten sums up a cultural materialist approach in saying that openly proclaimed tendency in art 'enables us to take our distance from official information'.

The jealously guarded liberal conceit of 'objectivity' must be re-appraised, for the objectivity desired by some can only exist in an unimaginably politics-free society. No information is context-less; information does not exist in a kind of vacuum-space antiseptically-free of mediation (and therefore corruption) by human agency. The phenomenon of 'objective information' is itself a hegemonic myth, designed to anchor populations in a unified view of the world. The concept of objectivity can still be important if it serves the primary purpose of helping to identify *levels* of information distortion, in a world where all information must be constructed by some interested party for someone else's consumption. As George Szanto notes: 'Objectivity as a (non-achievable) form, and relative reductivity, are valuable in quasi-opposition only when they lead to an awareness of the existence of limitations both in the tools for getting at information and in the kinds of

information available.'[18] The idealised continuum runs from utter and
obvious falsification through to allegedly distortion-free 'pure information' (guaranteed untouched by human hand). To believe in a *real*,
achievable objectivity is to rely on what Williams calls 'a fiction about
reality itself'.[19]

Any information agency will tend to elide the distinction between
'facts' and 'reality' (and hence between both those concepts and 'truth');
the more so as that agency *claims* objectivity. This elision can sometimes
result in the distortion of propaganda (which for present purposes is
defined as information with not just a tendentious orientation but an
institutional base – this makes it potentially dangerous, since the scope for
dissemination of distorted information is vastly increased).

Acceptance that, in all 'messages', an element of distortion is inevitable
(an acceptance which permits us to admit that both information and
plays do not exist 'out there', but always have an intended audience and a
reception-context) enables us to engage more profoundly with cultural
production at whatever point of production is, or was, envisaged. We no
longer have to pronounce on a play's 'universal' significance (we no
longer have to *seek* one); instead, we are freed to describe and account for
the nature of a play's intervention into a social and political situation.
With True Stories this is especially important, because (being closer to,
and in an overt relationship with, that which generated them) they
impinge more on the world outside the performance space. Potentially,
they can interfere with Faith in Facts; in reality widespread use of natura-
lism/social realism neutralises the dangerous document.

Unnatural naturalism, unreal realism

'THE DRAMATURG: Realism is less naturalistic than naturalism, though
naturalism is considered fully as realistic as realism' (Bertolt Brecht).[20] In
much documentary drama the faith in facts is confirmed by an adherence
to realistic modes profoundly unhelpful in laying bare the structures
beneath the surface of events. Promising truth and realism, True Stories
have often participated in the 'selective tradition . . . a version of the past
which is intended to connect with and ratify the present'.[21] A few lines
after the quotation above, Brecht's Philosopher observes that 'mere
photographic reproductions' of reality have become fatally confused
with the thing itself. The fact that the camera (the photographic repro-
ducer) has been able to effect this confusion partly accounts for the
pre-eminence of naturalistic acting techniques in all the dramatic media.

The other contributory factor has been the tendency to validate the individual over the group: a completion in the present century of that valorisation of the individual which began with the rise of the bourgeoisie as a class.

Techniques in which believable *individualised* behaviours are reproduced on stage and screen by actors and actresses are the mainstay of acting training in the UK, the USA, and the USSR; they are the staple style within which those actors and actresses are asked to work during their professional lives. These techniques efface the very processes of reproduction up to the point at which those processes seem to become invisible – or, literally, 'natural'. The art-that-conceals works to turn the unnatural (acting) into the natural ('life itself'). Acting and production techniques go hand-in-hand in this project; costume and set design in the theatre, continuity and location work in the cinema combine to provide that simulacrum of the world in which we all live, move and have our being which is more than just 'lifelike' – in some people's minds it is life.

'Realistic performance', then, is performance in which 'you can't see the join', in which 'real life' is re-presented before your eyes. The Fourth Wall of the theatre, made transparent by playwright, production team and performers, becomes in the cinema and on television the Camera Eye, through which the audience, beneficiaries of all this concealment, observe a world constructed as 'real'. The Camera Eye is our own organ of vision. Anything unreal, that is to say anything not easily constructed as real (like the figure of the camera operator, for example) is resolutely effaced. This set of formal conventions, constructed as a 'natural' or 'real' technique, is then collapsed into a 'truth' which is offered as an endorsement of a 'natural', commonsensical, view of the world. The denial of technique, the veiling of conventions, is what is most unreal and unnatural of all, but without it the entertainment industry would grind to a halt – it still 'constitutes perhaps the basic demand that our society makes of its film and TV representations' (Ellis, p.9).

If it's real, it must be true – drama and the hegemony

'Naturalism's images resulted in criticism of the real world,' opines Brecht's Dramaturg in *The Messingkauf dialogues*. His Philosopher replies shortly, 'Feeble criticism' (p.27). The hegemony will often allow criticism, the feebler the better. The term 'hegemony' refers to those social and political interests which exert control over the mass of people in a society. This control can be exerted in very obvious ways, but can also be exerted through less obvious economic and cultural means. Writers following Gramsci have contended that it is not to be understood simply in reference to those obvious displays of power which we can all recognise, but also in much more subtle forms. Hegemony, expressed through the full range of economic determinants, interpenetrates the very forms of a culture, permeates a society's very concept of 'common sense', and structures its sense of what might constitute an unproblematical 'reality'.[22]

The reality of most people's everyday social experience is inflected by ideological assumptions about which they may well be unaware. Such a saturation of the processes of thought could not be achieved without powerful cultural outriders, pressing in the boundaries of understanding so that no one will question the hegemony's decisions regarding their place in a social structure. Thus a culture, shaped by a society, inflects that society's future behaviour through its fictions, all of which are supported (in the case of all the 'Western democracies') by capitalist modes of production. Naturalism supports the dominant economic mode because it is a practice which validates individuals, then rewards their portrayers – who can sometimes become 'stars' (or even 'superstars') solely by virtue of their acted performances.

In drama, the discourse which has corresponded for most people to 'the reality of social experience' is naturalism/social realism (as a glance at the output of television drama will tend to confirm). The popular Australian afternoon soap opera Neighbours purports to show 'ordinary' life. Kylie Minogue, one of its 'stars', even observed in a recent UK television interview that its 'normality' was the key to the programme's success. (Elizabeth Wilson's phrase about BBC Breakfast Television springs to mind here; its pervasive normality, she claims, 'is such that it borders on the mad'.)[23]

The ideology of a programme such as Neighbours works serially (that is, not just in each episode, but over a period of episodes) to convince you, or reinforce your prior conviction, of the cultural validity of the bourgeois family and suburban neighbourhood. The very appearance of ordinariness (and it is only a very superficial appearance) sutures the 'dramatic' happenings which stud the careers of the denizens of Ramsay Street. Patriarchy rules in every episode; potentially contentious and disruptive issues of class, race and gender, if introduced at all, are drained of danger. An issue such as feminism can be raised in one episode, consigned to the trash can of memory, all difficulties effaced, in the next.

Soaps like Neighbours serve the hegemony as part of the entertainment-industrial complex; issues are their raw material, actors their work force, the production team their managerial staff. Their production lines manufacture the most cost-effective cathartic output in the history of capitalist drama. Children's almost universal liking for Neighbours is a profound indicator of the limits of its sense of the dangerous – it sometimes speaks excitingly of Monsters and Things that go Bump in the Night, but it also soothes and reassures in the promotion of the fiction that life isn't really that dangerous (and nothing that Madge and Jim can't sort out between them).

The currency of all such programmes is a form of naturalism which slides through the mind without difficulty, persuading audiences of a certain level of reality, and confirming them in the view that all is well in the best of all possible worlds. That this (capitalist) world transcends national boundaries is indicated by the ease with which Neighbours has transferred from Australia to the UK.

If it's true, it must be real – neutralising the dangerous document

'The claims to objectivity, neutrality, simple fidelity to the truth . . . we must recognise as the ratifying formulas of those who offer their own senses and procedures as universal,' (Raymond Williams).[24] Like 'Beauty is Truth, Truth Beauty', a tautology as well as a paradox inheres in the 'true/real' proof. The attempts made to replicate reality within a drama (and to be 'true' in that very limited sense) are sometimes mind-bogglingly bizarre; for example, a CBS 'drama-documentary' of 1980, The plane that fell from the sky, involved forty (presumably sane) 'real' individuals who were persuaded to re-live for the cameras their (presumably terrifying) experience of a near-disaster in which a TWA Boeing 727 plummeted 30000 feet from the sky over Saginaw, Michigan in 1979. Having emerged rubber-legged from that plane to contemplate life's continuance rather than the abrupt termination which must moments before have seemed inevitable, what could have induced those people to pretend to go through the experience again?

The answer is a powerfully persuasive mixture of cash, the apparently universal desire to be famous (which the camera can so easily seem to gratify, and which media people always count on in their dealings with 'the public'), and the belief that others might understand something or other by experiencing the replication of their collective experience (the project's closeness to the genre of the Disaster Movie so popular in the

1970s is surely significant). A television practice which encompasses this project on the one hand and a True Story addressing a 'social problem' like the 1966 tele-play *Cathy come home* on the other is, to say the least, various.

TV films like Channel 4's *Mandela*, or cinema films like *Cry freedom* (both 1987), are underpinned by a more 'serious' wish to understand. But the variety of impressions such films generate may not include much significant increase in knowledge. Dominant among impressions will almost certainly be a vague notion that individual 'human relationships', re-produced through film naturalism, are just as important to an understanding of political issues as economic, social and historical context (perhaps more so). True Stories, like most drama, are supported by the naturalistic fallacy that to be real is to be true (and that to be both you have first to be believably individual). The dramatic method of most documentary dramas is congruent with the fantasy that issues and ideas can be readily understood through identification with 'real' individuals (it's just that documentary drama's individuals, like 'serious' drama's, are claimed to be 'realer' than soap's). The objection is not to naturalism/social realism as *technique* – like any other mode of production/performance, it is only rendered problematical by association, and naturalism has become totally identified with the hegemony.

The opening up of a space between 'acted fictional art' and 'acted factional non-Art' enables us to come very close to the heart of capitalist cultural production. The True Story scratches away at an inconvenient cultural 'itch' concerning provision of, and access to, information in post-industrial societies. As Jacques Ellul has said, 'the mechanisms of modern information induce a sort of hypnosis in the individual' (p.87). The trance induced by the information barrage under which we exist is occasionally broken by 'the dangerous document' (or the release of unsanctioned information). The Clive Ponting affair in the UK, or the Oliver North Irangate scandal in the USA are good examples. Suddenly, that mostly reassuring steam of information which emanates from the Western democracies (and on which they so pride themselves) is revealed as a highly selective process. The True Story can also set the 'web of facts' within which we are trapped into sudden and vivid context. Even such a limp vehicle as *Cry freedom* was *dangerous* – otherwise the Botha government would not have suppressed it in South Africa (as they did in July 1988).

Uncontentious documentary dramas are the response of a hegemony which has also found it necessary (and continues to find it necessary) to efface the problem posed by the 'document' – a piece of manifest social reality, existing (literally, *materially*) outside the drama (even outside the consciousness of the makers of the drama). Documents are so potentially dangerous to a hegemony that access to them is carefully controlled. Even documents embedded within a drama pose a potential threat to a hegemony, unless a means for control can be found. That means has been readily available in naturalism, the hegemony's pre-ferred dramatic practice. Hence television documentary drama tends to be inflexibly naturalistic, depending on that convention through which it purports to show what is happening, *naturally*. Like the documentary proper, documentary drama's very posing of a 'problem' can effect a kind of closure to that problem.

I can identify with that – the hegemony strikes back

Hegemonies respond to any threat in a variety of ways. Responses available vary from crude suppression to more subtle forms of economic incorporation and value-led marginalisation. By 'incorporation', I mean the transfer into the dominant discourse of anything which can be used to its ultimate advantage; by 'marginalisation', I mean the consistent displacement of any errant (or profoundly 'untransferrable') form to the edges of critical approval and cultural practice (until it becomes not just an errant but an outlaw, a 'rogue', form). 'Suppression', of course, is achieved via acts of overt and covert censorship. Incorporation allows a hegemony to 'recuperate' (or restore to itself) things which might other-wise disturb its pattern of control. Thus naturalism, seen as a real danger to society at the turn of the century, was successfully incorporated over a period of time and is now itself an instrument of incorporation (other techniques having being marginalised). The best examples of the incor-poration of factual material form a defining alternative to documentary drama; they are the phenomenally successful television 'costume' drama series which began with the BBC's *Forsyte saga* in 1967.

A recent example of the incorporation of 'real' material into televi-sion's telling of the True Story of history was *The jewel in the crown* (1985). This dramatisation of Paul Scott's Raj Quartet novels coded its authen-ticity through specific historical 'markers', including authentic dress, locations, properties and settings easily received by viewers as histori-cally accurate. While 'documentary' in one (very limited) sense, such externals are rarely seen as important at all in novels. But when films of novels are made lavish attention is bestowed upon such supporting detail (the same is true for cinema equivalents – like David Lean's 1984 *A passage to India*). Freshly-washed and polished cars just out of their motor museum cruise by oh-so-casually while some impeccably accurately dressed 'character' individualises for us a post-Imperial issue (which the film makers believe will be otherwise impossibly complex). An 'authentic' background helps to validate the view of history being put up by the makers of the film, and is based on the premise that unless we can feel we are 'really there' (in Raj and post-Raj India) we cannot grasp anything at all. In 'cultural tourism', we see plenty, but are left none the wiser.

It is a fact of our culture that most film, and play, makers seem to assume no issue can be understood unless mediated through a Representative Individual with whom the audience can identify. This belief assists the twin projects of incorporation and marginalisation and may not even be conscious on the part of the programme/film maker or makers. He (and it usually is a 'he', women not yet having quite the same access to the means of cultural production as men) will have absorbed this notion as a pre-requisite for achieving a position of eminence within a broadcasting superstructure deeply imbricated into capitalist ideology. Naturalism, as it were, comes with the territory if you want to be a media power-wielder.

Louis Althusser's view of classical naturalistic theatre was that the totality of its meaning was reflected 'in a consciousness, in a talking, acting, thinking, developing human being'. The ideological limitations of this were clearest in those unquestioned 'transparent myths', that 'uncriticized ideology', through which 'a society or an age can recognise itself (but not know itself)'. For Althusser this was a mirror which society 'looks into for self-recognition, precisely the mirror it must break if it is to know itself'.[25] The deconstruction of the myths of both realism and individualism is a major priority in paving the way for a drama interested in issues and events at a supra-individual level.

In *Cry freedom*, the mirror is unbroken. Despite Donald Woods's worthy attempts in the book *Biko* to frame the account of his friendship with black activist Steve Biko with an analysis of South African history, Richard Attenborough (as successful media man) knew that this would not wash with the punters. What they needed was someone to whom they could *relate* (he didn't necessarily need to reason this, as a 'professional' he's grown up with the notion as a kind of given). An insight into the reorientation necessary when the film was made is given by Donald Woods himself in his Preface to *Asking for trouble* (one of *Cry freedom's* source books): 'While events concerning both families [his own and

Steve Biko's] are the foreground of the script, they are set against the background of major incidents of public record in South Africa during the time frame of 1975 to 1978,' (p.7 – my emphasis).

So Cry freedom, following the mostly unproblematical and routine sexism of the entertainment industry, gives the audience someone they can relate to (if male) or be attracted to (if female) – it gives them Kevin Kline's impersonation of Woods himself. Entertainment cinema's usual pride of place is ceded to the white middle-class male. Sitting in the cinema's powerful darkness (so akin to the psychic state of dreaming), we are invited to identify, not with a political situation, not with a black leader, but with a Courageous White (who is fighting back). It is but a short step to believing that we too are fighting back, simply by watching a film.

Reality testing testing

This book opposes the 'natural' collapsing of the collective object or event into the individual subject, and the needless mystification of the processes of Art. Recent critical theory has offered important perspectives on the products of 'culture', showing them to be, not transcendental works of quasi-divine inspiration, but the results of a complex interaction of social, economic, historical (in a word, political) factors. So-called 'works of art' are made as much by the historical conjuncture within which they appear as by human agency. This is not to deny a place for human agency in a sweepingly-deterministic way, but to place human agency firmly within those shaping forces by which artistic ideas, forms and genres come to have particular values ascribed to them by a society, and without which it is inconceivable that anyone would be able to shape an artwork at all. Art in general, and dramatic art (being highly social) in particular, does not just re-flect the society which produces it, it also in-flects that society with developed (and developing) meanings. Nowhere is this more evident than in the True Story.

A cultural materialist approach stressing the ways certain methodologies unsuited to the dominant hegemony are marginalised, incorporated or suppressed (while others easier to manipulate are promoted to saturation point) may offset that view of culture which states that only that which 'survives' is worth having. By locating True Stories within whatever supporting socio-historical conditions obtained at particular times, they can be addressed in terms of practice and consumption. This offers a release from a narrowly-judgemental approach, which will tend to downgrade them. The critical approach taken will seek comparisons and

B

correspondences, arguing that a discontinuous reading of its history will reveal much which has previously been hidden, or 'naturalised', about the True Story.

The True Story indirectly challenges the hegemonic myth that real art is independently created by a freely-choosing individual artist. The claim is therefore made that documentary drama is less 'free' than other kinds of drama (therefore less valuable) because 'editing' of material rather than 'creation' is the process involved. To be an 'editor' of material is, perhaps, to be at a different creative level from an 'artist'. As with most judgements of value, we learn a great deal about a culture from such formulations. What is obscured is the precise nature of the work involved in the two operations. The frequently collective nature of cultural production involving drama makes it all the more likely that collective processes will preponderate over individual 'artistry'. But the characteristic discourses of criticism will always tend to assume an individual source for a work unless persuaded otherwise. This seems part of an overall cultural determination to validate the individual over the collective. This is not simply a matter of convenience (i.e. that it is easier to talk in terms of individuals, because there is likely to be less argument), it is also a matter of ideology.

To coin a phrase, 'the art is in the edit' in any drama making use of documents; a clear editorial line provides the spectator with one half of a dialectic – it is up to the spectator to provide the other half. The inbuilt challenge to the Myth of Facts which documentary drama makes is difficult for audiences to ignore. The True Story (documentary-style) invites an audience to orientate itself to mater-real documents within the parameters of that audience's own subjective reality – the audience enters into a relationship with documentary material through a frame (the documentary drama).

The psychological effect of this is potentially far reaching; in 1969, an American psychologist examining documentary plays of the period wrote: 'A comparison of internal with external reality and a correction of internal reality, where it is in blatant conflict with the external one, is called "reality testing" in psychoanalytic parlance'.[26] This 'reality testing' exists at depth on an instinctual plane. With True Stories, we risk a reality test, but are usually reassured. Sometimes, however, we are not: Attenborough's 1987 *Cry freedom* turned into a reality test for South Africa in 1988, just as *Tumbledown* had been a reality test for the UK in 1987. Both films became controversial within the 'realities' promoted by the two states; elsewhere, they hardly mattered at all. *Tumbledown* was unlikely to be of interest in the USA because of its parochial subject, while *Cry freedom's* view of racist South Africa is so mild that it failed to make anything like the same impact in the UK and the USA.

This is why the documentary mode of the True Story can be so disturbing to audiences, so threatening to hegemonies. The audience is firmly implicated (consciously and sub-consciously) in a conflict over 'The Facts', in which fundamental tenets about those facts are criticised and challenged – their model of 'reality' is 'tested' and put under strain. As Althusser said of Brecht's late work, the play 'is really the production of a new spectator, an actor who starts where the performance ends' (p.151). In the twentieth century, Faith in Facts has produced a situation in which the accessing of documents, and their subsequent use to prove or disprove versions of the truth, has become an issue of the utmost importance. Drama making use of documentary material(s) intervenes in this debate. For some it chafes a sore spot; for others it illuminates a grey area; for everyone it disrupts the debate in an unexpected way, transgressing and disputing previously-held boundaries of cultural discourse.

The 'problematic' of documentary – True/Real Stories

This chapter has raised the *problematic* of documentary. Through a problematic, a term (in this case 'documentary') is rendered doubtful or questionable precisely by being located within the ideological framework without which it cannot exist. It is taken out of isolation, as it were, and placed in a context where it is 'interrogated'. The term 'documentary' has been utilised for widely divergent purposes during the brief period of its existence, but its use is an implicit invocation of Faith in Facts promising the truth, the whole truth, and nothing but the truth.

The documentary mode occupies a different position on the 'facts-truth axis' from most other drama, and it is this which makes it (potentially) dangerous to a hegemony under threat. Julia Kristeva has expressed the fundamental instability of the facts-truth axis in the twentieth century through her coinage 'le vréel', an amalgam of 'le vrai' and 'le réel' – the true and the real. The true, says Kristeva, 'has lost its former logical and ontological security, and is now expressed instead as the true-real'.[27]

Documentary dramas are True/Real Stories, characteristically working towards an articulation of publicly known matters which invites an audience to define or re-define its relationship to them. True Stories thrive upon that shock of recognition of the true/real which sometimes leads an audience to take issue with the facts as presented. The Myth of Facts is problematised by this area of cultural production, which cannot be analysed without an appropriate critical matrix. In the absence of such a matrix, value-judgements tend to fill the void – value-judgements which prioritise loosely-defined concepts such as 'objectivity'. Ultimately, the untheorised use of such concepts benefits only one segment of society.

It is worth reminding oneself that 'hard facts' are never likely to be in dispute (otherwise they would hardly be hard facts); the really interesting facts are those most buried, concealed, or disputed. It can never be a viable critical project to 'evaluate' selections of facts made in True Stories, since this activity presupposes an ideal template of facts against which to place any 'selection'; all that ought to be possible is the revelation of tendency, declared or undeclared. A documentary drama's insertion into social reality is always inhibited when there is a veiling of tendency and intention. But this veiling is the norm, and plays are still attacked as factually 'biased', which shows the power of the Objectivist Fallacy. When attacked at the level of 'entertainment', something of the strength of the Naturalist Fallacy is revealed.

At times a subversive form, at times profoundly subservient to the hegemony, the True Story has played an important role in disturbing one of the most treasured myths of the twentieth century, that 'facts = truth'. It is through such myths that a society recognises and confirms its collective model of itself. The potential to disturb such a profoundly hegemonic myth has sometimes placed the True Story in a Cassandra-like oppositional stance. The development, marginalisation, and recuperation of this potential can be seen most clearly through an examination of the 'two traditions' of documentary.

The clash of facts and entertainment: the two traditions of documentary

We have shifted responsibility for making the world interesting from God to the newspaperman. (Daniel Boorstin)[1]

Still harping on disasters

I have before me a magazine/book entitled *Disaster* which is the epitome of the notion that 'facts' can co-exist with 'entertainment'. Published in 1975, it is Volume 1 of a series calling itself 'The Library of the Bizarre and Extraordinary'. It is the kind of publication regularly to be found at airport and station bookstalls, appealing as it does to a kind 'there-but-for-the-grace-of-God' feeling which publishers clearly think is fairly universal, especially before a journey. An eye-catching angled strip in the bottom left-hand corner announces that the publication contains: '14 TRUE STORIES THAT SHOOK THE WORLD'. On the cover is the German airship, *Hindenburg*, burning as it docked in New Jersey, USA, after a transatlantic flight in May 1937. Other disaster-stories in the volume include the 1911 sinking of the *Titanic*, the 1929 Wall Street Crash, and the 1923 Tokyo earthquake.

The 'book' is remarkable for its assumption that there is a market for stories about mass death and destruction, an assumption amply confirmed, not only by the present-day news media's constant harping on disasters, but also by the way 'spectators' can be confidently expected to turn up at disaster sites. At one level, the True Story is all about this cultural compulsion (usually offered up as 'natural') to be 'shaken' by the 'truth', in an apparently-endless soap opera of desperate deeds and heroic endurance. The first confessional *True story* publication, capitalising on this desire to consume dangers vicariously, appeared in the USA as early as 1919.

All fourteen True Stories in *Disaster* are presented through a 'documentary' medium of photographs and/or 'reconstruction' drawings, juxtaposed with newspaper-like columns of prose laden with quotations from 'eye-witnesses'. The stories are classic examples of that 'photo-journalism' which both tells us and shows us its stories. There are frequent reproductions of actual newspaper front pages, as well as authentic news-photos and 'reporter-speak prose'. In many ways, the example is unremarkable; such sensationalised accounts, published in similar formats, abound in the USA and the UK. The photo-journalistic True Story has been naturalised over a period of time, until its tales of murder, robbery, love, war, and disaster have become quite commonplace, evidence of the cultural confidence placed in camera eye and I-witness.

Together, technological apparatus and on-the-spot human agent promise authenticity; next to 'being there' oneself, they offer the simulation of someone else's, 'I was there'. The 'picture/speech' format has become the *sine qua non* of reportage, a journalistic technique whereby the pictures alone will tell the story to the rapidly-glancing eye. This bears out Walter Benjamin's observation that the technological reproduction of reality has brought about 'profound changes in the apperceptive apparatus' of humankind.[2] Unless we see, we find it hard to *believe*. Yet seeing does not always facilitate understanding; there is a hollowness at the heart of the invitation to identify with the camera-I which can only be filled with demands for more and more sensation – hence publications like *Disaster* (and tabloid newspapers like the UK *Sun*).

The rise of photo-journalism signalled the reliable portable camera's arrival on the scene of the public (and private) event. This enabled the reporter-I and the camera-eye to seem as if they had merged and become one (at least as far as the *reproduction* of reality was concerned). The need to include photographic evidence is a quintessentially twentieth-century need. The real heyday of photo-journalism was the 1930s and 1940s (pre-television), when there was a burgeoning of picture magazine production worldwide. In the USA, *Life* magazine was founded in 1936, to be followed by *Look* the following year, and then by a host of imitators – *Click*, *See*, *Focus*, *Foto*, *Photo*, *Picture* (the names nearly always foregrounded the photographic element).[3] This pattern was repeated all over the world. In the UK *Picture post* was founded in 1938, and in Hitler's Germany the wartime potential of the medium was so well understood that foreign editions of its photo-magazine *Signal* were always established in conquered countries, until the circulation reached 2½ million by 1943.[4]

There was also an enormous upsurge during the period of the movie concomitant of photo-journalism – the newsreel. Here, a 'commentator-I' normally interpreted someone else's writing to supply the language through which audiences glossed the images of the movie camera-eye. Newsreels varied from 'news of the day' compilations produced both in Europe and by all the major Hollywood studios as a regular contribution to an evening 'programme' of films, to series like the US *March of time* which began on radio in 1931 and on film in 1935. Constructed like a newsreel, with free-standing 'stories' in a programme composed of a number of sections, *March of time* went so far as openly to 'reconstruct' its news stories, either persuading real participants in news events to 'go through the motions' again for the camera, or using 'look-alike' performers in actual (or simulated-actual) locations. The clear precursor of much television 'documentary' work, its makers significantly preferred the term 'pictorial journalism'. *March of time* even had a European office which employed many of John Grierson's documentary film personnel.

During the Second World War newsreels became important as a means not only of providing information, but also of raising morale (the latter function arguably predominating over the former). All this added up to a massive interest in 'photo-news', the re-production of 'actuality' whether in still, or moving, picture form. Essentially, this was an interest in 'entertaining facts' – offered as a kind of opposite to fiction.

Fiction's opposite

Photo-journalism and the newsreel are neither the end, nor the beginning, of the story of the interaction between modern technology (cameras, microphones, projectors, sound amplifiers) and human agents (speakers, performers, writers, directors). In 1930s America, 'the primary expression' of the times 'was not fiction but fiction's opposite' (Stott, p.xi); it was, indeed, True Stories that 'shook the world', not just America, between the two world wars – the range of cultural production offered by 'fiction's opposite' was enormous. All major events between the wars seem not only to have been filmed, but also accompanied by a piece of prose 'reportage', a documentary report/account seeing into the heart of things (like American John Reed's *Ten days that shook the world*, an 'eye-witness' account of the 1917 Russian Revolution).

But the term 'documentary' was coined primarily by film-makers (or in writing on film). If the Fact was powerful, the Visual Fact became even more so, and the activities of the documentary film movement placed the camera-eye centre stage in 1930s culture. In his review of Robert Flaherty's *Moana* (New York sun, 8th February 1926), John Grierson wrote: 'Being a visual account of the daily life of a Polynesian youth, *Moana* has *documentary value*' (Hardy, p.11 – my emphasis). This remark led to Flaherty's being dubbed 'the father of documentary'.

Flaherty's first film was *Nanook of the north*, made in 1922. Like *Moana*, it was a broadly anthropological study (of Eskimo life in Canada), and it inaugurated the tradition of American documentary film-making. A full account of even the early history of this would include the New Deal work of Pare Lorentz and Dutchman Joris Ivens, and the wartime films of John Huston, John Ford and others. The account of work in the UK from the same period would discuss Arthur Elton, Humphrey Jennings, Paul Rotha, Basil Wright, as well as Grierson himself. It would not be possible, either, to discount European influences such as those of Alberto Cavalcanti and Henri Storck, nor the contribution of the Russians Esfir Shub and Dziga Vertov. (If Flaherty was the 'father of the documentary', then Vertov was surely the 'father of *cinéma vérité*', with his 1920s concept of the 'Kino Eye'.)[5] The world of documentary film in the 1930s was sufficiently small for influences to percolate very quickly, and 'chicken-or-egg' arguments about who came first depend largely on the culture from which one views developments.

The major impact of the activity so roughly sketched here on the dramatic True Story was to intensify that belief in the unproblematical authenticity of the visual which was so much part of the shift in structures of feeling. Beyond the 'Promise of Fact' was a promise of 'Privileged Seeing' which was carried by Fiction's Opposite in film. Fiction's Opposite between the wars came to mean *seeing* the real. The promised pleasure of this 'seeing' motivated audiences worldwide in their mass consumption of the altogether-new movie experience. In the UK alone, a weekly average of 18 million people, nearly half the population, were going to the cinema by 1934. There was also a vast expansion in the building of cinemas, or 'Picture *Palaces*', as they were known between the wars. What people 'saw' in those factories of simulated experience included regular packages of Fiction's Opposite, which contributed their distinctive discourse to the major social occasion which was pre-War movie going.

Depression authenticity

The newsreels' 'controlling' images of 1930s life still determine and define our historical constructions of the period. One of the central images is of the 'welfare' kitchens of the USA, where bedraggled down-and-out Americans of the Depression years following the Wall Street

Crash went to stave off starvation. The 1932 E.Y.Harburg/Jay Gorney song 'Buddy, Can You Spare A Dime?' epitomises the class location of such people. Once they 'built a railroad, made it run/Made it race against time', now they are unemployed; without the dignity their work once conferred on them, they are reduced to abject beggary. In the UK, a controlling image of the same period is of the 1936 Jarrow Hunger Marchers, trooping their banner through some rain-swept English town on their way to London from the North-East to petition the government.

Unemployment in the 1930s galloped to previously-unheard-of levels. In the UK, it reached 2½ million in 1932; in Germany, it was 5½ million; in the USA, 13½ million. In the face of such figures it was impossible to keep social deprivation off the political and cultural agenda. The appearance on the screen, in novels, and on stages of a class largely ignored or stereotyped in previous representations could not but be noticed. Social problems were reported and recorded in 1930s cultural production to a new and unprecedented degree, especially in the new documentary movement. The arts in the UK and USA in the period between the wars were reflective of a growing compulsion to open up the respective societies involved to underclasses of various kinds. Grierson even felt, towards the end of his life, that he was, 'the first guy to put the working-class on the screen'.[6]

But there were plenty of other accommodations of working class life in 1930s culture. Many young intellectuals (politicised by Depression economics and influenced by left-wing philosophy) attempted, just like Grierson and his associates, to assert the importance of a social democratic politics which would speak for (and to) all classes. There was even a certain *cachet* in being a left-wing artist in the 1930s (as there was again in the 1960s), and, then as now, those who got the economic backing were often those who least rocked the political boat. Ultimately, it is always easier to *establish* practices 'urging a paternalistic social democratic view of non-conflictive politics under a "strong" but "benevolent" state', as Don Macpherson has remarked of Grierson's project.[7] It is much harder to establish more radical practices (as UK film maker Ralph Bond tried to do in the 1930s, for example).

There were many less obviously 'serious' screen works which pictured the working classes in the period between the wars. They were not 'serious' in the same way documentary films were, but they must be seen as part of the same ideological thrust. They include the very popular films of Gracie Fields and George Formby in the UK, and the equally-popular 'rags-to-riches' musicals of Busby Berkeley in the USA.

Berkeley's *Goldiggers* of 1933 contains two classic Depression songs, 'We're in the Money' and 'My Forgotten Man'. The former was choreographed with the chorus waving giant coins and bank notes around, the latter is a song not unlike 'Buddy Can You Spare a Dime?'. It tells the story (with appropriate dance-action) of men marching away to war, then returning to the dole queues and soup kitchens of the Depression – this in spite of the fact that relatively few Americans were *actual* forgotten former First World War soldiers.

The music hall (UK) and vaudeville (USA) traditions, reaching back into the nineteenth century, had been portraying the working class for a very long time in sketch and song, and they form a 'spine' supporting popular entertainment of the period. Hegemonies adapt themselves over a period of time in terms of 'accommodations' to such traditions, which demonstrates some sensitivity to changed structures of feeling. Like the licensed Fool of medieval times, the modern artist exists through levels of permission which close off some activities, and sanction others. Documentary film was one accommodation, Berkeley's musicals another, Harburg and Gorney's 'Buddy, Can You Spare a Dime?' yet another. While one is constructed as 'serious', the others as 'entertainment', both exist in the same spectrum of cultural trans-formations of the 'problem' of the Depression. In the 1930s, the arts were just one expression of the claim for wider social inclusion brought about by economic collapse; the hegemony had to acknowledge this claim or face the consequences. Cultural production of the period can be 'read' as shifting the boundaries of social inclusion, even as it defused potential revolution.

In 1980s UK, the re-production of that doughty British cultural monument William Shakespeare offers a paradigm. As Terry Eagleton has pointed out (in another volume in this series), Shakespeare is 'the quintessential commodity, at once ever-new and consolingly recognisable'.[8] The Royal Shakespeare Company constructs itself as the main producer of radically challenging readings of Shakespeare, but is inevitably compromised by its licensed location within a hegemony keenly interested in monumentalising the Bard. Whatever the *individual* motivations of its artists, the institutional frame within which they work anchors any oppositional meanings they might make to a debate defined by the hegemony. Increasingly, the RSC is becoming brand-leader in the theatrical drive for tourists and exports (Praise the American/Japanese tourist and pass the Penguin Shakespeare). Cultural production is often used thus, appropriating potentially dangerous material and thereby consolidating the dominant order's position. The 'arts' are sometimes class war by other means, just as sport is nationalist conflict by other means.

Wherever possible, political argument is displaced to an arena outside politics (where there would be a risk of conferring *real* power). The arts are a particularly convenient arena for politics to be discussed at a distance. The challenging 'artwork' can be a preliminary to actual political recognition, of course, and it has been claimed that the documentary movement was instrumental in forming a climate of opinion which ultimately led to New Deal welfare policies in the USA and Welfare State socialism in the UK. But cultural activity alone is no more than an indication of an agenda, not evidence of effective change (or even evidence that change is about to take place). Cultural production is a necessary, but never a sufficient, condition for change – a hegemony's hand needs to be forced in other spheres too. Shifts (or even earthquakes) detected by the cultural seismograph are all too easily constructed as the formation of new solar systems.

The Russians are coming – fear of revolution

Capitalist hegemonies of the 1930s can be seen with the infallible wisdom of hindsight to be successfully *resisting* calls for social change, as well as making some accommodations. The appearance of 'art-with-a-social-conscience', often read as a positive indication of British and American society's basic sense of responsibility, was also part of the moment of containment. The 'sudden' surge of documentary work was only sudden if one choses to 'read' the history in that way. Accounts of cultural change privileging individuals (i.e. the usual kinds of cultural account) tend to obscure the fact that individuals do not exert as much leverage on events as is popularly supposed; they choose to participate in the development of pre-existent modes fully as much as they invent them. They may inflect a cultural movement by their specific practices, but to suppose that they do more than select from discourses made available through much wider shifts is to privilege the individual unduly. It is merely a convenient historical fiction to say that Grierson 'invented' the use of the term 'documentary', or that Flaherty was the 'father of the documentary'. It displaces questions about the nature of cultural material, modes of production, and access to those modes.

One can oppose this view even at its own level – indeed, the academic industry thrives on such opposition. It would be theoretically possible to suggest other 'originators' of documentary, including the Lumière brothers themselves. Or what about Boleslaw Matuszewski, a cinematograph operator in Warsaw who, in 1898, proposed a museum for the collection of film 'of a documentary interest' comprising 'slices of public and national life'?[9] But who calls him 'the father of the documentary', or first-coiner of the term? The reasons why the reader almost certainly has not heard of Matuszewski are cultural; we accommodate most easily that which is within our own (often parochial) culture, and this is communicated as cultural history. We cannot cope so easily with global cultural issues, nor with a more global politics of change. Our wish to find 'onlie true begetters' lies partly in the difficulty of accounting for the real complexities of culture as material production in a political process. This would mean accounting for a more usually effaced economic and political dimension unsuited to one of the founding notions of bourgeois culture – that the 'great' individual wields the lever of change, whether cultural or otherwise.

The advent of Fiction's Opposite in the period between the two world wars was part of an ideological counter-thrust to Russian communism. In this (largely successful) initiative, the capitalist hegemonies of the UK and USA succeeded in rescuing their construction of the world from potential destruction, and re-imposing it on a mass consciousness which (they feared) had been made unstable by the re-drawing of political boundaries in the USSR. A whole anglophone culture was mobilised against the potential crisis of working-class revolution, symbolised in the western world by the Russian Revolution of 1917. This event so concentrated the minds of the rulers of the West, that accommodations 'suddenly' became possible, amongst them those examinations of socially-disadvantaged lives which were made by Grierson *et al*.

The much-vaunted 'documentary movement', with its New Improved Realism, was merely one manifestation of a subjugation of a documentary impulse which could have become dangerous. Photo-journalism, documentary film, the newsreel, the documentary novel, all were successfully incorporated, and particular examples have subsequently been read as standing 'the test of time'. Even crueller than being marginalised in your own lifetime must be the experience of being erased from the later historical account: that was the experience of a generation of socialist artists (the achievements of people like Ralph Bond and Ivor Montague are only now coming into the light again). The potential effects of their practices were deflected by the elevation to importance of practices easier to control. Hegemonies could accommodate almost any

number of revolutionary artists as long as this meant avoiding revolutionary masses.

Reporting and recording – the 'two traditions' of documentary

'History,' claims Terry Eagleton, 'is not a fair copy but a palimpsest,
whose deleted layers must be thrust to light, written together in their
episodic rhythms rather than repressed to unruptured narrative'.[10] Marginalised in any account of documentary which insists on regarding it
simply as a new and better realism is another ideological thrust, through
which documentary material was used to expose the political causes
underlying social conditions. There have been (and still are) two clear
'traditions' through which documentary and dramatic elements have
been mixed in the twentieth century, and there are fundamental
differences between them which are part of cultural history's 'deleted
layers'. The recovery of these layers is of vital importance if the tragic
history of the 1930s is not to be repeated in the 1990s as grim and ugly
farce. The 'unruptured narratives' of the history of any art must be
contested wherever they occur, if only to assert that other possibilities
have been, and still are, possible and available in signifying practices.

The dominant tradition of documentary is the liberal/conservative one
which holds that facts and information are in themselves liberating, and that
a responsible, democratic society will see to it that its citizens are sufficiently well-informed to make judicious moral and political decisions.
Indeed, the responsible, democratic society habitually pictures itself to
its citizens through its licensed cultural production as bending over
backwards to accommodate whatever 'problem' might be nominated.
There is a tendency in this tradition to see facts and information as
'objective' entities, free from all 'bias' and equivalent to 'truth'. Assemble
enough facts, and truth will automatically precipitate out as 'naturally' as
in a chemical reaction. This tradition belongs to a liberal/conservative
ideology because the image it gives of itself (in order to perpetuate itself,
as dominant ideologies always attempt to do) is one of evolutionary
improvement, of a society gradually becoming fairer through the honest
efforts of honest men. From time to time it will even admit women and
ethnic minorities to this exalted circle of the Great and the Good, and
what could be more accommodating than that?

This tradition is a recording one; that is, it believes that the effacement of
the subjective creator(s) of cultural production will produce an 'objective' account. This literal 'record' of the event/activity is placed at the

service of a universalised 'public good'. Film and television, initially confident in their ability to capture and fix the living moment, have made most use of the 'recording' tradition. Cultural producers have claimed to use documentary material without imposing themselves on it directly, mere 'flies on the wall', incapable of disturbing what they record. Their texts are claimed as transparent mediators of a reality which, although reproduced, is routinely constructed as 'natural'. The very fact that such texts are produced at all is an additional earnest of good intentions, part of a society's cultural bona fides to its citizens.

The alternative tradition is a radical/revolutionary reporting one, which recognises that facts and information can never come value-free, and that the responsible film/theatre piece will make this clear. Whereas the 'record' of an event is presented as transparent (but is in fact mediated), the mediator in the 'report' is, to adapt McLuhan, also the message. The first tradition is 'compensatory'; it constructs a citizen who must be compensated for his/her lack of knowledge by a programme maker who automatically becomes superior – part of an informational élite. This is partly why this tradition is more popular with the 'benevolent state', (which must always know better than its citizens). The second tradition assumes knowledge and allows the citizen access to the makers' own place in the mode of production (on the assumption that s/he will be able to cope with the notion of mediation). Just as a newspaper reporter's account of events is 'framed', and therefore contextualised, by people's knowledge of the journal which contains the report, so (in the reporting tradition) cultural production is framed by the declared perspective of its creator(s). The information it contains is 'enabling' rather than compensatory. This tradition has been more evident in the theatre and in radio than in the 'photo-media'.

Exposure of the all-important context behind information has most often been achieved through 'montage' techniques. Montage is a cinematic term (deriving from the French monter, 'to mount') meaning the cutting and subsequent joining together of pieces of film, often disparate in themselves, such that they form a unit of meaning which can be perceived, or 'read', by a spectator. The entertainment cinema has worked hard over the years to construct a film narrative which will conceal montage; it is the hidden motor which drives the realist film.

A good example is the staple action/reaction point-of-view shot. Here, a close-up of a face (say, the 'hero's'), looking deeply affectionate and saying the line, 'I love you', will almost inevitably be followed by a cut in the film, and a join to the next piece of film which will show what he is seeing – in this case (since the entertainment cinema is pretty inflexibly heterosexist) probably the suitably-grateful and reciprocating expression of the 'heroine', also in close-up. Few consuming this clichéd piece of montage will question the 180-degree switch which has taken place in the point-of-view of the camera. This will be effaced along with any awareness of the effects of 'cutting' (not to speak of the on-set re-staging which will have taken place in the 'real time' of filming). The audience will accept the cut as a totally 'natural' viewpoint, and will assemble the moment in 'film time' as simultaneous. So naturalised has this kind of technique become that the join is to all intents and purposes 'invisible' to spectators experienced in decoding the technique.

This linkage montage is a basic technique; it makes, in current critical parlance, a suture between the real and the imaginary in the viewer's mind which has little relevance to the literal join in the film negative. The suture enables the film both to construct narrative (at the imaginary level) and to seem 'natural' (at the symbolic). The theatre, too has its linkage montage: whereas, in the nineteenth century, quite long gaps in a performance for scene changes were not difficult for an audience to sustain, today's theatre audiences will become restive if a scene change lasts more than ten or fifteen seconds. Modern materials and equipment in stage design, lighting, and sound solve the potentially disruptive problem of the modern scene change. Designers create adaptable sets, modern lighting instruments provide clearly focused area lighting, cross-fades and fades-to-black-out – all permit scene changes rapid enough for an audience to 'bridge' the implied gap and link the narrative.

Although montage at its lowest level denies itself in order to construct realist narrative, collision montage can present an event and an attitude to it simultaneously. Here, the more disparate the items, the more evident the montage becomes to the spectator. There is a healthy (although by no means valorised) tradition of collision montage in theatre in which 'joins' are not concealed at all. Collision montage was a vital formal element in the Epic Theatre of the period between the wars (in the USSR, Weimar Germany, and the USA). This formal accommodation of a 'problem' in apperception was, on numerous occasions, 'documentary' – but not at all in the conventional 'objective' sense.

Documentary drama/'Documentary Theatre'

The distinction being made between documentary drama and documentary theatre is not offered in an effort to provide transcendental definitional keys to the door of the problematic of documentary, but as a further, indispensable, step towards recovering the history of the use of documents in drama. The present, 'naturalised', use of the term documentary is the result of conscious and unconscious choices between modes of production in historical conjunctures other than our own. The term 'Documentary Theatre' can be conveniently given capital letters, because it is much easier to establish as a coherent (and self-defining) signifying practice. It highlights a tradition opposed to realism, and signifies in particular the Brechtian/Piscatorian Epic Theatre, in which access to the means of production is granted to an audience expected not to consume passively, but to engage actively with the material being presented.

To extend the distinction between 'drama' and 'theatre' made on the first page of this book, 'documentary drama' will be used to describe the full range of dramatic practices in which the True Story invokes the special power of the document. Documentary Theatre will refer to one segment of documentary drama production, comprising those pieces of work written, devised or compiled first and foremost for theatrical presentation, and in the theatrical style pioneered by Meyerhold, Brecht and Piscator. Styles other than naturalism have been consistently selected as the rule rather than the exception in Documentary Theatre.

If the term 'documentary' has most frequently been used in one tradition to head off any dissenting argument about the 'truth' of a particular play's content (as if the very factuality of a play renders it in some way more 'real', therefore more 'true', than other created works), in the other tradition it has been used to question the very notion of a single and univocal 'truth'. Formal techniques in this tradition have made it possible to insert radical critiques of dominant ideologies into stage performance; from the outset, it has been a multivocal approach to drama.

The dominant tradition remains pretty inflexibly set in the concrete of a naturalistic/social realistic dramatic rhetoric which is one part of the battery of techniques used to justify, ensure the continuance of, and further the power of, the hegemony. This supercharged reality, bolstered by finely-honed naturalistic acting techniques, is always particularly useful at those times when a culture is under pressure from self-doubt (thus the national traumas of Vietnam and of Loss of Empire have been 'explained' through documentary dramas in the USA and the UK, and in post-glasnost USSR, we find the Chernobyl disaster addressed through Vladimir Gubaryev's 1986 documentary play Sarcophagus).

When addressed through the dramatic technique of a naturalism/
social realism which can quite easily recuperate the problem discussed
for the dominant ideology, the tendency is to make it appear as if,
basically, everything is under control. This is also the project of all
governmental information agencies. Documentary *drama* tends to be
complicit with this project, but the period between the wars was also a
conjuncture which favoured alternatives, one of which was Documentary Theatre. This emerged at the point at which art in the Soviet
Union attempted to come to terms with the profound changes wrought
by the Revolution of 1917, a period in which Russian film and theatre
employed new methodological 'hinges' on which to swing the cultural
'door'. In the years following the Revolution, the new Russian cinema
(with directors like Pudovkin, Eisenstein and Dovzhenko) was influential in its use of collision montage. Originally a pupil of the radical theatre
director Meyerhold, Eisenstein in particular developed the concept,
elaborating his views in the Moscow arts magazine *Lef* in 1923:

Instead of static 'reflection' of an event with all possibilities for activity within the
limits of the event's logical action, we advance to a new plane – *free montage of
arbitrarily selected independent* (within the given composition and the subject links that
hold the influencing actions together) *attractions* – all from the strand of establishing certain final thematic effects – this is montage of attractions.[11]

Eisenstein's emphasis on a narrative construction non-reflective of the
surface of life (freed, that is, of the confines of an event's surface 'logic',
and driven instead by an interior rhythm of related but contrasting
'attractions' which comment on an action), prefigures much of the later
thought of Brecht and Piscator in the German theatre. The principle of
montage as an alternative means of structuring a dramatic piece was vital
to the development of Documentary Theatre as a new genre.

Documentary Theatre is predominantly events- and/or issues-centred.
If events/issues are to be articulated on stage in something approaching
their full complexity, a *presentational* mode is required which allows them
expression independent, if necessary, of any human agents in those
events/issues. In order to escape the imperative of the bourgeois theatre,
which requires the understanding of any issue to be funnelled through
an understanding of a single individual's relation to it, the revolutionary
theatre of the USSR needed to be able to make connections not governed
by the temporal and spatial logic of a single individual's experience –
montage supplied that capacity, and Meyerhold and Eisenstein were vital
figures in its practical and theoretical articulation, not least because they

were able to theorise in a way which disseminated their ideas beyond
the USSR.

The 'new gigantic actor'

The impact of the technological media of the twentieth century, with
their apparent ability to replicate complex 'actuality', lead to a recognition by Bertolt Brecht and Erwin Piscator that theatre could gain a good
deal of cultural leverage in the twentieth century by judicious use of film
and photograph montaged *within the theatrical frame*. Piscator produced a
series of plays in Weimar Germany in the 1920s which were issue-based
and which investigated the interface between theatre and technology,
drama and politics.

Some of his plays, like the 1927 *Rasputin, the Romanovs, the war and the people
which rose against them* made conscious use of a range of documentary
sources, including photographs and film projected on to screens above
and at the side of the stage. His plays broke new ground precisely
because the actuality film could be contextualised through stage action,
and vice versa. A 'deconstruction' of the actuality film was made possible
through Documentary Theatre, which deliberately destabilised and
undermined photography's apparent authority. Piscator wrote in 1929:

> It is not by chance that the factual substance becomes the main thing in each play.
> It is only from the facts that the constraints and the constant mechanisms of life
> emerge, giving a deeper meaning to our private fates. For this I need some means
> of showing how human-superhuman factors interact with classes or individuals.
> One of the means was film.[12]

Having called in 1927 for 'a great epic and documentary theatre', Brecht
also thought film could play a part in this theatre, pronouncing it to be 'a
new gigantic actor that helped to narrate events'. By means of film,
'documents could be shown as part of the scenic background'. He
realised that there was a sudden exciting possibility of 'simultaneous
events in different places' being seen together.[13]

Film in plays, then, was capable of three things: it could provide a
discourse of factuality with which the human performers could interact;
it could also transform stage space in an important way. Finally, it was
revealed as mediation in a reflexivity which challenged the audience to
think as well as emote. It was, almost literally, an 'actor' in the drama.
Brecht explained these functions of film further in an essay written
around 1936; film worked on stage, he said, 'by recalling other

simultaneous events elsewhere, by projecting documents which confirmed or contradicted what the characters said, by concrete and intelligible figures to accompany abstract conversations, by figures and sentences to support mimed transactions whose sense was unclear'.[14] Piscator used film in order to demonstrate 'the link between events on the stage and the great forces active in history' (p.93).

A discourse which maximised the characteristic rhetorics of the new photographic media while not being enslaved by them allowed flexibility; Piscator distinguished three functions for his technological devices in *Rasputin*:

Didactic film presents the objective facts, up-to-the-minute facts as well as historical ones . . . broadens the subject in terms of time and space.

Dramatic film plays a part in the development of the action and is a 'substitute' for the live scene. But where live scenes waste time . . . film can illuminate the situation in the play with a few quick shots.

Film commentary accompanies the action in the manner of a chorus . . . It addresses itself directly to the audience, speaks to it . . . It draws the audience's attention to important developments in the action . . . It levels criticisms, makes accusations, provides important facts, indeed, at times it carries out direct agitation. (pp.237–9)

The function of this 'technological actor' was, then, interactive and multi-levelled.

This highly-sophisticated use of film/slide has no real theatrical model; the most useful entertainment models are the cabaret and music hall traditions of nineteenth and early twentieth century Europe.[15] The use of *direct address* in this tradition (by which a *conférencier* or master of ceremonies would comment to the audience) was an important technique, and it was one extensively 'borrowed' by Documentary Theatre. An additional model was the newspaper; at the level of research into, and dissemination of, information, Documentary Theatre has a good deal in common with journalism (the three functions of film adduced above could be summarised as 'Headlines', 'Articles', and 'Editorial'). The reporting tradition of documentary, whose mediation is no secret, is *multi-vocal*, and mixes forms unashamedly.

'Complex seeing' in the new media

The most obvious feature of popular films, silent or otherwise, is the pace and movement of the story-line . . . The experience of movies has led the popular audience to expect a certain level of invention and intensity and movement from a good piece of entertainment: and taught them the shorthand, the elliptical language of narrative necessary to maintain such a pace. (John McGrath)[16]

The new media radically altered the manipulation of time and space on stage; in theatre's 'real time' it was impossible to conceal those manipulations of time and place so routinely erased in film narrative. Brecht, amongst others, recognised that collision montage opened up new possibilities. In his Epic Theatre's handling of stage time, such essentially cinematic principles as montage and cross-cutting of scenes proved to be vital components of the disruption of the representation of time. Brecht proposed an 'exercise in complex seeing' in the arts in connection with the medium of radio (which, because of its non-visual nature, has always had the potential to disrupt 'naturalised' conceptions of reproduced reality). In 1929, Brecht called for 'a kind of resistance' by listeners to radio, which would lead to their 'mobilization and redrafting as a producer'.[17] Here we see, in the context of his thinking about radio, Brecht's characteristic concern with spectators being permitted to engage in an active, not passive, relationship with the material presented to them – enabled, not compensated.

In the UK, from the 1930s onwards, there existed a very vigorous tradition of radio montage documentary which can be set against the Griersonian idea of film documentary. The work of A.E.Harding was instrumental in introducing statistics, facts and information into radio 'entertainments'. In three programmes broadcast on the National Programme in 1929, 1931 and 1932, Harding laid the basis of a radio montage documentary tradition. Paddy Scannell (writing about the 1931 *Crisis in Spain*) observes, 'By foregrounding the role of the modern media, the narrative achieved a complex cross-cutting between events taking place in Spain and their simultaneous retransmission round the world'.[18] Moved by Reith to Manchester in 1933 (after the controversial 1932 *New Year over Europe* had provoked complaints from the Polish Ambassador in London), Harding (with D.G.Bridson) produced more remarkable radio features in the period up to 1939. Joan Littlewood and Ewan MacColl were involved in many of these, and the disciplines they learnt were to prove crucial in the work of their Theatre Workshop company. 'Facts', in the work of the BBC Northern Region under Harding, were montaged with music, song and narration in the presentation of serious subjects to listeners who had to work towards their own construction of the elements offered. As with newspapers, the editing policy restricted any 'free' choice in this construction, but no concealment of technique was involved.

The use of a narrator, narration through song, and the notion of the 'actuality' field recording are some of the continuities present in UK radio documentary. They are visible post-World War Two in the work of Charles Parker, whose first 'Radio Ballad' (made in 1958 in collaboration with MacColl) montaged actuality recording, narration and song to tell the story of an heroic locomotive driver. *The ballad of John Axon* is remarkable for many things, not least the way the explanation of the breakdown of a component in Axon's locomotive (which led to the train wreck in which he died) is carried in a song – an unthinkable procedure in conventional documentary work. The important point in all this is the use of montage as a dialectical means of approaching issues and events. Radio has proved itself capable of 'redrafting' the spectator through a montaged clash of discourses which permits 'complex seeing'. In the song explaining the fracture of a braking system steampipe in *The ballad of John Axon*, we have technical detail defamiliarised to a degree which virtually ensures concentration on this one, vital, issue.

The new photographic media demonstrated a capacity for the representation of reality which gave them an apparent advantage over the theatre, but Documentary Theatre 'borrowed' discourses from the new media and demystified them. Pieces of film run through the projector during performance, or recordings reproduced over a loudspeaker, themselves acquired the status of a document and had their apparently unproblematic relationship to reality challenged. This 'montage of attractions' is impossible to reproduce in printed textual form; it must remain part of the performance text, along with the acting styles employed, the quality of any musical input, and so on. Documentary Theatre directly challenged the concept of 'objectivity'. Many present-day televisual manifestations of documentary drama are deeply inscribed with the attitude of the documentary programme-proper; they are still locked into the view that no 'shape' must be evident in something carrying the 'documentary' label, it must be unhampered by any 'interference' between material and maker. With the assistance of various formal devices, something essentially 'created' is designated in a viewer's mind as 'factual', and is accepted as such.

A key 'validating' device in the documentary-proper is the 'voice-over', which is in almost universal use, and which rarely changes in essence. It supplies the programme's aural editorial gloss, but purports to be value-free information. Most documentary television favours the voices of *actors* for such voice-overs. The relative rarity with which actresses are called upon to do them should alert us to the culturally-conditioned nature of the device. The quality, as well as the sex, of the voice heard against the visual images is also of some significance; the well-modulated

tones characteristically preferred by producers (the voice of the nineteenth-century novel's omniscient narrator translated into twentieth-
century technological terms) are simultaneously authorial, authoritative
and reassuring. They become more so as an audience grows accustomed
to the genre (as they acculmulate experience of documentaries). The
voices of those who so urbanely take us by the ear and guide us through
the material being viewed frequently belong to actors who are just the
unfamiliar side of being household names, so we are comforted but not
distracted.

There are important cases where this 'rule' does not apply. International television co-productions, especially those concerned with the
subject of war, require a different order of performance; hence Michael
Redgrave's Shakespearian delivery of the commentary for Correlli
Barnett's 1964 BBC series *The Great War*. Colin McArthur observes that on
these occasions the 'rhetoric of narration in tele-history' comes close to
'more heightened, stylised forms of verbal discourse such as blank verse
and other *dramatic* forms'.[19] But still the narration is almost always, to
quote McArthur again, the 'guarantor of truth', as it (apparently) orders
and organises the various discourses within the programme, giving the
dominant position from which the visual information is to be decoded.
The US/UK television co-production *World at war* in the 1980s used that
doyen of traditional acting, Lord Olivier, to provide the commentary –
who better to provide a blank verse editorial?

In contrast, Documentary Theatre's 'complex seeing' provides a
number of contexts through which to view events, because each single
context is disrupted through the montage, no one position achieving
pre-eminence for long enough to acquire the reassuring tone of the
voice-over commentary. The theatre, as John McGrath says 'is the one
medium that forces, by its very limitations, that confrontation between
an abstraction and a person, between a system and a group of individual
people, between social history, or political theory, and the actual life of a
man or woman' (p.86-7). Documentary Theatre's power is most
obviously located in 'confrontation'; the degree to which it is able to
confront is, however, conditional upon its audience's capacity to accommodate confrontation. In the USSR and Weimar Germany in the 1920s,
and to a lesser extent in the USA of the 1930s, audiences' capacity for
Documentary Theatre's confrontational stance was particularly marked.

Even when under threat from censorship Documentary Theatre of the
period could confront. One scene in Piscator's 1927 production of
Rasputin irked the former German Kaiser, now exiled in Holland. By

taking legal action, the ex-Kaiser succeeded in restraining Piscator from portraying him on stage. Had *Rasputin* been a naturalistic play and not a montage documentary, this would have posed severe problems; in the event, Piscator adopted the simple (and formally appropriate) expedient of replacing the Kaiser's lines with an on-stage reading of the legal writ. Thus the *subject matter* of the scene was retained, even if the form in which it was presented had to be adjusted. This is a good example of what is possible in Documentary Theatre. Even *in extremis*, the montage documentary can not only cope with hostile criticism, it can incorporate it within the debate which constitutes the play. This is conflict, as we are often told drama must be, but it is conflict at the level of issues not individuals.

Radical theatres, conservative societies

'The living newspaper grew out of the necessity to use as many as possible of Federal Theatre's greatest asset: unemployed people,' (Karen Malpede Taylor).[20] If theatre workers using radical practices made a cardinal error in the period between the wars, it was to assume that societies in Europe and America were ready for more radical change than was really the case. In the USA the unemployed became an asset not a threat, and too zealous a pursuit of a socialist ideal usually meant an eventual appearance before the 'House Un-American Activities Committee' (where once a committee member inquired whether Christopher Marlowe was a communist).[21] In the USSR and Weimar Germany, exile, imprisonment, even death (as in Meyerhold's case) could result from misreading the runes. Western societies do not have the monopoly on conservative practices, and a good deal of radical theatre practice was expunged from Russian theatre history in a Stalinist period of 'Socialist Realism' in the arts.

The international sense of themselves that Marxist groups had, allied to the considerable extent of emigration which took place as Germany in particular became more repressive from 1933 (following Hitler's rise to power), ensured a fragile continuity in alternative theatre practice in which practices developed in the USSR of the 1920s were imported into Germany late in the decade, then transferred via immigrant communities to the USA. Information from all three sources percolated into the UK by both 'front' (European) and 'back' (US) doors. In the USA and the UK, the distances (both ideological and geographical) from the European epicentre of World Revolution ensured that, while political reverberations were not entirely absent, they were slight in comparison to the European experiences. The Second World War had the long-term effect of driving all radical artistic practice to the margins, as various nationalisms (always tinged with conservatism) held sway. Eventually cultural practitioners everywhere have had to 'recover' radical practices from the margins of cultural experience or (as happened in the 1960s) *reinvent* them.

In the USSR, the 'Blue Blouse' groups with their *zhivaya gazeta* (or 'living newspapers') toured the country in the aftermath of the Revolution, instructing and informing a population unused to thinking for itself and frequently unable to read printed newspapers anyway. There were film shows on river-boats and on trains, all developed under the auspices of the Soviet Department of Agitation and Propaganda from 1920. Acting on the theory of revolutionary artists like Mayerhold and Eisenstein, these touring collectives perfected a style of theatre designed to inform and energise the population. During the period of civil war, shows were composed of disparate elements montaged to provide a coherent account of, for example, the Red Army's battles with the White Russian forces. Subsequently, performances were used to publicise and explain Soviet government policy and to enhance morale (the perennial project of the arts in times of hardship).[22]

All these practices, both of the largely anonymous Blue Blouse groups, and of the internationally famous revolutionary artists, were made available to Marxist artists from other countries. Piscator visited the USSR on a number of occasions, as did Brecht, and as did Americans like theatre/film director Joseph Losey, and originator of the Federal Theatre Project Hallie Flanagan. A Blue Blouse company toured Germany in 1927, seeding its production methodology into the practices of German left-wing groups already well-established since the early 1920s. This was important since, with the policy of 'socialism in one country', radical practices went rapidly out of favour in the USSR in the early 1930s. The cultural 'trigger' provided by all this work produced a brief flowering of Documentary Theatre in anglophone culture in the US 'Living News-paper' of the 1930s. This was yet another aspect of the almost-universal interest of the time in Fiction's Opposite.

In the wake of the Wall Street Crash of 24 October 1929, the USA, leader then as now of the capitalist world, experienced a deep social crisis. The crash was an issue which involved American society from top to bottom. It is difficult to believe that the widespread shifts in cultural production and consumption which were eventually achieved under the New Deal would ever have been effected without this powerful social and political driving force. The coming to power of F.D.Roosevelt in 1932, and his proclamation of a 'New Deal' policy from 1933, ensured a set of circumstances which, for a few years, occasioned a proliferation of documentary theatrical techniques not seen again until the 1960s.

Discernible in the American documentary movement were the dialectical montage style, and 'realistic' techniques favouring actuality material; they often worked with the same social and political material. The drive towards more realism in the arts was evident in a conservative/liberal tendency which favoured documentary realism, setting out to observe the social system, record 'objective' information about it, and set American society's conscience in motion. The radical tendency utilised montage more, seeking to expose a social system which produced poverty as a consequence of producing wealth. The two tendencies had adherents in almost all the arts: for example, the 1930s novels of John Steinbeck (*The grapes of wrath* – liberal 'documentary realism'), and John Dos Passos (the *USA* trilogy – radical montage, including actual 'documents'). Steinbeck's novel began as a 1938 research assignment into the 'Okie' community for *Life* magazine.

The Federal Theatre Project Living Newspaper Unit was a celebrated manifestation of dialectical montage theatre. The Project itself (which began in 1935 as part of the WPA, or Works Progress Administration, arm of Roosevelt's New Deal) was an institutionalised movement, carrying a significant degree of government funding; within it met workers' theatre personnel, theatre professionals, and academic radicals. The Living Newspaper Unit, also formed in 1935, produced a style of Russian/German Documentary Theatre (a *New York times* review of the 1936 Living Newspaper *Injunction granted* even noted its 'Moscow stylization') which became both celebrated and influential beyond American shores.[23] There was, however, a vital difference between the USA and Europe in the lack of any coherently collective revolutionary spark in American society itself. Hallie Flanagan could be called many things, but she was not a revolutionary, and in the USA there was no sufficiently widespread revolutionary movement. The New Deal's central motive 'was to preserve the American socioeconomic system by reforming it' (Stott, p.241). The Living Newspapers demonstrated that formal radicalism alone will not achieve significant political change. Flanagan had travelled in the USSR, but she was not a communist; under her leadership the FTP was a broad church which she kept together by temporising if necessary. For example, when there were problems with *Injunction granted*, she wrote a memorandum to its co-creator Morris Watson which she quotes in her memoir of the FTP years, *Arena*: 'Morris, I want you and Joe [Losey] to be clear about this. As I have repeatedly said I will not have the Federal Theatre used politically. I will not have it used to further the ends of the Democratic party, the Republican party, or the Communist party' (Flanagan, p.73).

The Project was first and foremost part of a liberal relief programme, designed to give quasi-employment, in this case to out-of-work theatre personnel. These people constituted a major asset, given that the cost of employing them under 'normal' commercial circumstances would have been very expensive indeed. Since the Living Newspapers 'employed' out-of-work newspaper staff also, it was phenomenally successful in its labour-intensiveness, even more so than all the other types of FTP production. Although she wrote in 1938 that the job of the Living Newspapers was to expose 'the conditions back of conditions' (O'Connor and Brown, p.26), Flanagan was a liberal democrat, not a revolutionary, and the flavour of her quintessentially American (indeed, Rooseveltian) idealism can be detected in her claim that the Federal Theatre was 'a pioneer theatre' engaged in a 're-thinking, re-building and re-dreaming of America'.[24] This 're-dreaming' notion connects resonantly with the fact that the Depression had been experienced as a painful demolition of the American Dream.

Part of the popularity of the New Deal philosophy was that it undertook to reform America from within, to *re-make* the Dream. It was predicated upon a belief in American democracy which is evident in the view that there was nothing wrong with America which could not be solved by American (and that meant liberal) reform. Initially, this worked to the good of the FTP in terms of the support (financial and other) that the Project was able to obtain, and in the short term there was an astonishing out-pouring of theatre activity. The reliance on fact, 'on the objective logic of events rather than upon subjective emotion'[25] in the American Living Newspaper, the major exponent of the 'reporting' tradition in the USA, is further evidence of the importance of Fiction's Opposite.

Facts as 'hit entertainment'
– the flowering of the Living Newspaper

Flanagan was an academic whose initial reputation had been created through an on-campus experimental theatre at Vassar College. She was able to feed continental ideas into America both as a theatre practitioner and commentator. At Vassar, she put European ideas into practice in her own verse documentaries (such as the 1931 *Can you hear their voices?*). What was destined to become the rhetoric of the Living Newspaper (the rhetoric of charts, graphs and statistics, of loudspeakers and slides, the rhetoric of the 'speaking setting') was fully present in these early examples. The two major hallmarks of the American Living Newspaper were to be the use of electronic technology (e.g. loudspeaker systems and slide projectors) interacting with stage performers, plus the meticulous referencing of items used in scripts. Flanagan's understanding of *zhivaya gazeta* forms, and of Meyerholdian/Piscatorian technological formalism, was highly influential.

Scripts for Living Newspapers were generated as a collective enterprise by a large group of newspaper worker/researchers (up to fifty), and a second group of theatre workers (a much smaller writing committee). In 1938 Flanagan described the organisation as 'like a large city daily, with editor-in-chief, managing editor, city editor, reporters and copy editors' (De Rohan, p.vii). The first FTP Living Newspaper, *Ethiopia*, was an analysis in montage documentary form of the Italian invasion of Ethiopia, and the response to this act of aggression by other nations. The Federal Government acted quickly against what it saw as a potentially embarrassing portrayal on the stage of Mussolini (defined at that time as the head of a friendly state) and the play was not performed.

Subsequent Living Newspapers were more careful; having been told what was and what was not permissible by the Government – no foreign policy, domestic subjects only – they followed a line defined by Hallie Flanagan's 'Address to the American Federation of Arts' (12 May, 1937): 'Living Newspapers seek to dramatize a new struggle – the search of the average American of today for knowledge about his century and his world; to dramatize his struggle to turn the great natural and economic and social forces of our time toward a better life for more people'.[26] The New York unit was especially prolific: the 1936 *Triple-A plowed under* examined the Depression from the agricultural workers' point of view, the 1937 *Power* celebrated the formation of the Tennessee Valley Authority (one of the New Deal's most significant social and civil projects), in 1938, *One-third of a nation* exposed the poor housing conditions obtaining in New York, using as its title President Roosevelt's own words from his Second Inaugural Address. Living Newspapers were highly popular, and were produced by local units in California, Oregon, Iowa, Chicago and elsewhere. The Living Newspaper was a Grierson-style compensatory social project designed to inform the average citizen about their rights; 'conditions back of conditions' were only examined up to a point. Harry Hopkins (chief WPA Administrator) called *Power* 'propaganda to educate the consumer' (O'Connor and Brown, p.13). The Living Newspapers were 'the biggest hits of the most popular New Deal project' (Stott, p.108); for 1930s America, the Fact had undoubted Entertainment Value.

Flanagan's acknowledgement of European, left-wing, sources is interesting given the fact that persecution of FTP was already in the air by 1938. Writing in 1936, Morris Watson was able to give a broadly socialist context to the Living Newspaper, as he compared it to *March of time*; the latter was, he said, sponsored by a rich magazine (*Time/Life*) and a rich advertiser. The Living Newspaper, however, was 'written, edited, staged and acted by people who struggle for their living' (K.M. Taylor, p.154). But by 1938, editor/writer/director Arthur Arent found it expedient to deny the revolutionary provenance of his production ideas: 'What are the sources of this technique? As far as I know, there aren't any. At least if there are, we didn't know about them'.[27] This disingenuousness has to be seen as self-protection – only Flanagan had a sufficiently safe establishment platform openly to acknowledge Russian and German models. Even she, by December 1938, was having to defend the Project before the philistinism of the House Un-American Activities Committee.

The Living Newspaper was a 'union of popular entertainments with people's theatre' (K.M.Taylor, p.146). Its particular version of montage documentary was partly based upon the kinds of spectacular stage effects perennially delightful to audiences, and to which they were becoming accustomed through the movies. In *Power*, especially, new standards of audience expectation were set by the use of projected scenery and of film. The use of a translucent curtain (called a 'scrim') for projection of film, slides, and visuals like graphs and statistics was evident as early as *Triple-A plowed under*. This common scenic device of the 1930s was used by the musical film-maker Busby Berkeley (in the 'My Forgotten Man' sequence in *Golddiggers of 1933*, mentioned earlier), and also by Noel Coward in his 1932 play *Cavalcade*. In both examples, lines of men become shadows as they pass behind a scrim, receiving rifles and army hats and 'becoming' soldiers marching off to the First World War. In the Busby Berkeley film, they 'return' to become the 'forgotten men' of the Depression. The scrim could be at once this 'Shadow-graph', when back-lit, and also a screen for projections; it became participative in the action of the play, after the manner recommended by Brecht and

Piscator.

The narration device of the Loudspeaker (very like *March of time*'s own sepulchral 'Voice of Time') became a kind of 'trademark' of the Living Newspaper. When first promulgated in *Ethiopia*, it was, according to Arthur Arent, 'a kind of non-participating dateline which introduced the various scenes' (Arent, p.58). In other words, it was a disembodied recorder of fact. The Loudspeaker gradually developed as a character in the drama, becoming antagonist, in the classical sense, to the 'Little Man' protagonist of the Living Newspaper. The problem of continuity, likely to beset any Documentary Theatre presentation, was solved by the development of the 'narration-dialogue', a symbolic dialogue-inter-action between a kind of Everyman 'ordinary person' (the Little Man) and the faceless institution (the Loudspeaker Voice).

In its use of a wide vocabulary of technical devices, the Living News-paper has obvious connections with the radical theatrical movements in Europe. There was the agit-prop attention to information and the non-naturalistic styles of rapid transformation which originated with the peripatetic troupes of the USSR and Germany; there were the cross-cut-ting techniques of cinema, and the montage structures of European cabaret/music hall brought into the theatre by the likes of Meyerhold and Piscator. The Living Newspaper succeeded in theatricalising issues, and (by theatricalising them) made them 'entertaining'. The Living News-papers of the FTP considerably developed a tradition of theatrical 'dia-logue' (in the broad sense of the word) alternative to the great dialogue tradition of the naturalist theatre. Mordecai Gorelik's description of Piscator's Documentary Theatre could apply equally to the FTP Living Newspaper; this, too, was 'a theatre of fact in movement – a theatre not of static facts but of facts in conflict, facts in mounting progression' (Gorelik, p.426).

Documentary Theatre's 'powerful enemies'

The force of the Federal Theatre Living Newspapers' theatre of 'facts in movement' was, of course, that it would enable the 'little man' (and, presumably, woman) citizen to understand their country's social prob-lems better. The intended effect was to mobilise citizens in support of Federal initiatives already attempting to solve the problems adduced in the entertainments. The show itself, after all, was an earnest of the Federal Government's good intentions; its New Deal policies brought the American people both the theatre event and the attack on social problems. The Living Newspaper was a long way from agit-prop theatre, which attempts 'to rouse its audience and society to active ends' (Szanto, p.9). Ultimately, and inevitably, the Project was compromised, mortgaged to its economic base. Precisely by incorporating alternative theatre strategies so well, the FTP put them on the agenda for suppression at the point at which they ceased to serve the purposes of the hegemony. This point duly arrived when the New Deal appeared to have deflected the worst aspects of American poverty in the late 1930s and, of course, when a war-time economy necessitated increased production and a united front in the American nation.

While the Living Newspapers were a relatively small part of the FTP's overall operation, their use of facts was *dangerous*. 'Facts are high explosives, and hence any plays based on fact must be carefully documented and handled with judicious restraint', wrote Flanagan (p.72). She tried to cope with the inherent instability of the fact by a meticulous attention to the substantiation of all facts used, footnoting *everything* in published texts. But this methodical procedure failed to save the Living Newspaper. The claim of unimpeachable authenticity alone, however well proven, has never saved a play from the depredations of a political system inimical to it. The Living Newspapers made 'powerful enemies' who were 'instrumental in the final closing of the project' (Flanagan, p.221). It is not the authenticity (or otherwise) of the True Story which offends, it is its closeness to potential trouble – the hegemony's licence to entertain will only extend so far.

Theatre does not lead a society; it is a more or less dynamic means of reflecting some of that society's most crucial tensions. The tensions surrounding facts and their use in presenting arguments are exacerbated when facts collide with overtly fictional forms. In 1930s USA, the whole documentary project tended eventually to validate the effectiveness of the political *status quo*; like a great deal of cultural production in the 1930s, the documentary 'began as a way of calling attention to America's failures and ended by celebrating its successes' (Stott, p.237).

During the period of the war the relatively uncritical recording mode of documentary held sway virtually everywhere. For example, the resistance of Stalingrad during 1942-3 was celebrated in the USSR by a True Story play *The people of Stalingrad*. The author, Yuri Chapurin (a war correspondent attached to the Red Army) claimed that speeches in the play had been taken down 'word for word' from the soldiers involved.[28] In the USA and the UK, film makers were also 'war correspondents', their True Stories often turning pre-war tensions on their heads and making them into wartime strengths. The characteristic American True War Story, for instance, habitually portrays the USA's racial diversity (normally a 'problem', as in peacetime 'race riots') as a strength. From John Huston's 1944 documentary *The battle of San Pietro*, through Lewis Milestone's 1946 *Walk in the sun*, to Cornel Wilde's 1967 *Beach red*, to Oliver Stone's 1987 *Platoon* this has been the case. What is occluded, of course, is any real recognition that, in the main, it is poor whites and blacks who fight America's wars. In the UK, similar closing of social ranks produced war documentaries like the 1940 *London can take it*, and True Story consensus movies like the 1941 *The foreman went to France*.

The Living Newspapers of the FTP appear to be the most obviously successful manifestation of Documentary Theatre, so it is instructive to consider the extent to which they failed. A melancholy illustration of the degree of failure is the lack of permeation of Living Newspaper techniques into post-war American theatre. In their subsequent careers, many FTP personnel (actors like Burt Lancaster and Arthur Kennedy, directors like Joseph Losey, stage managers like Nicholas Ray) went on to become establishment figures in the arts. Almost all of them were incorporated into an entertainment industry even more compromised than FTP ever was by its economic base.

By making the very compromises which ironically secured its four years of activity, by addressing superstructural issues instead of structural ones (Flanagan's 'conditions back of conditions'), the FTP created a space which the American Right were eventually able to exploit. Karen Malpede Taylor sees in the failure to address the hidden structure of American society the most serious shortcoming of 1930s theatre: 'Exactly where the plays failed, the House Un-American Activities Committee took over. The process the plays could not explain, HUAC perverted into a grotesque parody of itself' (p.198). For the USA, system-validating social realism could not begin to 'expose the conditions back of conditions', and system-validating social realism became the norm. Trusting in the historical conditions of the Depression, and in the gathering menace of European Fascism, to politicise their proletariats, theatres of the Left tended to misread the capacities of the capitalist hegemony to recuperate, marginalise or suppress their critiques.

The Living Newspaper of the USA, then, suffered a similar fate to Documentary Theatre in the USSR and Weimar Germany, perishing through a mixture of implacable opposition and a set of working practices (collectivity, labour intensiveness) basically inimical to the capitalist entertainment industry. Thus, although the term 'documentary' can be invoked in the cause both of more and less realism in dramatic art, people are in the main familiar with the term through the realist, recording tradition and its use in the photographic media. The paradox is worth holding on to, however, and can be traced to that bifurcation in the use of the term in the late 1920s/early 1930s, which lead to markedly differing expectations when the word was used in the context of film or theatre. One effect was to validate the document even more, in the sense that a desire for unfettered access to information led to something of an 'unfreezing' of information sources. (The new mass broadcasting media had a certain faith in the social efficacy of the well-informed citizen, leading at the BBC to the Reithian assurance of broadcasting 'objectivity'.) But Documentary Theatre techniques were disseminated sufficiently widely to make the kind of impact which is only now beginning to be acknowledged – the fragile between-the-wars radical tradition was not entirely broken.

The broken tradition –
montage documentary theatre
and post-war change

Oh What a Lovely War was an elegy not just for two-and-a-half million dead, but for a revolution which never happened. (Ronald Bryden)[1]

Introduction – revolution revisited

The 'revolution' to which theatre critic Ronald Bryden was referring had nothing to do with plays or films. He was talking about the revolution which might have taken place in the UK after World War One, but which ultimately atrophied after the failure of the 1926 General Strike. Had tens of thousands not perished in the trenches of the Western Front, would a revolution have been more likely? In terms of long-vanished historical possibility, a revolution in the UK could well have been part of that World Revolution towards which communists of many nations looked in the 1920s. After all, a revolution had taken place in Russia, had almost taken place in Germany, and fear of such developments had led to important concessions by power-elites in the USA between the wars, and in the UK after World War Two.

As well as a trace of this first 'possible revolution', traces of a second potentially revolutionary moment (that of 1968) remain in dramatic practices in the UK, and they remain in large measure through the crucial intervention of Theatre Workshop, and in particular its production of Oh what a lovely war in 1963. As a result of this play (and the kinds of activity it generated) a tradition of radical, reporting documentary continues in our culture, in addition to the more high-profile recording one. The radical tradition's continuity may have been interrupted, it may be compromised, but it has never been completely occluded; it is as present, and as important, as we care to make it.

Dramatic practices which fed off the methodological model of Lovely war became especially important after 1968, when the theatre became

overtly politicised in the aftermath of the so-called 'student revolution' of
1968. This is still an important historical conjuncture to analyse,
especially for the Left. Was it, as those who actively participated in it
claim, a moment when the fates of European capitalist hegemonies hung
in the balance (the Paris *évenements* did, after all, bring down a French
government)? Or was it a kind of *rite de passage*, in which the sons and
daughters of the privileged (a class much extended by post-war social
and educational change) played out a version of revolution unconnected
to any revolutionary power-base, in order, as it turned out, to 'discover
themselves' – their early energy eventually dissipating into a myriad
'causes' bereft of the single, unifying, cause of revolution?

During the summer of 1988 the British media, ever hungry for broad-
castable anniversaries, gorged itself upon audio-visual reminiscences of
that potentially-revolutionary time. Revolution-twenty-years-on provided opportunities to dust down actuality film of the period, and to
interview ageing revolutionaries (some predictably grown into the very
fat cats they once despised). The tendency in such programmes, equally
predictably, has been for a persistent draining of issues into the ultimate
capacity of individuals to sustain them over time. Of course, individuals
on their own will find it very difficult to sustain ideas which run against the
social grain. The end result, most predictably of all, is a discrediting of
radical ideas, and the further promotion of the truism that 'you can't
change human nature'. Whatever the 'moment' *might* have been, it has
been somewhat sanitised and re-packaged as a trip to Revolution Land,
during which a new generation can amuse themselves in contemplation
of a far-off and quaint culture.

Such activity is part of a process of *recuperation*, in which the hegemony
not only asserts its values in the present conjuncture, but also
repossesses the past. The hegemony has always recuperated in this way,
but part of the price paid for its part-accommodation of oppositional
ideas (however 'successfully' they are recuperated) is that unaccommo-
datable elements remain. These are *displaced*, but not expunged. Anything
which cannot be used by the hegemony is certainly detached from that
which can be used, but this does not, as it were, 'dissolve' and then
disappear – it remains in 'trace' form at the margins of a culture. Such
traces can, and do, re-combine into new oppositional modes.

Collision montage, apparently 'detached' from theatrical practice at
the end of the 1930s, re-emerged in the 1960s, carried forward into a new
conjuncture mainly by the theatrical practice of Theatre Workshop. The
radical European montage techniques developed and used by

Meyerhold, Piscator and Brecht were 'secured' for a new radical generation by *Oh what a lovely war*, and the imitations of that production which proliferated in the late 1960s and early 1970s.

The 'Piscatorian Tradition'

'Montage, with its polymorphic possibilities, allows for the articulation of the spectator's own interests and judgements vis-à-vis artistic representation,' (Roswitha Mueller).[2] Only in Epic Theatre is montage as critique consistently foregrounded as 'collision montage', and only in the 'Piscatorian tradition' are True Stories using such techniques consistently told. This tradition has rarely been given the kind of coherent support which would lead to its becoming a dominant mode of production, because its political project is unsuited to the wants and needs of the *status quo*. Instead, the favoured style of True Story (especially in film and television 'documentary drama') has been 'life-like' social realism, in which performers quite literally 'look like' their real-life models and stage or film sets fetishise the external emblems of surface reality.

True Stories in the Piscatorian theatrical tradition can be distinguished from 'True-props-sets-and-costumes-Stories' by the following elements:

i) They may use *projections of actualities* (in the form of photographs and films) to which the stage action refers.
ii) They may quote from printed 'documentary' sources (projected via slides, written on placards, spoken by performers).
iii) They may *address the audience directly* from the stage (performers may do this in their own right or via loudspeaker systems).
iv) They may utilise *music and song* in order to provide an element of critique (rather than a supportive 'atmosphere').
v) Their performers may employ that 'cool' acting style associated with Brecht's *Verfremdungseffekt*[3] in order (for example) to play several roles, rather than a single naturalistic 'character'.

All these elements were present in *Lovely war*: for this reason, it was an excellent model of practices otherwise unavailable to theatre practitioners in the UK.

The purpose of the 'collisions' which result when such 'attractions' as these are assembled is to be found in their manifest difference from the 'believable' techniques of naturalism and realism. Since the techniques of True Stories Piscator-style are so deliberately 'un-believable', the active calling of the spectator's attention to technique shifts more of the burden of construction of meaning on to the audience. Attention moves from

externals like props, sets and costumes to a more *situated* view of events.
The playwright Peter Weiss saw the spectator being drawn into the action
in Documentary Theatre, in a process operating 'against the tendency of
the mass media to keep the population in a state of stupefaction and
bewilderment' (p.41). The spectator in True Stories of the Documentary
Theatre is, at least potentially, *empowered* by being granted access to a more
usually effaced context to events.

'Oh what a lovely war' – a theatrical Trojan Horse

'We knew all about Bertolt Brecht in the thirties. On Broadway and
Shaftesbury Avenue he's still a novelty in the sixties,' (Joan Littlewood).[4]
Oh what a lovely war (a Brechtian 'novelty' when first performed) offered a
way out of the *impasse* caused by an identificatory model of theatrical
consumption. Like the best Brecht, it did this, not by eschewing identification altogether, but by subordinating the role of feeling in a process
committed to understanding rather than emoting. Its methodology foregrounded theatricality; like its Piscatorian models, *Lovely war* called attention to its montage of attractions in order to mobilise understanding. It
accepted that it was necessary to be didactic – to use, and to mediate, facts
and information in order to provide a framework within which feeling
and emotion could function productively.

There is an inherent risk in any commitment to the didactic by a
dramatic work. Being didactic in modern culture is always tantamount to
being boring; any play which seems to incline towards overt teaching is
in serious danger of being constructed as unentertaining and boring (this
naturalised view of the didactic has permeated education, too, in the
form of the 'child-centred' philosophy). Worst of all, such plays lay
themselves open to the blanket condemnation that they are 'ineffective
drama'. And yet, the equating of the didactic and the dull is a *very* recent
phenomenon. Only since the rise of the cultivated gentleman in the
nineteenth century (and lady, provided she accepted the gentleman's
terms) has there been an active splitting-off of the 'literary' and the
'didactic'.

As the reading of 'literature' became a pleasant diversion for a leisured
class, so the reading of 'non-literature' (the 'factual') became increasingly
constructed as onerous. This was compounded by changes in education
which gave rise to the factual (and boring) 'text-book'. The legitimation
of the 'time-filler' (literature) led, in other words, to the de-legitimation
of the 'utile text' (discursive writing of non-fictional kinds). This has led

to the unproblematic division of reading into the 'pleasurable', but ultimately undemanding, activity of consuming 'entertaining' books, and the brow-corrugating 'difficulty' of 'serious' literature. This is a pity, not least because it wipes out at a stroke a vast tradition of *popular* discursive writing, beginning with the sermons so frequently printed in the Elizabethan and Jacobean era. Listening to, or reading, 'serious' work has not *always* been constructed as unentertaining-because-boring – instruction and diversion have not *always* been cultural opposites. The documentary idea was one attempt to put non-fiction back on the artistic agenda; *Oh what a lovely war* was a notably succesful part of this attempt in the UK.

As with all True Stories, arguments about *Oh what a lovely war*'s interpretation of the facts which contribute to its 'truth' may occur, but no one seriously doubts that the events mentioned actually took place, in roughly the manner described by the play. *Oh what a lovely war* 'documents' relatively straightforwardly certain events of the 1914-18 World War, or more specifically the trench warfare of the 'Western Front' which ran from the coast of Belgium to Switzerland. The story of the series of battles which constituted the first 'modern' war of powerful long-range artillery (and, with the tank and aeroplane, a degree of mechanisation) was mediated through several layers of signification far more problematical than the play's deployment of facts.

At one level, this True Story was told through popular songs of the period. The company had access to the songs mainly through Charles Chilton, a BBC radio producer with a background in 'light entertainment' and 'features' rather than radio drama. He had an almost encyclopaedic knowledge of British popular music, gained in the 1930s through work in the BBC Gramophone Library. Subsequently he deployed this knowledge in many programmes which mined British and American popular culture. Chilton had produced a radio show called *The long long trail*, first in 1961, then again in 1962 (with the variety artist Bud Flanagan reading the narration). The songs used included patriotic recruiting songs ('We don't want to lose you, but we think you ought to go/Your King and your Country both need you so') and 'instant history' ('Belgium put the kibosh on the Kaiser/Europe took a stick and made him sore'). The former was used in 1914 to persuade men in music hall audiences to come on stage and sign up; the latter was briefly popular when the Belgian Army held up the German advance (for a few days of August, 1914). Other songs ranged through comic accounts of army life to bitter parodies of hymns, and the 'gallows humour' of men about to die. Songs

were mixed with narrated information about the Western Front, meticulously researched by Chilton and his wife.

Chilton brought all this material with him when invited to work on the
show that was to become *Lovely war* in early 1963. The songs alone
provided atmosphere, information, and occasionally critique – as they
had done in his radio programme. To these, the show added contemporary actuality photographs, projected on to a screen behind the acting
area, depicting a shift similar to that of the songs, from the hopeful and
boastful jingoism of 1914 parades to the grim reality of post-1916 mud
and death. At still another level, a ticker-tape 'Newspanel' above the
proscenium arch gave periodical 'newsflashes', often statistical accounts
of the 'cost' in human lives of battles on the Western Front.

To have accounted for three levels of signification existing in a stage
show and still not to have mentioned acting, character, or plot is
remarkable enough in itself, but a further remarkable element of *Oh what
a lovely war* was its mix of acting styles. The *Lovely war* performers were
costumed as pierrots, those artists of rapid transformations from the
ancient tradition of the Italian *commedia dell'arte*. Their set, framed with
fairy lights, reflected this, as well as having the more recent Piscatorian
elements of slide-screen and newspanel. The acting style made full use of
performers' skills of instant characterisation, often at the kind of emble-
matic level which was the hallmark of the Blue Blouse or FTP groups. But
there were also scenes in which Stanislavskian 'psychological reality' was
important – this was truly *international* theatre. It reflects the curious fact
that the company were always more celebrated abroad than at home.
They were a manifestation of that unusual phenomenon, the British
institution more European than British. It is remarkable enough to
conquer that narrow xenophobia which is 'British and Proud of It'
sufficiently to take in a foreign culture; it was far more remarkable to be
recognised by that culture. And from Paris to Warsaw, in Eastern and
Western Europe, Theatre Workshop were so recognised.[5]

On the stage of *Lovely war* were not performers-pretending-to-be-peo-
ple, but performers-pretending-to-be-pierrots-pretending-to-be-peo-
ple (or even 'things'). Sometimes they were real historical figures (such as
Field Marshal Earl Haig), sometimes 'ordinary' soldiers on the Western
Front, or 'munitionettes' on the Home Front; at other times they transformed into the personified abstractions of agit-prop theatre (such as
'Germany' and 'America'). In Act One alone, the reasons for the war were
explained via a 'Circus Parade' in which the personified combatant
nations 'introduce themselves' to the audience via statements of

foreign policy; a two-dimensional comic scene depicted a meeting between Allied generals in which communication is hampered by language problems; and a 'realistic' scene showed the arrival at Waterloo Station of the first British wounded of the war. In the climactic sequence of the Act, a *segue* (or musical 'splice') simultaneously ran two scenes together and illustrated the continued jingoism of the Home Front while introducing the most realistic scene in the play – an evocation of the famous 1914 Christmas Truce on the Western Front. This scene's dialogue was drawn substantially from spoof newspapers produced by front-line troops in the Ypres sector during 1916.

Such montage elements as these 'spoke to' each other in 'dialogue' of frequently devastating richness. Rather than *characters* in dialogue with each other, *Oh what a lovely war* set elements of a theatre machine in conversation – Eisenstein's 'attractions', interesting in their own right, were montaged so as to create a coherent argument. In the second act, the collage of material included soldiers' bitter parodies of hymns, in which 'Onward Christian Soldiers' could become:

We are Fred Karno's army,
The Ragtime Infantry,
We cannot fight, we cannot shoot,
What bleeding use are we?[6]

This song was given 'straight', within the context of a religious service before a battle. But the religious service was invested with irony via the counterpointed parody. Thus it was *both* serious and entertaining, an ironic statement of the soldiers' feelings and a hymn 'properly' sung. Elsewhere in the second act, an agit-prop scene using personified nations dramatised the commercial nature of modern warfare in an account of war profiteering. In the final moments of the play, projections of 'real' soldiers, weary from battle, formed both a literal and a metaphorical backcloth for the 'real' Pierrot soldiers to sing a grim valedictory (And when they ask us, how dangerous it was,/Oh, we'll never tell them, no, we'll never tell them' – p.107). The absent-present (the photographs) combined with the present-absent (the Pierrots-pretending-to-be-soldiers) over time (the song) to give the audience a layered reality (composed of differences rather than a flattened reality of sameness) expressive of 'experience of war'. The show did not pretend that you could be *there* through art; it fostered *recognition* of a particular experience rather than its *expropriation*.

Oh what a lovely war made an enormous impression, even before its 1964

West End run (when it went on to achieve an even higher profile than it might have otherwise done). It introduced Brechtian/Piscatorian 'collision montage' from an essentially European theatre tradition into a country which had largely marginalised such practices. Although this mode of production remains marginal in mainstream theatre, on both sides of the Atlantic (but especially in the USA), that it is present at all is due to a very considerable extent to Littlewood and her company. John Russell Taylor was among the first critics to see a post-war 'revolution' in the English-speaking theatre, and many writers since his 1962 *Anger and after* have followed him in dating this revolution from 1956. But for many people, it was not *Look back in anger* in 1956, but *Lovely war* in 1963 which was the theatrical event 'marking then off from now' (J.R.Taylor, p.9). John McGrath is one important theatre practitioner who acknowledges that *Lovely war* had 'an extraordinary effect on British theatre', via a 'new generation of young actors who played in it, sang the songs, and heard how Joan's actors had worked on it.' Theatre Workshop, McGrath concludes, instituted 'a whole new set of attitudes to making theatre' (pp.48-9).

Theatre Workshop's original production was very highly skilled in wiping the smile of delight (caused by its constant capacity to entertain) off the spectator's face (with the force of facts deployed within a theatrical frame). Like the best productions of Brecht, *Oh what a lovely war* was didactic *and* entertaining. It was the Trojan Horse through which a set of critical attitudes, and a European theatrical methodology capable of sustaining a critique of issues and events (rather than personalities) was smuggled into the cosily-conservative world of British theatre. Some would say that this was no great compliment: Brecht is still discussed as if he were a humourless German who followed the 'wrong' political philosophy, and allowed politics to interfere disastrously with play-writing (writing indigestible quantities of that 'theory' which is such anathaema to the True Brit). In *Theatre inside out* (a thoroughly unpleasant book by a former drama critic for *The spectator*), Kenneth Hurren articulates an all too common mainstream theatrical attitude when he refers to Brecht as 'that Teutonic plague' (p.69); contemptuously he finds a 'monumental' banality in Brecht's work. (Perhaps Hurren's fears of the 'Fringe', nurtured into confrontational being by Brechtian techniques, partly account for his almost pathological dislike.)

The 'anonymous' author – models of collectivity

The coming into being of the notion of 'author' constitutes the privileged moment of *individualization* in the history of ideas, knowledge, literature, philosophy, and the sciences. (Michel Foucault)[7]

Lovely war was constructed upon a collectivist principle as unlike dominant modes of composition as can be imagined. The controlling notion for Theatre Workshop was that *all* aspects of production, including writing, were essentially *collective*, a concept born in pre-war days. In order to ensure that even writing remained part of a process in which, for the overall health of the enterprise, the contribution of the individual should not be valorised, extreme measures were sometimes taken. At Stratford East, it was writers' as well as actors' egos which were sacrificed to the common cause. This attitude is reflected in a remark by Ewan MacColl, who was one of the most important early influences in the company. MacColl (a major figure in British folk music too) believes that songs in the folk tradition should articulate a collectivity which is, almost inevitably, *anonymous*. 'My ideal,' says MacColl, 'was the anonymous author, the anonymous song-writer, and you only achieve anonymity by becoming part of the whole.'[8]

This model of collectivity put Stratford East in touch with a form of theatre which pre-dates literature as we know it, and which harks back to a time (the Elizabethan and Jacobean period) when performance texts rather than printed books were the acknowledged raw material of the theatre. The 'Stratford East method' sought to replace the characteristically individualistic means of production which has tended to hold sway in theatres and publishing houses for many centuries (and which, as Foucault points out above, coincides with the post-Enlightenment bourgeoisification of culture) with a collectivist version in which the individual effort is still fully present, but is firmly subordinated to a whole which is greater than the sum of its parts. Arguably, one of the reasons why *Lovely war* was so successful was that its collectivity was so manifest in performance, offering a potent theatrical emblem for another sense of collectivity – that which helped to sustain the 'ordinary' soldier of the Great War.

Oh what a lovely war was 'a theatre machine to think with', actively encouraging the spectator to think events through. Thought was not divorced from enjoyment and from feeling, but was properly *contextualised* by them. The constituent parts of the machine can be itemised, but to do so is to deny them their collective force, which derived from the process of theatre rather than from its eventual product. The dominant ideology's cultural certainties are disrupted by theatre projects substituting process for product, and collectives for individuals. *Lovely war* was proof that alternatives to the unitary text and the univocal mode of production existed. 'Alternative' theatre's understanding of these things brought about a real theatrical revolution in the UK, which had nothing to do with the cosmetic alterations of the Osbornes and the Pinters in 1956. The collective methods, and European tradition, of Theatre Workshop were taken up by seminal 'Fringe' companies like 7:84, Red Ladder, General Will and Joint Stock, and also by innovative repertory theatre directors like Peter Cheeseman of Stoke. This was all theatre created against the odds – in the present conjuncture, we are in danger of losing this tradition once again.

'Mainstream' and 'alternative' – the effect of 'Lovely war' in the UK

After the 1960s, there was something of a bifurcation into 'mainstream', and 'fringe' or 'alternative' theatres. Even such a self-confessedly bourgeois critic as Sir Harold Hobson has begun in recent years to acknowledge that Joan Littlewood and Theatre Workshop 'revolutionised the British theatre'. He doubts, in fact, whether 'there would have been any fringe without Joan' (Goorney, p.179). What he gives with one hand, of course, he takes away with the other: his determination to find an individual source for Theatre Workshop's excellence, while validating 'Joan', simultaneously occludes and effaces the collective Anonymous Author. It was the *company* (with Joan Littlewood a demonstrably important *member*) which introduced the European Epic Theatre methodology into British theatre through the success of *Oh what a lovely war* and other productions. Once this foothold was established, the tradition of social-democratic British documentary (of Grierson *et al*) merged with it to produce a documentary mode which has been a staple technique for a considerable sector of British theatre production post-1968.

This sector has had very little to do with the bright lights of Shaftesbury Avenue, but it has been significant none the less – fulfilling several important functions. Documentary Theatre True Stories (with declared purpose and factual base) usually have one or more of the following purposes – they are:

  i) *Reassessments* of the past
  ii) *Celebrations* of the past
  iii) *Investigations* into 'topical' events and issues.
  iv) *Explanations*, in a didactic sense, of social, historical and political phenomena.

While examples of all these functions exist in the mainstream, they have been far more evident in alternative settings. Pasts reassessed and/or celebrated can be national (and, to that extent, general), or local and specific. Documentary Theatre has shown a tendency especially to re-claim pasts, and presents, which have become 'hidden', for whatever reason. Documentary True Stories (in all media) may propose one or more of the first three projects, but they only rarely address the fourth – that is more usually the province of alternative theatre.

Oh what a lovely war provided insight into all four purposes, hence its crucial importance as a 'Trojan Horse' for committed, political, theatrical practices. It manifestly 'reassessed' the Myth of Victory in the Great War, accusing war leaders such as Haig of incompetence. It 'celebrated' the collectivity and tenacity of ordinary soldiers who had to compensate with their lives for official muddle. It 'investigated' a largely undeclared past of international war profiteering. Finally, it 'explained' the War through the direct mediation of statistical information. This latter was particularly audacious, given statistics' apparent potential for being constructed as 'boring'.

Use of the Lovely war methodology has been discernable in both major areas of theatre production and consumption in the UK. Mainstream work included West End 'commercial' theatre; provincial 'Repertory' theatre; and the work of the two big post-war institutional theatres (the National, and the Royal Shakespeare Company). 'Alternative' (or 'Fringe') theatre, which developed post-1965, included touring companies, small building-based operations, 'community and constituency' theatre, and 'Theatre-in-Education'. All these modes of production and consumption have made extensive use of the documentary methodology. Within a few years of Lovely war's first production, several other documentary plays were produced. One (US – 1966), came from a celebrated company (the RSC) and a celebrated director (Peter Brook). In the Repertory Theatre, Peter Cheeseman began his influential local documentaries at Stoke with The jolly potter in 1965. The Fringe's first documentary productions began in the late 1960s, with such politically committed work as that of Red Ladder. The first Theatre-in-Education companies and productions began to appear from 1965 onwards, Documentary Theatre providing their staple technique.[9] With the advent of Repertory theatre 'studio spaces' in the 1970s, and as types and locations of alternative theatre continued to burgeon, documentaries flourished.

An English version of Piscator and Brecht was readily available which had established continuity with an otherwise 'broken tradition' of political theatre.[10] This broken tradition (perennially masked from and marginalised by anglophone culture because it originated from outside the narrow world of the British and American theatre) has hung on not just because of *Lovely War*; Brecht's Berliner Ensemble tour of the UK in 1956 was crucial, and there was input from Piscator himself in the 1960s. But within British culture there has been inadequate recognition both of the significance of *Lovely war* and the importance of alternative theatre; the two things are not unconnected.

The Stoke documentary method

The belief that we ought to be doing something about our own district, that's the most *powerful* motive for our documentaries! (Peter Cheeseman)[11]

The most significant and influential development for the True Story in mainstream British theatre took place in a provincial setting. In Stoke-on-Trent, in that unfashionable Midlands once part of the heartland of British industry, the 'Stoke documentaries' were pioneered by director Peter Cheeseman. They helped give overt expression to provincial theatre companies' legitimate aspiration to 'situate' communities culturally and socially, and to provide alternatives to the inexorable 'London-centredness' of British culture (especially marked in the world of professional theatre). Of the large number of theatre directors of the 1960s acknowledging a direct debt to Joan Littlewood, none is more important to the fashioning of theatrical True Stories than Peter Cheeseman.

His method of producing documentaries at the Victoria Theatre, Stoke foregrounded factual source material, via a structure making extensive use of music and demanding multiple competencies from its actors and actresses. Like *Lovely war*, the Stoke method made use of the vocabulary of the 'new media', particularly radio. In the Introduction to *The knotty*, Cheeseman acknowledged his debt to 'the didactic Left Wing theatre brilliantly extended by Joan Littlewood out of the German and American documentary traditions', and also to the Charles Parker Radio Ballads.[12]

Since his Victoria Theatre was a 'theatre-in-the-round' (and it was there-fore difficult to use screens) Cheeseman was constrained to make much greater use of sound tape, in a kind of extension of the 'Loudspeaker Voice' of the Living Newspaper.

In many ways, the Radio Ballads (1958-1963), which extended the tradition of radio documentary of the 1930s by further developing the use of folk song and actuality tape, were as important to Cheeseman as the European theatrical tradition. Like the Radio Ballad team, Cheese-man and his researchers used sophisticated tape recorders capable of producing broadcast-quality sound. This added the presence of an aural 'technological actor' to all the Stoke documentaries. In *Fight for Shelton Bar* (1974), this led to scenes as interesting as those in *Lovely war* in which 'real' and 'non-real' performers interacted. At the end of Part One, for example, actor Graham Watkins (playing local steel works Union leader Ted Smith) ceased talking and the taped voice of the real Ted Smith took over. At the end of the play each evening, the real Ted Smith actually came on stage to give an up-date on the latest position in the battle to keep the local steel works open.

Cheeseman's use of a folk music style was based on two premises, one aesthetic, the other pragmatic. Firstly, he believed that such songs are 'accessible and attractive to more sections of the public than any other kind of music' (p.xvi); and secondly, he recognised that the music hall style of *Lovely war*'s songs was beyond the competence of the majority of his performers, trained in the predominantly Stanislavskian tradition of the drama schools. Whereas Theatre Workshop performers had variety artists' skills, Cheeseman knew he could not rely on his performers having such skills. In addition, Cheeseman's liking for, and connection with, the Radio Ballad team of Charles Parker and Ewan MacColl, made the use of folk music even more likely. Both the Radio Ballads and the Repertory documentaries can most usefully be seen as part of the same historically specific cultural continuum.

Early local documentaries (in Sheffield and Bolton, as well as Stoke) concentrated on that decline of industrial Britain which had already given rise to visible waste and decay in the industrial heartlands of the UK by the 1960s. The End-of-Empire revaluation of the Imperial past (so apparent in *Lovely war* itself), was clearly visible in cultural attitudes taken to the UK's industrial past. The folk-song revival of the time, which gave the local documentary its distinctive musical style, had a somewhat romantic vision of a kind of 'green', pre-industrial, past in which local communities really had been communities. This past, it was thought, had been fatally disrupted by the Industrial Revolution. The structure of feeling evident in this view was determined by much more than local factors.

The Stoke acting style required a good deal of subordination of the individual will to the collective purpose. The actor was the 'instrument' through which the factual material was disseminated; Cheeseman saw the actor as 'the means of exposing factual material'. He believed that performers had to have 'a totally candid and honest basic relationship with the audience' in the first place:

> It is almost as if this permitted the audience to trace on him the shape of each character when they could see it so clearly standing out against his own openness. There needs to be considerable restraint and objectivity in the playing of each part. (pp.xvii-xviii)

Littlewood had a reserve of performers able to cope with her 'English Brechtianism'; Cheeseman, on the other hand, had to deal with a theatre profession still 'cursed with the currency of psychological realism' (p.x). This 'new' style was a means of combating the performer's naturalised assumption that s/he will always be playing a 'character', and that nothing is intelligible without that individuation.

As well as shifting scenes through the 'technological actor', Cheeseman also used a non-naturalistic costuming convention which allowed for speed of scenic transformation. This theatrical 'shorthand', as unlike social realist convention as can be imagined, permitted 'modification for different characters by superficial changes of hat, neckwear, or jacket' (p.xviii). This theatrical communication through emblem is part of Left Theatre tradition, and has clearest affinities with the agit-prop Blue Blouse. As with Lovely war's pierrot costumes, performers are able simultaneously to be both themselves and (simplified) characters through this strategy. They can exist for an audience on at least two declared levels; this can have profound implications for the construction of meaning.

Other companies using the local documentary were not as fastidious as the self-confessedly 'puritanical' Cheeseman about their use of sources, but, in any case, it is doubtful whether the phenomenon of the Local Documentary is most usefully described through its relationship with facts. It is better described through its highly public statements about locality and community. A survey in New theatre magazine in 1973 found between 60 and 70 local documentary plays over a nine year period since the Stoke production of The jolly potters in 1964. They shared 'a family resemblance in their focus on community and social issues rather than domestic and psychological crises . . . ultimately it is the similarity of the statements these plays have made to their local audiences that defines the genre'.[13] This essentially celebratory project continues in the present historical conjuncture via 'community plays' of the type pioneered by Ann Jellicoe in the West of England. These plays habitually mix theatre professionals (writers, directors, technicians and 'lead' actors) with amateurs (usually the bulk of the performers).[14]

'Overcoming the past' – influences other than 'Lovely war'

Almost as much has been made of 1968 as a year in which the mould of a period was broken. As with accounts of 1956 (*Godot, Look back in anger*, etc.), a fundamental alteration in patterns of thinking, especially among the younger generation, is frequently adduced as the factor lying behind a theatrical (and in the case of 1968 a wider) 'revolution'. Catherine Itzin is representative of many writers who claim that 1968 'marked the coming to consciousness – to political consciousness – of the war-baby generation', and that the movement resulting from this consciousness, 'did not remain random, but became a movement of the political Left, appealing (however confusedly) to Marx as a symbol of the revolutionary transformation of society' (Itzin, p.3).

Virtually all accounts of the emergence of the 'Fringe' in 1968 pay due tribute, as does Itzin, to the Paris *évenements*, the war in Vietnam, the Soviet invasion of Czechoslovakia, amongst other elements in a political situation which engendered that 'oppositional' stance which became associated with the radical 'student movement'. This politicisation was reflected in theatre in the formation of 'arts labs' (in London and elsewhere) and travelling groups (like Portable Theatre), the appearance of lunchtime theatres (like the King's Head, Islington) and small 'experimental' spaces (like London's Open Space). The sudden interest in American theatre groups using performance styles of rapid transformation generated through improvisation (like La Mama), and in experimenters (like Polish director Jerzy Grotowski), can also be linked to the widespread spirit of revolt.

More recent accounts attribute the power of the theatrical movement of the late 1960s as much to *despair* at the political situation which obtained, as to any hope of a new political future.[15] This view (of a theatre recording a revolutionary moment lost) is congruent with Ronald Bryden's notion that *Lovely war* marked the English revolution that might have been. As Sandy Craig has rightly observed, the Fringe became (still is) 'a social seismograph … registering long-buried underground pressures well before they rose to the surface of social life' (Craig, p.9). A narrative structuring of history which seeks 'watershed' dates will almost inevitably tend to 'tidy up' the process of history, turning it into a seamless 'continuum' of progress, dominated by the actions of individuals. This process tends to ignore those 'continuities' which do not fit, or which seem in some way unworthy – these become 'discontinuities' for any official account.

The radical theatrical tradition, enshrined in Theatre Workshop's style (and especially in *Lovely war*), is one such 'discontinuity'. It formed a bridge between radicalism of the 1930s and the 1960s, looking (Janus-like) backwards and forwards. It affected attitudes and practices in the arts, often in such a general way that young theatre workers of the late 1960s could use some of the techniques of the tradition without necessarily knowing their origin. In the 1960s, many young performers, writers and directors had to learn techniques, not from existing practical models, but at this remove.[16] Survival has depended upon what seem to be quite random occurrences, like the tenacity of Theatre Workshop and the success of *Lovely war*. But the continuance of Documentary Theatre was also partly facilitated by the post-war re-emergence of another aspect of the broken tradition.

In West Germany in 1963, there was another event which gives further cause for regarding that year as one of profound significance – Erwin Piscator's production of *The representative* (sometimes translated as 'The deputy'). This was one of a series of documentary plays by German dramatists, which were highly influential in the USA. All these plays had a similarity in one crucial respect; they used factual material in a dramatic form in order to reassess and investigate important 'hidden' elements of the recent past. The attitudes expressed in these plays were profoundly critical, they can be seen as challenges to the very notion of political consensus at least as much as *Look back in anger* can. This challenge did not start in 1963, or 1956, or indeed in 1945 or 1918 – it had been part of the political fabric throughout the century. After 1945, particular sets of circumstances caused a sharpening of oppositional attitudes: these can be seen in the UK, in West Germany and in the USA. As would be expected, a metaphorical 're-writing' of history was an important aspect of the oppositional approach. The project of these post-war documentary plays is enshrined in Piscator's comment that *The representative* was a rare contribution to 'overcoming the Past'.[17]

In the post-war world, the German past which Piscator wanted to

'overcome' (or reassess and put into meaningful context) had to do
with the bitterness and guilt of the Nazi experience (1933-1945). This
disaster was not simply on the material plane of defeat in the Second
World War; in fact Piscator's major objection to Adenauer's West German society of the 'economic miracle' was that only the material dimension of the nation's illness was being treated. The major German failure,
he contended, was a moral and spiritual one – the past to be overcome
was the past of the death camps, of Auschwitz, Belsen, Dachau. By
addressing this past (when the subject was more usually avoided), Piscator hoped to reverse the desire to forget and to re-establish the theatre 'as
a moral institution'.[18]

The trial in Jerusalem of Adolf Eichmann (1961-2) provided a platform
for this re-establishment. The subsequent Frankfurt trials which Peter
Weiss used for his The investigation (1965) drew crowds of young West
Germans, showing that the Holocaust had been for too long a proscribed
subject. In Heinar Kipphardt's In the matter of J.Robert Oppenheimer (1963), the
subject addressed was the nuclear threat – that most final of Final Solu-
tions. Whether these plays were Epic or not, Piscator made them so in his
characteristic collision montage style (with plentiful use of actuality
slides). Such things had been his trademarks since the 1920s.

He believed that he had also found the vital ingredient missing from
his former theatrical practice – plays suited to his particular notion of the
Epic Theatre. For him The representative was 'an epic play, epic-scientific,
epic-documentary; a play for epic, political theatre, for which I have
fought for more than thirty years: a total play for a total theatre'.[19] Despite
his evident faith in the play (which was written in a kind of free verse
which he believed avoided naturalism), Rolf Hochhuth's play was very
different from Piscator's earlier dramatic vehicles. Characterisation in The
representative was determinedly individualistic, for example, enabling one
commentator to observe that its overall effect was 'to abase history to the
level of personality'.[20]

The furore generated by the play is evident in Eric Bentley's 1964
collection The storm over 'The deputy'. The articles and critiques collected
over just one year by Bentley are a vivid indication of how easy it was to
displace Hochhuth's intended critique of the Vatican's institutional culpability in the Holocaust into a defence of the individual character of Cardinal
Pacelli (Pope Pius XII). Hochhuth sought to make Pacelli 'representative'
of a widespread complicity with the Final Solution which involved the
leaders of many European states; so widespread was the complicity that
to try to make any one person the focus was to miss the point. The

channelling of issues through an individual's relation to them (in the form of three-dimensional characterisation by which an audience 'identifies') is a trait of that naturalistic theatre from which Piscator had formerly tried to escape; Hochhuth's play did not permit this escape.

The documentary element in Hochhuth's play was not as much embedded in the performance text in the characteristic way of the stage documentary as it was concealed in *extra-dramatic prose* in the published text. The lengthy 'stage directions', for example, are often not stage directions at all, but discussions of source material which run for pages at a time; the 'Historical Sidelights' section is an important, contextualising 62-page editorial insert – parts of which would make an appearence on stage in 'real' Documentary Theatre. Ultimately, Hochhuth's interest in Documentary Theatre was minimal, documents were 'merely the raw material, the bricks with which one builds a play,' he wrote at the time, adding: 'I still maintain a belief in the autonomy of the individual and that the individual can make some impact on the world'.[21] As a consequence, documentary elements used in production, such as projections or film, tended to seem like justificatory 'add-ons'. This seems to have been the case with Clifford Williams's London production. Reviewing for *Plays and players* in December 1963, Charles Marowitz and Hugh Leonard were in agreement: the newsreels were 'the production's great misjudgement' (Marowitz); they were 'no more than emotional blackmail' (Leonard). Such elements had not been 'added on' in the 1920s – they had been central.

Piscator seems not to have noticed it (perhaps as a result of his enthusiasm for the subject-matter of the play), but *The representative* was a very traditional play. It was quite conventionally characterised and plot-ted, and, as Robert Brustein said in *New republic* in March, 1964, 'Hoch-huth's tendency to make the individual accountable for the failures of the institution is a heritage of his German idealism' (Brustein, p.205). *The representative* was in some ways quite an unsuitable vehicle for the tech-niques of Documentary Theatre; *Oh what a lovely war* was much more the inheritor of the 'Piscatorian tradition' of epic-documentary.

American perspectives – 'Theatre of fact and cruelty'

In the USA, *Oh what a lovely war*'s effect was negligible as a carrier-forward of the Piscatorian Documentary Theatre tradition (although the play was much performed on the American college circuit). Its lack of impact, despite a New York run in 1964, may well have been due as much as anything else to the USA's relative lack of interest in the subject of the Great War (the USA joined the conflict late on, and did not have anything like the same numbers involved in the war as other combatant nations). Nor did Brecht have much effect, being regarded as perennially-bad box office. In the USA, Piscator's protégés Hochhuth and Weiss were all important; The representative and The investigation were the Trojan Horses. It was not only in Germany that The representative in particular became controversial; in the USA, the play caused a huge fuss, mostly over its depiction of Pope Pius XII. The publication of The storm over 'The deputy' is indicative of the play's impact, bringing Piscator's work to the attention of young, radical American theatre workers. Whatever its limitations as a play, The representative drew American attention to the Documentary Theatre method of telling a True Story.

The impact of even an imperfect example of Documentary Theatre like The representative on public consciousness in the USA is testimony to the enduring ability of the stage documentary True Story to raise the temperature of public debate because of the way it raises the truth-claim stakes. As with the 1920s and 1930s, Documentary Theatre became a way of dealing with crisis. The changing politics of the new historical conjuncture brought a new cross-fertilisation of ideas in the 1960s which can be compared to that which occured in the 1930s. America, like the UK, had its theatrical 'revolution' to go with its student revolution. Emergent social movements in the USA of the 1960s produced a great many distinctive theatrical offerings in the US version of the Fringe – 'Off Broadway'. The formation of Black, Chicano, womens and gay theatre groups (all of whom used documentary methods) mirrors in American culture the 'opening up' of discussion agendas which I have argued was such a feature of UK culture. Open Theatre's tour to the UK in 1967 was as influential an occurrence as the Berliner Ensemble tour of 1956. The La Mama troupe, who produced Paul Foster's Tom Paine at the 1967 Edinburgh Festival, were similarly important and influential. So, also, was the work of Julian Beck and Judith Molina's Living Theatre company (this group's prominence arguably increased after their 1963 production of Kenneth Brown's The brig, a piece of staged documentary realism about life in a US Marine Corps prison). These groups, with their charismatic directorial figures Chaikin, O'Horgan and Beck, influenced improvisational approaches to True Story material in the USA of the late 1960s and early 1970s.[22]

Amongst the many US theatre True Stories of the period, Donald Freed's 1970 documentary play Inquest provides a sort of 'state-of-the-art' example.[23] Not only was Freed's play closely based on the facts of the trial and execution of the 'spies' Julius and Ethel Rosenberg in 1953, it was also *Lovely war*-like in its use of on-stage technology and Epic Theatre methodology. Its 'documentariness' was even evident *outside* the theatre space (in a foyer display of newspaper material and sound tape, and a sidewalk 'happening' with documentary projections). All this was illustrative of Freed's view that his True Story was a demystifying 'anti-myth', challenging the audience to avoid the overwhelming conclusion that the Rosenberg trial was a kind of ritualised sacrifice conditioned by politics and not justice. Freed argues that the work of Peter Weiss and others had produced a synthesised Theatre of Fact and Cruelty which could combine the best of Brecht and Artaud. 'The two new theatres of Fact and Cruelty,' he writes, 'provide a grammar, at last, for a popular drama of the twentieth century' (Freed, p.4).

The evidence that Freed's ideas were something of a false dawn is encapsulated in his own re-emergence in 1986 with the limp star-vehicle *Circe and Bravo*. This play featured Faye Dunaway as an (imaginary) President's wife with an alcohol, and hence a security, problem. Miss Dunaway was, of course, applauded at her first entrance (when I saw the play in London's West End) in that self-congratulatory ritual which so typifies the bourgeois theatre audience. The only other time there was a similar sign of life from them was in a curious example of art-imitating-life-imi-tating-art; the actress briefly reproduced, within the context of Freed's play, her 'Bonnie' characterisation from Arthur Penn's 1968 film *Bonnie and Clyde*. She recited the 'Ballad of Bonnie and Clyde', much to the delight of an audience (many of whom were quite probably there only because of that film, and its subsequent establishment of Faye Dunaway as Star).

The compromising of the Fringe

In the USA, the production of the musical *Hair* in 1968 signalled the recuperation into the mainstream of La Mama's Tom O'Horgan, who was to go on to direct stage and film versions of the equally appalling *Jesus Christ superstar*. The American Fringe stood revealed through such developments as a kind of theatrical 'nursery slope'. Just as the Federal Theatre Project had been thirty years previously, so Off-Broadway had become the place where talent could 'develop'. In a similar way, main-stream theatre in the UK assiduously recuperated what it could from the Fringe from the early 1970s onwards. Since 1968, oppositional theatre groups and workers have almost entirely been, either incorporated into mainstream theatre, or marginalised further than would have been thought possible at the height of revolutionary hopefulness in the early 1970s. The new drama became a *product* in a wider, economic, sense because of its success. The inertial power of the characteristic economic determinations of the dominant ideology made it difficult for individuals, even for groups, to withstand the inexorable imperatives of the recuperative process.

This is especially true of the dramatists who worked with the pioneering English company Portable Theatre in the early 1970s. Then as now, these writers must be regarded as leaders of the pack. Nothing sums up the process of incorporation so clearly as the reflection that the 1971 *Lay-by* and the 1972 *England's Ireland* (written for Portable Theatre by teams of writers) provide, not only a 'who's who' of 1970s alternative theatre, but also a checklist of 'major' mainstream writers of the 1980s. Howard Brenton, David Hare, Trevor Griffiths, Stephen Poliakoff, Brian Clark, Snoo Wilson, David Edgar (all of whom worked on one or both the plays in question) have since gone on to write for the National Theatre, the RSC, the Royal Court, the West End, and the cinema and television – just as Osborne, Pinter and Wesker did before them in the late 1950s/early 1960s. It is easily forgotten that in 1968 these dramatists were young *men* who had their way to make in a chosen profession whose economics rendered their progress extremely uncertain (it took *women* nearly another decade to be in anything like a similar position of power, of course).

The tightness of the control exercised over theatre productions by managements on the one hand, and over entry into the profession by Equity on the other, ensured that, then as now, the theatre was a very difficult business to 'break into' (a revealing phrasal verb, if ever there was one). The Fringe offered work which was for a time outside the legislative boundaries of both theatre managements and unions. By the mid-1970s, when the word 'Alternative' had supplanted 'Fringe', this was formalised to a degree which enabled the major theatrical institutions to recover their power. The opening up of a wholly-new network, in a profession otherwise somewhat starved of opportunity, ensured that there would be no lack of performers, directors and technicians ready to undertake Fringe work. Since it became clear that it was also work which could claim with some justice to be re-drawing the parameters of theatrical possibility, Fringe theatre acquired even greater prestige, to the extent that, by 1971, 'name' performers were eagerly seeking lunchtime theatre work, if not the rigours of 'the road' – even for the comparatively well-known, 'Fringe Theatre' had become a useful shop-window.

The rather provisional 'managements' of the alternative circuit were from the outset in a potentially anomalous position: while rejecting the institutionalised power structures of the capitalist, 'official' theatre, they found themselves in a position of undeniable power vis-à-vis their ability to offer people interesting work. This partly accounts for the agonies over 'company democracy' entered into by the likes of Red Ladder, General Will and 7:84 in the early 1970s. Red Ladder (whose documentary agit-prop style made them very similar to the Russian and German groups of the 1920s) were particularly insistent on a collective policy, rather than domination of the group by an individual or individuals. A different member of the company chaired discussions each day, even if the 'discussion' was actually an argument in a van on the way to a venue. These were conscientious attempts to break out of an economic mould imposed by the theatre profession, bolstered by the individualistic ideology of capitalism, and underpinned by the inertia of a large entertainment industry. The debates over who should control what were in part a recognition of that inexorable force, that 'continuity', which ultimately seemed to be compelling even 'alternative' groups to operate an economic structure just like that of the mainstream, but on a more reduced scale. The debate can be seen as a philosophy of collectivity taking arms ('however confusedly', to borrow Itzin's phrase) against individualism. But the more fundamental issue of control of the product (or of, both literally and metaphorically, the means of production) was eventually displaced to the margins by a capitalistic job market which, as ever, divided and ruled.

Recuperation was also facilitated by the very thing that kept the Fringe alive after its initial burst of energy, by the very thing which transformed its early ad hoc nature into the institution of 'Alternative Theatre' – that is, state subsidy. This played a part, not only in sustaining the energy of the Fringe beyond the late 1960s, but also in determining its subsequent trajectory. The apparent blessing of subsidy, alleviating the frontier economics of the earlier period, has often proved problematical over the last twenty years, no more so than now when groups are being saddled with the concept of 'project funding'. This device seems likely to destroy the continuity of much alternative work because it knocks away the prop of continuous funding (which, of course, goes some way to securing continuous artistic policy). This is especially important for Documentary Theatre, because it is highly labour intensive. It is difficult in the present climate, for example, to imagine theatres being able to afford the luxury of a lengthy research period for a play. Yet this is exactly how the local documentaries and 'verbatim plays' of Peter Cheeseman and his disciples worked.

As we move towards the Peter Palumbo Arts Council of the 1990s, the boundaries are being redrawn in order to exclude such working methods, and to silence dissenting voices of the 7:84 and Foco Novo kind. Arts subsidy is now in the charge of what John McGrath has called the 'Persuasion People': this 'army of PR men, administrators, experts, consultants and managers' are the stormtroopers of the new enterprise culture.[24] Ruthlessly they efface difference, and erase opposition through those hallowed 'market forces' which effectively level everything down to a blandness they can easily control and sell (and which is guaranteed non-dangerous).

The privatisation of culture

Although the Fringe brought new ideas into an essentially stolid commercial theatre operation, it could not but be compromised from the start by the kind of society within which it was situated. The nature of the Fringe's provisional institutions, and their subsequent incorporation (into a mainstream only marginally changed as a result) ensured the continued dominance of saleable drama which valorised the actions of the 'freely-choosing individual' over the 'shaping context' of events and issues. But masses of people, not individuals alone, consent to or oppose the propositions of their rulers. Cultural consumption is one of a variety of ways of doing this, and cultural consumption is partly contingent upon what is available at any given time in signifying practices. Culture is a site of political contestation, and this is particularly important to us now, as we approach the 1990s – we need the 'guerrilla' technique of Piscatorian documentary.

For, ultimately, what use we are supposed to make of a mainstream dramatic art which still only requires identification to ensure comprehension, in spite of the experimentation which has taken place? The 'liberal humanist' view, which has been under consistent attack for some time but continues to resist, believes that we are made 'better people' through the surrogate experiences which, for them, constitute all literary 'art'. This view claims that 'second order' experience can be turned into something as good as (indeed, better than) 'real' experience through great art. In the theatre, the elitist wing of this liberal politics is still largely in control of cultural institutions like the RSC, the National Theatre and the West End. Unless there is some palpable alteration in our patterns of thought (as well as evidence of our capacity to empathise), the social efficacy of art cannot really be claimed, much less proved. A 'utile' art must subordinate the effects of identification to a more consistent ratiocinative process.

In a book which could be taken as a cultural marker for this debate, *A clockwork orange* (1962), Anthony Burgess depicted a hooligan youth indulging in a spree of violence to a mental score composed by Beethoven. How could such violence and ugliness be accompanied by, even be engendered by, such beauty? What right had a novelist to yoke together, as effect and cause, violence and 'great music', a supposedly 'civilising' thing (for such is still the belief of most European education systems)? The effects of recent world history on the ways feeling can be structured (in and out of art) offers one possible answer to such questions. In this recent history, concentration camp commandants could organise holocausts while reserving some potential victims to play classical music for them. The 'best' brains (and not just those of science) could be complicit in the project of inventing, deploying and excusing weapons capable of hitherto unimaginable destructive power. How could 'educated', 'cultured' people do this? What price the civilising influence of art in such a conjuncture? What price the ritual genuflections towards élitist art forms of governments committed to policies of 'defence' which incorporate strategies of global destruction and pollution?

The easy answer to this paradox is that education and culture alone cannot prevent people acting in an uncivilised manner, but the more interesting and more complex argument is that both education and culture are complicit in the very processes of distributing power (and are now subordinated to the Persuasion People – even education being sent off to find sponsorship). They are more complicit in sustaining the *status quo* than notions of the 'neutrality' of education and culture would readily admit. Responses to 'art' are just one site of a surveillance which ultimately determines who shall and who shall not be entrusted with roles in the power élite. While at one level it may seem that only minor roles in the power structure are at issue here, they are all-important in the task of ensuring cohesion and continuance.

Say the 'right' things about plays, novels, poems and films and you will qualify for a place in that class fraction which is 'upwardly mobile' towards the professional managerial classes, and likely to wish to sustain the hegemony in its dominance. Of course, culture is a potential site for contestation as well as surveillance, but the present vogue for 'sponsorship' of the arts demonstrates just how much the Persuasion People have taken over. One of Thatcherism's not inconsiderable achievements has been its effective 'privatisation' of a culture which it has already helped to commodify to an almost-undreamed of point. In a recent RSC newsletter of summer 1988, for example, history, culture and food are all 'conceptually' packaged in the 'Henry Platter' obtainable from the RSC restaurant after one has seen the current productions comprising Shakespeare's *Henriad*. The 'Henry Platter', it will surprise no one to learn, is roast-beef-based.

Any piece of cultural production perceived as a challenge to those modes which can be safely 'ghettoised' as 'art' (culinary or otherwise) is normally castigated for precisely those reasons which elsewhere sustain the hegemony's real power. Thus the violence of a society whose representatives felt justified in de-stabilising the democratically-elected government of Salvador Allende in Chile in 1973 is as nothing compared to that society's reaction to violence in films. Stanley Kubrick's 1971 film of *A clockwork orange* concerned societies not vastly bothered by Burgess's book, one must note; but the film was blamed for much 'copycat' violence by individual criminals. Its director refused, and still refuses, to grant re-release or video rights on the film in the UK, so irked was he by the debate on 'screen sex and violence' that it engendered. The attempt to assert an equation between screen violence and people's behaviour in 'real life' can only be drawn when the pre-eminence of the 'choosing individual' in society is accepted as unproblematical, and screen/stage behaviours are constructed as 'naturally' comparable. Dramatic art on screen and stage promotes this view consistently, and in True Stories it does so through a concept of the 'real/true' which further buttresses a society's project to contain (or efface) anything 'difficult'.

Documentary Theatre (like Piscator's productions in the 1920s, like the Living Newspapers of the 1930s, and like *Oh what a lovely war*) also portrays what is manifestly 'real'. The difference is that Documentary Theatre does not necessarily portray the real realistically. I have taken issue already with the way commercial film and broadcast television drama promote a particular kind of realism, through an aesthetic which is ideological even when it claims not to be. Such drama, it was claimed, is *especially* ideological at those times it claims to be least so (that is, when it is just 'entertaining'). Any dramatic work which tries to confront issues without first passing them through that most important mechanism, characterisation, runs a risk of being immediately branded as 'unentertaining'.

It is as if our full engagement with a dramatic work is deemed impossible until and unless our understanding and our capacity for feeling are united through identification with a 'performance other'. This is not necessarily the process of alterity it appears to be on the surface, it can also be one more refinement of egoism, for in order to identify at all, our sense of self is being flattered and inflated – comp-li-mented rather than comp-le-mented. The stage or film 'other' is not only 'ourselves writ large', so to speak, s/he is often a glamorised, wish-fulfilled self – 'ourselves as we would like to be'. For this reason 'film stars' of both sexes do not tend to deviate from fashionable concepts of what is 'good looking' and 'attractive'.

In its way, an emphasis on alterity is a manifestly good thing, encouraging as it does the recognition of what George Eliot would have called 'alternative centres of self'. Without such recognition, it is difficult to imagine a society working *at all*. But the emphasis has been distorted through an apotheosis of the individual in late twentieth-century capitalism which is, quite literally, unrealistic – our 'individualist materialism' just cannot seem to take the strain. The issues and events which ultimately determine our lives are fashioned at root by *masses*, not individuals. In society, *collectives* hold sway whatever may be said to the contrary by right-wing governments. The government of the day in the UK tacitly recognise this through their sustained attacks on civil liberties (evident during the 1984 Miners' Strike, represented by the infamous Section 28, and seen in 1988 in the punitive action against Trade Unionists at Cheltenham GCHQ). These attacks come from a government preaching the autonomy of the individual, its Prime Minister the high priestess of an individualism freed from the interference of the State. And yet legislation like Clause 28, taken on behalf of a collective of about 40-45% of the nation, underlines the fact that some individuals are more equal than others – especially if they belong to the collective of the powerful.

Whenever dramatic art depicts the moral fragmentation which results from this 'devil-take-the-hindmost' philosophy, whenever Thatcherite 'individual responsibility' is shown for the double-speak it is, it gets blamed in a kind of judgemental Catch-22. Hence the little-publicised (but sustained) attacks which have been made on 'Alternative' theatre, via the cutting-off of resources from groups opposed to the right-wing politics of the Conservative Government. This has taken from the cultural scene groups like 7:84 (both the English and Scottish companies) and

Foco Novo. The Persuasion People are undoubtedly good at selling, but ultimately they are only interested in one market – the largest and blandest available. Even a play quite mildly critical of Thatcher – David Hare's 1988 *The secret rapture* – could not attract sponsorship at that flagship of the tourist industry the National Theatre.

It must be said that the situation in that part of the English-speaking world even more geared up to exploit 'economic opportunities' is far worse. In the USA the likelihood of the sustained exploration of issues and events through radical theatrical practice is even less likely now. Donald Freed's career has already been taken as a benchmark – how much more regrettable is the disappearance of the highly-talented Paul Foster, the La Mama dramatist who really was exploring the interface between Brechtian and Artaudian ideas in the late 1960s.[25]

The world of film production, dominated by American finance and influence, is most indicative of what happens when money calls the tune: sooner or later the genuinely provocative is sacrificed for the simply saleable. In 1969 Richard Attenborough made a film version of *Oh what a lovely war*; it was a worthy, even conscientious, attempt to transpose Theatre Workshop's play onto the screen. The film was a 'star vehicle' (how else would Attenborough have got his finance?), so the upper echelons of the British theatrical profession were wheeled out (Olivier as French, Mills as Haig). A prettified Brighton Pier was the major location; the Christmas Truce scene was in 'real' trenches with synthetic snow and 'real action' replaced actuality slides. It is possible to watch the film and hardly be aware of the statistics so much foregrounded by the stage show. For the US market, a major moment in which the 'Yanks Arrive' was grafted on a stage script in which the USA was hardly mentioned (apart from an Act Two statistic – '21,000 Americans Became Millionaires During War').

The film could never hope to reproduce the absent-present/present-absent dimension of theatrical collision montage in the Piscatorian tradition, but it could have sought a filmic alternative. Film's undoubted capacity for dialectical collisions could not be achieved by 'copying' a theatrical methodology alone. As John McGrath has commented, 'If you want to see how to make a disgusting mess of the same material, go and see Richard Attenborough's film . . . See what some truly bourgeois confusion, and a great deal of American money, can do to destroy something strong and valuable' (p.48). For anyone who saw the Theatre Workshop original, Attenborough's film is a cautionary reminder of how the hegemony's recuperative power can operate where 'production values' replace political commitment.

Re-producing realism
– tales of cultural tourism

. . . through a car window everything you see is just more TV. You're a passive observer and it is all moving by you boringly in a frame. On a [motor]cycle the frame is gone. You're completely in contact with it all . . . the whole thing, the whole experience, is never removed from immediate consciousness. (Robert Pirsig)[1]

Introduction – looking in and looking on

When she recommended the eating of cake as a substitute for bread, Marie Antoinette was not, it is now thought, displaying an aristocrat's natural contempt for the class at the bottom of the social heap; to imagine she was says far more about the twentieth century than about Revolutionary France. She was, in fact, so totally without an operational concept of what it might be like to live and work in grinding, Third World-style poverty that she genuinely could not conceive of a life where there was nothing *whatever* to eat. If there was no bread in the households of her poor French subjects, then surely they could have cake instead? That's what *she* would have done in their situation. Hers was the innocent, inevitably off-centre reaction of a committed cultural tourist, who *thought* she understood but (disastrously) didn't. This woman (who regularly played shepherdesses in an idyllic, custom-built, rural 'village' at the corner of her Versailles estate) had no effective knowledge of how *real* villagers lived – just outside her palace walls.

Marie Antionette's celebrated piece of cultural aphasia should be cautionary for those engaged in the reproduction of 'realism', for that is what Louis XVI's wife *thought* she was doing in her Versailles 'village'. Since its inception, the documentary has displayed a liberal social conscience, and has assumed the cultural responsibility of both finding out about and showing 'social reality'. It has mediated messages about poverty in particular, in both the developed and the underdeveloped worlds. Documentaries have been telling us pretty consistently over nearly sixty years that some people in our world are (literally and meta-phorically) without bread. From Arthur Elton and Edgar Anstey's film *Housing problems* (made for the Gas Council in 1935), through to *Cathy come home* in 1966, portraying the living conditions of the poor (who are, of course, always with us) has been a legitimate aim of socially-concerned film, and play, makers.

None of them has been stupid enough to counsel the eating of cake, but the consistent marketability of the 'social problem' says something about the 'taste' for such things which manifestly exists. The danger is that audiences consume social problems as individuals, and by so doing displace the collective will to alter conditions. As with Marie Antoinette, what the individual human being can *do* with increased knowledge is partly contingent upon what that human being's social location has prepared them for. After all, she now knew that the poor had no bread, it was just that her answer to the problem was inadequate. Similarly, cultural producers may inadvertently confirm our lack of understanding while increasing our knowledge.

The compensatory social project in film was mainly approached pre-war via a recording tradition of documentary, in which cultural production has done its job simply by *showing*. In drama-based True Stories, especially on post-war television, the staple technique for this socially-committed work has been social realism, linked to a docu-mentary discourse of factuality. This is being termed 'cultural tourist' – 'tourist' because problems must inevitably be perceived at a distance, whatever immediacy is claimed by such mediations. The dangers inher-ent in that distance are grave ones; the very immediacy-claim masks a distance which (potentially) distorts. Paradoxically, the recording tradi-tion both tells us about issues and, as it were, un-tells us. While the discourse of factuality is helping to legitimate the fiction, issues are draining away into an exaggerated 'human interest' which is (ultimately) unproductive. It is as if, like Robert Pirsig's car drivers, the 'reality' seen is being re-shaped even as it is seen. The window through which it is presented is distorting, not transparent; it grants an illusory access.

This was the case with *Cathy come home*, the Ken Loach/Jeremy Sandford tele-film of 1966, a piece of cultural production which has been much celebrated as typical of the 'crusading' artwork. The argument that televi-sion fulfills a social role has often been pressed by appealing to such examples as this; as Edward Lucie-Smith once remarked, 'If you want to defend the medium to its detractors, mention *Cathy come home*'.[2] Loach (with Tony Garnett as his producer on many projects, and writers like

Sandford, David Mercer and Jim Allen) has an excellent track record of 'socially-committed' work, all of which links a social realistic acting style with the filmic discourse of factuality (location rather than studio filming, hand-held cameras, voice over narration, on screen statistical information). Besides *Cathy*, the Loach/Garnett team have produced other teleplays (like the 1975 *Days of hope* – a review of the history of the British labour movement), and films (like the 1971 *Family life* – about the treatment of mental illness). Loach and Garnett's work fully justifies the label 'committed'. It is not my purpose to 'trash' such work, but I do want to suggest that there are unintended implications to 'looking on' through 'looking in'.

The cultural tourist

'The cultural producer is keenly interested in the proliferation of wants which will lead consumers to seek out the commodities sold to satisfy those wants,' (Terry Lovell).[3] When we are tourists (in the commonest use of the word), we go on 'holiday' to new places, sometimes far-off and exotic. Once there, we may actually 'work' quite hard, looking at the sights, checking off particularly famous corners of foreign cities in our itineraries, making sure that we have that all-important photograph of the view of/from a famous landmark or surviving emblem of historical significance. We may be overtly 'cultural' as we trek round the Uffizi or the Louvre, we may be 'historical' as we look over the Pyramids or the Acropolis, or we may be happy to deep-fry in sun-oil on 'paradise beaches'. What we are really doing of course, whether we are sun or sight worshippers, is *consuming* a very heavily marketed product, the benefits of which are much mythologised. It behoves us to consider this carefully, on the simple basis of suspicion (if someone's making a lot of money, isn't someone else being exploited somewhere along the line?).

The First World is well-attuned to the commercial activity of tourism, and perfectly capable of ripping-off fully as much as it is ripped-off. Who, exactly, is exploiting whom in the Greek *taverna* on Rhodes or Corfu (intertextual with the film *Zorba the Greek*)? It is difficult to say, but quite likely that both tourists and 'ethnic entertainment' understand each other. But Third World countries are different. Indigenous populations on Caribbean islands (those archetypal 'tropical paradises') used to object quite strongly to being photographed by American and European tourists; they believed that part of their *soul* was being stolen in this act of appropriating their faces. The tourists laughed at the patent absurdity of this; they coaxed and cajoled, sometimes they even parted with money in their attempts to get these reluctant subjects into frame. Eventually, in most places, they have got their way, and market traders who trudge in from out-lying parishes to set out the literal fruits of their labours now smile obediently for the importunate lenses of the tourists.

But the previous, apparently primitive, reaction of the islanders had a point: photographs have a subject in more senses than one. The act of tourist photography converts indigenous *subjects* into consumed *objects*, objects to be possessed (at one remove, it is true, but possessed in important ways). The resultant objects are passed into a kind of currency back in the camera owners' home countries, where they become indicators of economic power, or sophistication, or of well-travelled knowledge of foreign lands, or of all these things in conversations and slide-viewing sessions. If the Grand Tour was an index of nineteenth-century sophistication, foreign travel is just as important now. Tourism is an expression particularly of American and Japanese economic supremacy. The Heritage industry in the UK has recognised this very clearly; in the absence of competitive manufacturing industry, the Brits fall back on that which cannot be taken away from them – the past (or carefully selected versions of it). This is a commodity which sells particularly well to a nation, the USA, rather troubled by its relative lack of a past, and ever-eager to find it in Europe. The present UK government is even now seeking to hi-jack secondary school history syllabuses for precisely this Heritage purpose.

But there is a wider 'cultural tourism' which takes consumers on a 'trip' across the borders of *experience* (for the purpose of saying, 'We've been there!'). Media tourists consume issues as if they were the sights of tourist itineraries. In the wake of the urban riots of July 1981 (according to one apocryphal story), a social worker in Camden was suddenly contacted to provide a guided coach tour of poor districts of north London for the mixture of 'professionals' who tended to form the 'task forces' set up to advise the government. Although these people lived and worked in London, they stared with a mixture of horror and amazement at the conditions they needed a coach tour to learn about. Marie Antionette is alive and well, and living in certain well-heeled areas of London? Some True Stories can be seen as coach tours for the privileged.

Cultural tourists, then, visit unfamiliar territory over which they hold economic power, and they go for specified periods in order to consume 'ways of life' different from their own. Having done this, they can collect information, they can claim knowledge, they can make authoritative pronouncements about this territory. As with 'real' tourists (who often claim to 'know' foreign countries on the basis of short acquaintance), cultural tourists may well gain a particular experience which is of use and value; the problem is that they will often believe that this is all that is necessary. The necessity of setting 'experience' into an over-arching social and political context for observer and observed will not always be recognised. If knowledge and information has to be inferred from dramatic True Stories in a social realistic mode, the claim for second order experience (through the empathy of 'involvement' with 'characters' portrayed on the screen or stage) seems even stronger.

Cultural production of the tourist kind is so widespread that a full list of examples would soon become tedious. Almost every issue, every 'problem', has been mediated through a True Story. Nuclear power and its dangers? See Mike Nichols's *Silkwood* (1983). Human rights in fascist dictatorships? There's Costa-Gavras's *Missing* (1982). In post-colonial situations? There's the Biko case and *Cry freedom*. Apartheid? That has been a particularly 'hot' issue in the 1980s. The horror of war? Such films are legion (pun intended). On UK television, the output of material dealing with Eastern European opposition to the USSR (and especially with the Polish trade union Solidarity) has been quite remarkable – a list would include *Three days in Szczecin* – ITV, 1976; *Invasion* – ITV, 1980; *Two weeks in winter* – BBC, 1982; and Tom Stoppard's *Squaring the circle* – ITV, 1984.

Of course, addressing such subjects as these is rightly taken as an index of the continuing 'conscience' of the artistic enterprise. Without such efforts society would be considerably diminished (if nothing else, they provide some insurance for the artist against charges of fiddling elegantly while the world explodes). But they are also potential salves to the conscience of the consumer, who can show by evincing a taste for such things that s/he is not solely interested in bread-and-circuses. Real tourists can (and do) justify themselves on the basis of the foreign exchange they bring to other countries, and on the increased understanding they achieve and bring back with them. Cultural tourists frequently believe that their increased 'understanding' is likely to contribute towards ameliorating problems. The more this way is specified, of course, the likelier this is to be true, but in most cases it remains at the level of unspecified (therefore vague) 'consciousness-raising'.

What is being marketed and consumed is an *attitude* of concern, a quasi-religious moral feeling partially-assuaged at the point of production, which relies on the religion of fact to which I drew attention in Chapter 2. In many cases, cultural production may contribute as much to keeping a 'problem' in place as it does towards shifting it. The crucial question is: what happens *after* a social problem has been elevated on to the arena of public debate? In the absence of real political will, shaped by collectivity rather than the 'choosing individual', all the individual tourist can do is withdraw his/her support. Individually, you can only decline to holiday in Sun City, but you won't abolish it on your own – to do that, it is necessary to join an organised collective, which will take *action*.

The major interest for the student of cultural production is the means by which (and the means through which) mediation of problematical issues takes place. Like the Caribbean islander, many 'subjects' are in danger of further impoverishment through the appropriations of institutionalised cultural production. This is especially true of that most consensual of mediums, television. True Stories are a *necessary*, but never *sufficient*, index of commitment in art.

'Cathy come home'

'When *Cathy* was written there was little information available in print. Now there is a lot. And there seems no end to Britain's housing crisis,' (Jeremy Sandford).[4] The individualising of issues through social realistic techniques has a tendency to scratch the cultural itch rather than treat the social inflammation, *displacing* rather than focusing issues and encouraging the tendency to 'taste' issues touristically. The example of *Cathy come home* has often been used to demonstrate how a piece of cultural production can have *direct* influence on the events of which it treats. The first screening of *Cathy* in 1966 led, we are sometimes told, to the formation of the organisation Shelter (dedicated to helping the poor with housing problems). Jeremy Sandford noted with pride that, 'It is good to know that I have altered, if only by a very small bit, the conditions of life for others in my own society' (p.14). But within a few years he was saying the pessimistic opposite, as can be seen from the quotation at the beginning of this paragraph.

It is as well to be cautious in attributing any social change directly to a dramatic work; Shelter itself, as its founder Des Wilson has subsequently observed, would have been formed with or without *Cathy*. The tele-play undoubtedly contributed to a climate of opinion; in that sense it *did no harm*, and may well have done some good, but it was not *instrumental*. Stoke's local documentary *Fight for Shelton Bar* is sometimes held up as an

Did GITM produce support?

example of what campaigning theatre can achieve, but Peter Cheeseman is the first to acknowledge that it was the organised *efforts of the workers* which saved the local steel works (for a pitifully short time, as it turned out). As has been remarked before, dramatic art can uniquely re-flect and in-flect, but real change is an altogether larger matter. Theatre, film, TV and radio can make a *contribution* towards change, but only where a climate for change already exists. Why commentators on cultural production should want to claim more than this is revealing of them in particular, and of society in general.

If *Cathy* is approached initially through formal analysis, it is clear even from the published screenplay that what John Fiske and John Hartley call 'overlap in code networks'[5] is a feature of the piece. There are frequent occasions when a discourse more usually associated with other (non-dramatic) kinds of programme is used to frame straight-forwardly 'dramatic' action. For example, about a quarter of the way through, a montage section described as 'general shots of life in the area' (in which Cathy and her husband Reg live) is accompanied by Cathy's reflective voice saying:

I fell for it, all the parts round here, these streets, they looked rough, and there was rats but life was quite good here. Some of the places was boarded up, with the upstairs windows empty, others was stuffed, crammed full with people and kiddies. Once I heard sounds coming out from one of the boarded up houses, sounds of a baby crying. (p.53)

The 'general shots' of working-class streets and houses have both a *diachronic* function (following, through time, Reg and Cathy's downward spiral in the housing market, which leads eventually to the pitiless 'Part III Accommodation'), and a *synchronic* function (as ironic, and simultaneous, counterpoint to Cathy's hopeful monologue). This fragment is part of an extended 'voice-over' and shot-montage sequence, following an extended meditation by Cathy on the significance of 'love' and 'nice surroundings' for a child. The voice-over commentary is more 'commonly associated with news and documentary programmes'; in *Cathy*, it 'is used to bring with it a sense of reality' (Fiske and Hartley, p.64).

As well as being 'straight' information, Cathy's words are also 'artful': they have been composed to reflect the speech patterns of a representative working-class girl. The writer attempts the kind of *replication* which will convince at the level of factuality. Crucially, the sequence is presented as if it were part of a documentary. Carol White, the Cathy actress, used her technique as a performer to bolster this illusion. The concern is not whether working-class girls really speak like this, but whether this speech-pattern will induce the audience to *believe*. If it does, it inevitably supports the programme's 'truth claim' by reinforcing the apparent-reality. True Stories routinely alter facts if it is thought 'necessary' to the truth-claim to do so, but any challenge to the citadel of believable behaviours is to be avoided.

In his personal memoir *Asking for trouble*, Donald Woods gives details of four 'real' occurrences which were not included in Attenborough's film *Cry freedom*; all were excluded because the film-makers feared they would not be *believed*: 'Sir Richard Attenborough explained that translating true stories into film involved not only the transmitting of true facts to the screen but facts that, no matter how true, would not *strain the credulity of the audience*,' (pp.8-9 – my emphasis). The four incidents included one where the fugitive Woods, waiting tensely for his passport to be stamped at the South Africa/Botswana border, has to wait while the official takes a phone call. Although Woods fears it might be the Security Police, it turns out to be the man's wife on the line with instructions about the household shopping! This would be 'too much for cinema audiences to accept', thought Attenborough and screenplay writer John Briley. Woods concurred completely with this editorial decision because 'anything which detracted from the credibility of the real story would be counter-productive, and because . . . much of the power of the film derived from the fact that it tells a true story' (p.10).

It is instructive to observe which parts of stories are deemed truer than others. Attenborough's decision (at a professional level an entirely competent and understandable one) relates entirely to the fictional discourse, social realism, within which he and his film were trapped. His problem was not truth or otherwise, but that intertextuality which is part of every sophisticated viewer's baggage – it is this which makes the 'true' incident in question potentially 'false'. Anti-climactic phone calls at crucial moments in a realist plot are a too-good-to-be-true cliché because they seem to happen in every other film you see (though it's difficult when put on the spot to think of an actual example).

Sandford's first attempt at the 'subject' which was to become *Cathy come home* was a radio documentary called *Homeless families*, composed largely of montaged verbatim interview material. In *Cathy come home*, this provenance is evident not just in Cathy's own 'shaped' voice-overs, but also in the use of radio-style 'wildtrack' voices on soundtrack, in which some of Sandford's original material was used. It is difficult to show any of this on the printed page; in a credits page note, Sandford says that he has added 'some of the voices that were heard on wildtrack in the course of the film'. A good deal of this wildtrack 'consisted of the words of real people living in the various locations we shot' (p.15). Reaction to the radio documentary was 'virtually nil', Sandford tells us. But such 'truth' as *background*, that was a different matter – the documentary reality in the (successful) film provides an authenticating device for the drama. Carol White's performance as Cathy, location filming, the use of the soundtrack, the 'real people' extras, shot composition and montage, everything in the project overlaps with a discourse of factuality deriving from the documentary.

Camera shots replicated newsreel camera techniques; in an interview, Sandford commented: 'The newsreel cameraman who may have to run to get his effects brings a vividness to the screen that is often lacking in the overstylized and ossified techniques so often found in TV drama productions. Ken Loach wanted to get this actuality aliveness in and succeeded'.[6] The key words in this account are 'vividness' and 'aliveness': Sandford's understanding of the mediation of the issue of housing coheres around a concept of the observable 'real'. Just as bourgeois historians of the nineteenth century believed in E.H. Carr's 'Ark of the Covenant in the temple of facts', so twentieth-century cultural producers tend 'to pin their faith on actuality film' (McArthur, p.28). Documentary devices generate *belief*, as do the writing and acting techniques of social realism (or such is the almost universal understanding).

But this capacity to inspire belief, which constitutes one of social realist documentary drama's main 'truth-claims', exists in a very narrow theoretical band. Social realist drama's *rapprochement* with the recording documentary is relatively unproblematical; neither actors' realistic behaviours nor documentary's claim to reproduce reality are directly confronted (provided the film is competently done). There is intertextuality between the two codes, but never a clash – they are never 'competing discourses'. There is a mutual complementing which finally effaces difference. 'Realistic' acting and 'realistic' filming never call attention to themselves; they are elided, for all the world as if the one really were the other. At all costs audience 'credibility', once won, must never be challenged or 'strained'.[7] This was the formal problem Attenborough had with the deleted 'larger than life' elements of Donald Woods's escape. Besides the phone call, there was a border searchlight scene, like something out of a World War Two escape movie (Woods makes the comparison himself on p.348 of his account), there was a (new) car which inexplicably broke down, it was all much too good to be true. Like good tourists, movie audiences like to see new things (or, at the very least, old things in new packaging).

Sandford calls attention to Ken Loach's skill in doing the job of effacing difference; Loach has, he says, 'a wonderful gift for simplification', and the effect of his suggestions for change at early script meetings was 'to give the story a more simplified or classical shape' (Sandford, p.13). Sandford seems to mean here that Loach knew 'shorthand' ways of conveying the fictional narrative, and driving it along quicker. In the opening sequence of the film, for example, Loach simplified very specifically. In Sandford's original script this section, about Cathy's arrival in London, was much longer, but Loach got it down to a slick linkage montage sequence in which Cathy is given a lift by a lorry driver, while in voice-over she looks back, older and wiser: 'I was mad in a way in those days . . . suppose you could say I was bored, wanted a bit of adventure . . . some adventure,' (pp.23-4). The contrast is between a 'then-Cathy' (stage direction: 'freed at last from ties to her family, heart-whole, at the age of consent, but unconsenting as yet, exultant yet shy' – p.21) and a 'now-Cathy' ('I was mad . . . in those days . . . '). We see a pretty, care-less Cathy obviously being fancied by the lorry driver, we hear the voice of a care-full Cathy. The meaning we are intended to construct is that, during the following hour or so, we will find out how the one grew into the other. This is the narrative dynamic of a piece of film fiction, which establishes very quickly the simple fact that Cathy has left home. In the original script, Sandford wanted to explore the leaving, but Loach understood, perhaps more clearly than the writer, that the film was to be about the housing trap, and not about why young people run away to London. Time spent giving an account of the latter would mean time lost dealing with the more important former. So he has composed what Sandford rightly calls a 'classical' series of opening shots.

If we compare this filmic opening with the first page of a naturalistic play like Ibsen's A doll's house, we can see in both how the need for 'believable' exposition is met by the smooth deployment of a series of conventions deliberately intended to facilitate the flow of the narrative. In A doll's house, we read class location and economic circumstance off the setting, time of day from the lighting, and time of year from the properties even before any character has had to speak.[8] In Cathy come home, a similar range of signifiers helps us to 'read' the montage sequence and its accompanying voice-over; the sequence is unproblematical precisely because it is 'classical' – it is like any number of other realistic films on television or in the cinema.

The coding of this 'shorthand' has some drawbacks, notably the 'Sixties-sexist' portrayal of Cathy. Why does she have to be 'young, pretty, and with an air of excitement about her' (p.21)? Sandford himself seems to feel vulnerable about this, because he is constrained to say in his Introduction: 'People often tell me that Cathy was too attractive – a girl as attractive as that could never have become homeless. This is nonsense. I would say that, on average, the girls I've met in Part III Accommodation were more attractive than those outside, although I couldn't say why' (p. 13). This misses the point and is itself somewhat sexist in its chivalrous championship of an 'attractivenes' which is always only culturally relative, and expressive of male-dominance.

The point at issue is why a group of film-makers should feel it necessary to portray an attractive Cathy in the first place, and by so doing actively reject the possibility of telling the story of a notionally 'unattractive' Cathy. The answer must surely be that, like the lorry driver in the opening sequence, the male section of the audience must be attracted to Cathy through desire (a common fate for the female at the centre of play and film narratives, and reflective of dominant patriarchal and heterosexist cultural assumptions). Sandford indirectly acknowledges this aspect in his courtly defence of the Part III Accommodation female, a defence which partly commodifies her.

Cathy must now be read as a kind of 'Sixties Icon'. It is surely no accident that a Cathy-inflected pop song (the Beatles' 'She's Leaving Home') followed the film in 1967. Now much anthologised in school poetry books, this song just about holds together a 'sad girl/happy girl' opposition via the mix of sweet (McCartney's voice) and sour (Lennon's). What gives it away is its quasi-classical musical arrangement. Like 'She's Leaving Home', Cathy come home has become both a cultural and historical 'monument'. Both tele-film and pop song, with their versions of social conscience, have permeated the collective unconscious. In the 1980s, school children wrestle with the split-narration of 'She's Leaving Home' in 'English' lessons, and a 1988 tele-play The diary of Rita Patel is seen as a 1980s Cathy come home.[9] Rita Patel told a 'based on fact' story about an Asian family suffering urban racial harrassment. In spite of the invocation of Cathy (intended as glowing praise), Rita Patel did not gain anything like the attention in the 1980s which Cathy achieved in the 1960s, and one is forced to conclude that Rita's brown skin may have had more than something to do with this. Because a white audience is still the dominant one, cultural production is still limited in the way it feels able to address racial issues.

Keeping the lid on

'The effect of *The war game* has been judged by the BBC to be too horrifying for the medium of broadcasting,' (BBC Statement, 1965).[10] *Cathy come home* was not the only television True Story to become something about which it was necessary to have an opinion in the 1960s (even if one hadn't seen it). Peter Watkins's 1965 *The war game* was even more interesting because, at least in the first instance, very few people were able to see it *at all*. Made in 1965 and finally seen on television in 1985, *The war game* has been a *cause célèbre* for over twenty years. Its longevity as a site of controversy and conflict makes it highly suitable as a representative of those True Stories which have periodically disturbed cultural production and exposed contradictions within society. Lesser known examples might include A.E.Harding's *New Year over Europe*, and Theatre Workshop's *Last edition* (a 1940 Living Newspaper which caused Joan Littlewood and Ewan MacColl to be arrested and 'bound over' because of the play's 'unpatriotic' attitude to events leading up to the declaration of war). Better known television examples include Antony Thomas's 1980 *Death of a princess*, which so offended Saudi Arabia (with its reconstruction of an Islamic execution of an Arab princess and her lover for adultery) that a British Foreign Minister – Lord Carrington – even apologised to the Saudis about it.

The war game challenged the post-war establishment orthodoxy of nuclear deterrence for the first time, and it continued to be an embarrassment for a considerable period (unlike *Death of a princess*, which was controversial for a few months). Controversy of any kind foregrounds a particular cultural *dilemma* (or series of dilemmas); the nuclear deterrence dilemma has been both difficult to resolve and impossible to ignore. Societies will always have problems which are difficult to resolve, of course; the difference with controversial issues is that the unhappiness which exists as a result of particular problems creates a certain *turbulence* in society as a whole. It is this turbulence which ensures that problems have the high profile of controversy, and in turn ensures that they cannot be ignored totally. While some problems can be conveniently assigned to the margins on a permanent basis, others won't, as it were, go away. One site at which controversial problems tend to re-emerge is cultural production.

The policy of nuclear deterrence has never been easy to 'sell' to civil populations, and a 'dialogue' concerning its morality and its viability has been going on ever since it was first promulgated. A myth of deterrence has been one of the main planks in power-wielding nations' 'defence' and foreign policies ever since the onset of the Cold War in 1947. There has been an on-going establishment interest in sustaining the case for deterrence, but there has also been an accompanying minority opposition to those policies, which in the UK has been manifested notably by the Campaign for Nuclear Disarmament, formed in 1958. *The war game* can be seen as a product of that oppositional movement (as, indeed, can *Oh what a lovely war*). The fact that the BBC, the institutional guardian of a hegemonically-constructed 'consensus' in the important field of broadcasting, could not countenance the transmission of the film in the 1960s tells us much about establishment fears concerning the level of civil acceptance of nuclear deterrence. This is often the fate of 'sensitive' subject matter; you only know how sensitive it is when it gets suppressed.

The irony about *The war game* was, of course, that it was not entirely suppressed: the initial furore was followed by institutional realisation that withdrawal from the schedules was provoking too much attention (indeed, it all looked a little like censorship). This caused the BBC to allow a film made with their money, but rejected by them, to be shown to a hand-picked audience, on a restricted cinema circuit composed mainly of 'art' cinema clubs and university film societies. The patriarchal presumption of the large-scale institution is revealed through such an action. *The war game* was, as it were, 'licensed' to be shown to those to whom it was thought it could do no harm – both the means of production and also the point of consumption were manipulated. The selected target audience was composed mainly of those already educated, or in the process of being educated, into the very social group empowered to make future censoring decisions. There was probably no need even to formulate such a policy of licensed transmission; it emerged as a 'commonsense' solution to a thorny problem, a 'reasonable compromise' in a tricky situation. It was, in other words, an *ideological* decision.

The cosy circularity of all this reveals that the 'harm' feared was in fact to the system and not to the individual. Undeclared fears about the damage *The war game* might do to the policy of nuclear deterrence (in terms of its attack on the credibility of that policy) were neatly diverted into declared fears about individual sensibilities, and thereby displaced. At the 'protection of individuals' level, it was relatively easy to excuse the act of censorship. The extent of a hegemony's ability to introduce Catch-22 logic whenever push-comes-to-shove is remarkable; this logic allowed you to watch *The war game* provided you believed its case already, otherwise it was deemed 'too horrifying'. Like Dickens's Mr Podsnap, cultural watch-dogs at places like the BBC are vigilant in excluding from mass transmission anything 'calculated to call a blush into the cheek of a young person', but (again like Mr Podsnap) they reserve the right to be the final arbiter on all 'blush-factors'. A large part of Peter Watkins's original aims and objectives in making the film were nullified at the crucial point of consumption of his film, which was intended as *informational* – it was meant to lighten citizens' darkness. As ever, domination of the means of production (the BBC's ownership of his film through economic controls) provided ready tools of censorship which are more dangerous because masked.

Neither is it just the UK establishment which is prone to such dealings. France was unable to cope with Marcel Orphuls's *The sorrow and the pity* in 1969. Orpuls's film was different from *The war game* in that it was a 'documentary proper', with 'straight' interview material. It effectively deconstructed the French myth of the Nazi occupation (in which no one collaborated, everyone was a Resistance freedom fighter), declaring the hitherto occluded facts not only of a more widespread collaboration, but also of in-fighting between different resistance groups. Also made for television, this film too had to be shown first in cinemas, and it too generated terrific interest (especially amongst the student audience). Like *The war game*, it promised to force an unpleasant subject into a very public forum. In the UK in 1965 and in France in 1969 establishment answers to the problems posed were the same. The policies of minimum visibility followed in France and the UK are a triumph of institutional craftiness, limiting damage while sidestepping the accusation of overt censorship. Whenever such things occur, it is vital to press the institutions concerned, both at the individual and the collective levels.

Another sixties icon?

'It's with the proliferation from the late 60s of Dramatised documentaries . . . that the debate about categories and credibility really begins to bite,' (Leslie Woodhead).[11] The eventual transmission of *The war game* in 1985 does not mark the institution's coming to its senses so much as the release of the policy of nuclear deterrence from the 'protected category'. It was not, after all, as if there had not been periodic attempts to shift the film off the proscribed list during the intervening twenty years before it was at last released to a mass audience. The final decision was contingent upon shifts in global politics (which can be seen most plainly in the

Reagan/Gorbachev accords of the late 1980s). To put it bluntly, the film was no longer such an embarrassment; its transmission no longer mattered so much to the power-élite.

The pre-1985 effectiveness of The war game should not be discounted, however. According to the broadcaster Ludovic Kennedy, introducing the film on television in 1985, an estimated six million viewers worldwide had already seen the film. But this cannot make up for the fact that we will never know what its impact might have been, had it been viewed by a mass (and partially-uncommitted) TV audience in 1965. This fact was made that much more poignant by the evident 'Sixties-ness' of the film when compared to its modern equivalents Threads and The day after. The war game is another icon of the 1960s, that decade now become so much the territory of the cultural tourist (after all, so much was going on then!). It is one of a trio of British documentary dramas made in the middle of the 1960s which constituted the (then) boundaries of the admissible and the inadmissible in terms of both form and content. Culloden (a Watkins' film of 1964) and Cathy come home were admissible, The war game was not.

Culloden demonstrated that formal properties alone do not matter in the last analysis; it is the attempt to force particular issues on to the public agenda which is crucial. The filmic techniques used in Culloden are similar to those used in The war game, the real difference between the films lies in the comfortable remoteness of the historical period of the former, and the altogether-too-close proximity of the issues and events portrayed in the latter. Slaughter of Scottish innocents of two hundred years ago, however realistically portrayed, can be easily coped with; the simulated incineration of modern citizenry was deemed more likely to be threatening to the Young Person, and the broadcasting Podsnaps acted quickly.

Both Culloden and The war game were different from Cathy in their concentration on issues and events; they were less individualised pieces of cultural production. Their classic structure was intertextual more with documentary film-making, less with social realistic play-making. They made heavier use of the authoritative (as against the character) voice-over, and greater use of the 'purely' informational insert (of statistics, maps, graphs, etc.) – all evidence of a documentary provenance. Voice-over provided a continuous editorial gloss on visuals which were primarily illustrative and informational, as they tend to be in the documentary proper. The camera-style imitated that of the actuality-documentary; it was, as it were, 1960s state-of-the-art. There was a good deal of that shaky, hand-held camera-work which is typical of 'crisis' reports on TV news, and which was to become such a 'real' feature of US television coverage of the Vietnam War in the late 1960s. There was a consistent documentary correspondence between the commentary and the filmed subject, with periodic jump-cut shifts being sutured by the editorial voice.

To take an example: one of *The war game*'s first visual subjects is a worried-looking black woman on a bus. Unlike the opening of *Cathy*, the sequence in which she features is not *dramatic narrative*; there is no dialogue, no character voice-over, no point-of-view shots. *Cathy* is the filmed equivalent of 'Fourth Wall' theatre naturalism, with the audience unacknowledged; but the black woman in *The war game* looks directly at the camera. The omniscient commentary's indexical utterance accompanying this image runs, 'This woman has had to leave her husband.' We are encouraged to 'read' the sequence in the context of an earlier factual statement (which revealed that men over 18 will not be evacuated in time of nuclear war).[12]

The black woman is, in other words, not an actress engaged in the job of characterising, but a documentary 'specimen', designed to illustrate through representing. Because she is documentary object (and not *Cathy*-style 'character' subject) she can look at the camera without disrupting any 'illusion'; there is similarly no need for her to speak, she simply has to *signify* in ways determined by the editorial voice (hence the mournful look). We then see her descend from the bus in what we are told is a 'strange town'. The camera cuts to her just once more, after a white woman (a resident in the 'strange town', because filmed standing at the threshold of 'her' house) has said that she hopes no 'coloureds' will be billeted with her. The word 'coloured' is itself an eloquent verbal icon of an earlier historical conjuncture, mobilised here to challenge the audience in one more way. The whole sequence centres *audience* rather than character.

The action which unfolds is similarly dominated by a commentary designed to inform and challenge those *outside* the action; this drives the film along, and provides its distinctive dynamic. Unlike *Cathy*, where voice-overs and their accompanying visuals tend to be reflective moments sealed off from the narrative, *The war game*'s voice-overs are not structural embellishments, they are integral to the structure of the piece – they give contextualising information, they shift the scene, they explain. The point of identification is generalised and constantly shifting. There are, it is true, various figures who feature more than the black woman does (a police inspector, for example), and occasionally these figures are personalised to the extent of a name. But the audience is not asked to empathise with specific characters, the distinctive focus is not on *an* individual but on *individuals*. This is because the film's project is to demonstrate the likely plight of a generalised 'people' in a nuclear war. People in general, and the audience by association, are involved in the deadly 'game' of the film's title. The key player in *The war game* is the *viewing*, not the 'acting', subject.

The temporal sequence of *The war game* is therefore not marked out by an individual consciousness, but by the progress of nuclear attack. This too reinforces the powerlessness of people, totally at the mercy of the bomb and its subsequent effects. The film does not show the governmental decisions which led to nuclear attack, increasing the sense of powerlessness further; people accustomed to constructing themselves as active agents are shown in the process of becoming the things (the dead things) that are the consequence of 'defence' policies allegedly framed in their interests. The inexorable advance of the attack is communicated by direct and indirect means (announcements from the voice-over commentary, and montaged 'radio announcements'). Visually, 'realistic' camera-work (like the evacuation sequence) is montaged with 'vox-pop' street interviews in which people from outside the drama say what they know about nuclear war, and with rolling captions giving information.

Because the whole project of the film is not only to simulate but also to prophesy, many of the commentary locutions are conditional – 'should x happen, y could/would follow'. After the evacuation sequence there is a freeze-frame of a man who has just been threatened with imprisonment if he continues to refuse to take his quota of evacuees; over the freeze-frame image, the commentator/narrator says, 'Should Britain ever thus attempt the evacuation of nearly 20% of her active population, such scenes as these would be almost inevitable.' The interaction between this conditional statement and the *cinéma vérité* camera technique has the effect of privileging probability over possibility. After all, we are seeing what purports to be a manifest 'reality', we are used to de-coding images such as these as tokens of reality in our 'readings' of the news and the documentary-proper. The documentary image may depend upon a 'constructed equivalence' between real subjects and film objects (Fiske and Hartley, p.48), but, for most viewers, the constructed equivalence of documentary involves the least problematical effort. Thus, although the words make a condition ('Should Britain . . . '), the images work with an apparent reality (which is 'convincing').

The conditional element in the commentary is made more of a

certainty by a quasi-academic 'footnoting' technique which, again, derives from the documentary. This culminates in a full list of sources given in a kind of visual bibliography at the end of the film. Precedents are continually cited in support of the credibility of the (fictional) visuals. A sequence following the air raid shows the burning of corpses, then the camera cuts to a line of bodies being covered with quicklime to prevent the spread of disease; the commentator says, 'Everything that you are now seeing happened in Germany after the heavy bombing in the last war.' Japanese precedent is offered later; apathetic survivors are depicted in abject misery, their morale non-existent. 'This happened,' the commentator admonishes us, 'at Hiroshima.' But, like the Living Newspapers before it, authentication alone could not save The war game.

TV's cultural centrality consists partly in its 'good fit' with the way individuals perceive reality. Especially important is its apparently-human field of vision; thus when we are told something could happen, and we then see it happening before our eyes, we are less aware of the experience as mediation, and the overall effect is potentially very powerful – and convincing. The hi-jacking of documentary 'truth-claim' techniques for advertisements (consider, for example, how the authoritative voice-over has been appropriated) has had the effect of nullifying some of the effects used in The war game somewhat, with the result that the 'truth-claim' has now to be mediated in other ways. The conventionality of The war game has only become fully apparent as its particular use of conventions approaches the level of cliché (ie. with the passage of time). In 1985, the Mick Jackson/Barry Hines Threads, covering similar ground to The war game, dispensed almost entirely with voice-over, preferring a tele-printer graphic to mediate basic information. In the early part of the film, the only voice-over (used during the opening credit sequence) gives an essentially poetic account of a society's interdependence; these are the 'threads' of the title. The accompanying visual is similarly 'poetic' – a spider spinning its intricate yet fragile web.

Direct looks at camera were permitted in The war game in a way which would not be possible in the discourse of 'fiction film' favoured by Threads and The day after. Looking at the camera, even more speaking to it, would unhinge the illusion in fiction film, much as direct address would disrupt the naturalistic stage play. The war game's use of interviews is interesting in this respect. Early in the film, street interviews appear to be 'genuine'; a team of interviewer and crew seem to have gone out on a roving commission to find out what the public know about nuclear warfare. A familiar range of 'truthful' responses result, the degree of self-consciousness before a camera (on the part of the filmed subject) being an index of their truth rather than their ineptitude (which it would signal if they were trying to 'act').

Initially, there appears to be two main uses of the interview in *The war game*, one 'straight-documentary' and the other 'dramatic'. 'Straight-documentary' interviews stop people in city streets and ask questions like, 'Do you know what Strontium 90 is and what it does?'. 'Dramatic' interviews interrupt the action with more open questions. So, as the camera follows a Civil Defence volunteer leafleting a street of terraced houses, the off-camera interviewer suddenly says, 'Excuse me, what are you doing here exactly?' The interviewee, acting startled, turns and replies. But the participants in 'drama' sequences are in fact the same people as those used in 'documentary' interviews. This is not to say that 'genuine' interviews were acted, of course, because *The war game* used a largely civilian, amateur cast (British Actors' Equity objected to this at the time the film was made). The point is that the 'cross-coding' which occurs in *The war game* reveals very clearly the 'normal' degree of accept-able conventionalising in television documentary modes. The whole thing can be faked very easily, and it is a mistake to suppose that this is an unproblematically bad thing.

Another interesting collision between the 'could/might' and the 'did/shall' constructions of the commentary occurs in the 'fire storm' sequence. Firemen (the genuine, Kent Fire Service article) are seen trying to cope with the fire storm which is the second consequence of the bomb (the first being the horrific blast). We are told of the high tem-peratures in the eye of the fire storm (800°C) which convert into hot winds. The camera records the men being flung about by the force of the wind which is also taking away their oxygen; it closes in on gas-masked figures so that we see their agonised expressions. 'These men,' we are told, 'are dying both of heat-stroke and of gassing.' The shift to a present tense in the commentary is revealing, marking the moment the film transgresses the 'boundary' between drama and documentary; if *The war game were* the pure actuality of news film, this is indeed the tense which would have to be used.

Such transgressions have become increasingly problematical for film-makers, partly because of the extent of the compromises forced on them. And yet, one should not blame cultural producers for not fighting battles which are the proper preserve of more overtly political action. As the journalist John Pilger recently observed, tinkering with the mechanisms of society in the 1960s 'made Britain *appear* less divisive . . .

which held great benefits for the ruling order, whose power it reinforced'.[13] One can gauge something of this power through the changes wrought in cultural production since the Swinging Sixties.

Never mind the documentary, what about the drama?

By the time television on both sides of the Atlantic felt itself able to tackle the nuclear question head on, much had changed. In *The war game*, captions are plentiful, and almost always *read out* by one of the two narrators used in the film; in *Threads*, however, a tele-type graphic is used simply as a time/scene shift mechanism, and an editorial voice is totally absent. The 'teacherly' *reading* of captions is an option which probably never even occurred to the makers of *Threads* or *The day after*; if asked, they might well have responded that this is one of the least acceptable documentary techniques at the present time, and to have captions rolling on at the length used in *The war game* would not be nearly punchy enough for the modern viewer. There is a characteristic pursuit of information in both films which is documentary in its thrust, but *Threads'* major technique is that of social realistic performance. Its True Story rubric is assembled from a taxonomy of *dramatic* rather than documentary skills. The film's naturalistic continuity was uncoupled to some extent by the concluding vision of a nuclear-winter dystopia. While this added a surreal element, however, the camera was still in the process of mediating the conventions of realism even in this post-nuclear world.

In *The day after* the sustaining illusion is, not just individual-, but star-centred. Jason Robards (a doctor in the film) was followed throughout as one of a number of firmly-established 'characters' with whom the audience could identify. It was almost as if, like Dr Kildare, he would be able to work things out given time. Robards's eventual end, asphyxiated in a nuclear bunker, disrupted the expectations of the 'normal' fiction film with its myth of the 'competent professional' – to this extent the 'facts' of nuclear war were acknowledged in *The day after*. That apart, the most significant offerings made by this very expensive piece of cultural production lay in images difficult to obtain without a large budget. For example, the British nuclear holocaust films would have been simply unable to provide such a spectacular sight as a sky full of Minutemen missiles, deadly toys released at last from their underground silos. *The day after*, with American money, was the only film of the three able to present this point-of-no-return – the moment of launch itself – as *spectacle*.

Even doctors, then, whose professional competence is itself a sustaining late-capitalist myth, are powerless in these nuclear scenarios, as are the 'Experts' who have for so long sustained this same hegemonic myth. The experts of The war game in 1965 talked confidently – directly to camera; establishing shots mediated scholarly faces, and sound tracks expert 'tones of voice'. Only after such actualising mediation did a caption concede the fictional nature of the sequence. Thus, a priest talked of the morality of nuclear warfare; the caption which eventually appeared read, 'Based on the recorded statements of an Anglican Bishop'. This technique was repeated for a psychiatrist and a military strategist. The latter was given an interesting background prop – a blackboard covered with arcane mathematical formulae and impenetrable verbal fragments suggestive of his expertise, and helping to establish the 'reality' of his testimony (which became more than just 'based on' reality as a result).

The provenance of the character of the expert is an interesting one. In the UK, his (usually his) history reaches back to the era of post-war consensus, when society was being re-built in the image of the Welfare State. All kinds of benign expert-figures were marshalled into Ministry of Information films to demonstrate the unimpeachable logic of governmental decisions. The epoch-making Beveridge Report of 1942 was to a large extent 'sold' to the British people via such cultural production. Now, with hindsight, architects explaining why blocks of high-rise flats are a wonderful idea seems ironic in the extreme, but such characters carried great post-war significance. The knowledge which they represented constituted a challenge and a promise; it was a challenge to received wisdoms, and a promise to the previously 'un-knowleged' (this 'promise' was, of course, enshrined in the 1945 Butler Education Act). It is another indication of The war game's 'Sixties-ness' that it used these figures in such a straightforward way; in the 1960s, expert figures were still, potentially, enablers – providers of information who would help promote 'truth' and encourage the just society. But Threads and The day after used them not at all.

Like post-war experts explaining the brave new society in Ministry of Information films, The war game's editorial voice also made vivid use of graphics. This device gave information about the siting of aerodromes, the likely targets for Russian attack, and the drift of nuclear fallout. As with the other 'non-dramatic' devices mentioned so far, these techniques are highly reminiscent of 'reporting theatre'. Oh what a lovely war encoded its understanding of the Great War through the dialogue of elements of the montage, amongst which diagrams were included; the US Living Newspapers similarly made full use of illustrative techniques. Moreover, Lovely war's use of actuality slides can be compared to The war game's occasional use of news film (in the newsreel 'combat shots' which provided the visuals for the narrator's explanation of NATO's battle with the Red Army on the West/East German border). Threads used such material, but at one remove; it can sometimes be seen going on in the background (for example, on a pub television while other 'dramatic' conversation was foregrounded).

If Expert with his maps and diagrams is no longer such a trusted figure in Western societies, the ways of mediating True Stories have manifestly been so reduced since the making of The war game, that it stood up surprisingly well to comparision with the two 1980s films, made with far bigger budgets and far more 'impressive' personnel and technology, when eventually transmitted. The realist styles of Threads and The day after are indicative of the ruthless foreclosing of artisic possibility (and its concomitant – rational investigation of issues) which has resulted in the twenty years since The war game.

In the wake of the 1980 controversy over Death of a princess, Sir Ian Gilmour, then Lord Privy Seal, said in the House of Commons (24 April 1980): 'The so-called dramatisation or fictionalisation of alleged history is extremely dangerous and misleading and is something the broadcasting authorities must give close attention to';[14] and this warning is merely the tip of an iceberg. Foreclosure of a range of possibility (and its concomitant, the privileging of an essentially narrow stylistic range) reinforces both an alienated society's tendency towards cultural tourism and an authoritarian government's tendency towards censorship. The latter has become more obvious in the late 1980s, with the sustained attack on broadcasting institutions; the former can be illustrated in the example of the transfer of a play from theatre to tele-film.

The end of the 'Road'

In 1986, the London Royal Court Theatre presented Road, a debut play by a young playwright called Jim Cartwright. The trajectory of Road's success is interesting. Opening in the Court's 'alternative' space (the Theatre Upstairs) in March, it transferred to the main auditorium in June. By the end of the year, it was being performed on tour (with the erstwhile rock star Ian Dury in it); it then went on to New York. Made into a tele-film in 1987, it was popular/controversial enough to be repeated the following year. In the transition from stage to screen it changed from a challengingly discontinuous theatre play into a piece of television with 'real' people (Andrée Molyneaux, the TV co-producer, was even able to find 'a great spirit of survival' in the characters).[15]

Cartwright's play is a bleak, observant and savagely-witty evocation of life in a Lancashire street at poverty-level. Intertextual with the major TV soap *Coronation Street*, it takes the opposite line to that consensual effacer of class difference and lower-class poverty. Where *Coronation Street*, locked into its soap logic, is irrepressibly optimistic about 'the people' and their funny/tragic/feckless/admirable ways, *Road* presents a brutalised world whose denizens, even when hopeful, seem pre-determinedly doomed. *Road*'s social realistic style was highly selective in the theatre version, with doubling-up of roles and direct address evident. The audience were given a 'guide' to the brutalised world of the poor, in the character Scullery, who addressed them directly: 'Wid' your night out yous chose to come and see us. Wid' our night as usual we's all getting ready and turning out for a drink'.[16] As a guide to a mean street, Scullery was exemplary; he knows that his theatre-going audience are cultural tourists, he tells them so frankly, and he treats them accordingly.

One could have wished for more insight into the political reasons for the grinding poverty of *Road*'s inhabitants, but this is carping criticism given the very considerable achievement of this kind of contextualising frame. Scullery joined the action periodically, reminding us of the frame; always outwardly friendly, he knew the distance between himself and his audience was not simply that between stage and auditorium. It was his voice which concluded the play with the sardonic line, 'If you're ever in the area call again. Call again' (p.35).

Narrator Scullery disappeared entirely from the television version, which mediated instead a kind of 'documentary sur-realism'. The film crew took over a derelict area in Darlington just before it was due for demolition. Director Alan Clarke used new technology to follow characters around this blighted landscape. The revolutionary 'Steadycam', although hand-held, has a balancing mechanism which compensates for the operator's movements and allows long, but steady, takes of moving subjects. As a result, the characters did, indeed, take us into their 'road'; we walked beside them, they turned to talk to us.[17] But, unlike the stage *Road*, this was all in the service of a sur-realism which did not so much erode the positioning of the cultural tourist as re-package it. The television audience were brought in, when they might have been held at a more critical distance.

The realistic project penetrated actors' thinking; one actress noted that, whereas she had had to play other characters in the stage play, in the tele-film, 'I had more time to concentrate on Carol . . . so I think there are maybe a couple more dimensions to her character which is really nice to work on.' Although director Alan Clarke made a particular point of invoking what he called 'the actuality of the real environment' to support his claim that Road was realistic, he vehemently denied that it was any kind of 'documentary'. Like many makers of drama in the 1980s, he wanted to efface the documentary connection. As with Threads, issues must be held at arm's length; the 'reporting' techniques of The war game go to the wall at the same time the Thatcher government erodes the power of the documentary proper (as happened in 1988 with the ITV documentary Death on the Rock).

The Royal Court's radical stance has always been predicated upon that most marketable of assets – moral outrage. This is an asset which has been relatively easy to appropriate in past as well as present conjunctures. The Court has, of course, been central to the development of post-war British drama, but this centrality has always been based upon the kind of social realism which made Road quite easy to bowdlerise in the televising. The theatre and television Roads are like Robert Pirsig's comparison between a motorcycle and a car journey. Both stage and television Road travel through Manchester Moss Side, but in one 'that concrete whizzing by five inches below your foot is the real thing' (Pirsig, p.4), while in the other the cultural tourist has the car heater and radio on full blast.

A major feature of the extremist politics of the present UK government is that organisations like the Royal Court have had to define the nature of their radicalism more carefully. The Court's director, Max Stafford-Clark, is currently being forced into doing this precisely because the Tory Government have simplified issues by knocking away the economic props. Desperate to secure financial survival, but unpopular with the business world, the Court must modify or die. Stafford-Clark recognised this in a recent interview in the Daily telegraph.[18] The Court's function, he told journalist and reviewer Benedict Nightingale, 'is to ensure the British theatre remains a major vehicle for social debate', with discussion being provoked, 'generally from a stance I'd call non-specific Left, meaning we're a very broad church.'

The sub-text of this could run, 'Don't be afraid of us, we're not Loony Lefties', and it emphasises Stafford-Clark's sense of the Daily telegraph audience. This was reinforced by Nightingale's own homiletic concluding sentence: 'After all, wouldn't our democracy be worse off without that nonconformist enclave in Sloane Square, with its crises, its heretical plays, its turbulence on and off the stage?' This masterpiece of patronage suggests, of course, that oppositional movements can be trusted never to get their own acts properly together ('turbulence on and off stage'). More importantly, it acknowledges that real democracy (not the Thatcherite imitation) is under threat. Any cultural institution with a left-wing reputation will have a problem with sponsorship; the government of the day know this full well. Their 'policy' towards the arts therefore stands revealed as the censorship it really is.

The institutions the Government might be willing to recuperate are also revealed – for a Tory newspaper to speak up for the Court as a needful element in democracy is remarkable. This is a real index of the times, one reinforced when the Editor of another Tory paper, the *Mail on Sunday*, recently made the astounding discovery that the British police have a tendency to abuse their power.[19] In the past, the consensus which sustained the hegemony was sutured precisely by the accommodations which were possible between such people as Stafford-Clark (representing a non-conformist, even leftist, 'artistic' institution) and Nightingale (representing a highly-conformist right-wing newspaper, but committed to the notion of 'the arts'). It was indeed possible for 'broad churches' (i.e. a consensus of people) to acknowledge social criticism, work for amelioration of society, and in general *agree* across party-political lines about social issues. This consensus has been ripped apart, and a certain amount of 'trimming' has resulted on both sides (as can be seen throughout the Nightingale article). In Marxist terms, we can see the operation of 'historical necessity' on both men, and more importantly on the institutions which they represent.

The effect of this problematising of the Court's institutional stance has been to accentuate the cultural tourism to which it has always been dangerously prone. As with advertisements on television, those texts which support the central, 'artistic', enterprise are most revealing of all – the publicity material on *Road* stressed a conceptual link with the 1930s 'Mass Observation' movement, something else which once tried to establish what the 'real' lives of Britain's lower classes were like. Jim Cartwright's credibility as a 'real' person, who knew what it was like to live in such a street as he describes in his play, was similarly stressed. Like a newspaper correspondent from a foreign land (or, more accurately, a foreign war) his observations can be *trusted*, then incorporated vicariously into his audience's 'experience'.

But this elision was nothing compared to the television experience, which takes belief to be a function of sight. As with tourism proper, cultural tourism's hold over the social and political structures which bring people to the condition we observe them in is in danger of being marginal to the experience offered. Such structures as these are, of course, less marketable commodities. The elision of cause and effect takes place to the point where only effect (realistic action) is visible, and this is taken as sufficient. The relatively comfortable (even, perhaps, *comforting*) feelings of moral outrage which are the stock-in-trade of the social realist film are not to be dismissed, since they do have the function of keeping issues on some kind of public agenda. Cultural tourism exists not because of authorial, directorial or even receivers' *intentions*, but as a partial result of foreclosed *possibilities*, which are themselves a consequence of political shifts. A modern audience constructed pre-eminently as observers with a thinly-defined responsibility towards problems finds re-action easy, action difficult. Empathy, a strength of the 'great' Naturalist dramatists Ibsen, Chekhov and Strindberg in their own conjuncture, has now become a means of displacing an audience's attention away from the root causes of issues (while being simultaneously a means for establishing a work's credentials of 'seriousness').

The camera eye's phantom objectivity – norms and alternatives in film

> A possible definition of the real is: *that for which it is possible to provide an equivalent reproduction* ... The real becomes not only what can be reproduced, but that which is always already reproduced: the hyperreal. (Jean Baudrillard)[1]

Introduction – the Holy Grail of realism

As Chapter 1 argued, the very provenance of the term 'documentary' places it in close proximity to an equally problematical concept of 'objectivity'. In film documentary, the camera's intervention into 'reality' was part of an on-going naturalist/realist project in which the still and movie camera appeared as the latest refinement in a process steadily evolving towards the perfection of unmediated intervention into a 'reality' often seen as an idealised absolute. The objectivity of film thus became especially valorised because the eye of the camera was taken to be an objective observer, recording events from a position of privileged omniscience; its images not only reflected reality, they were that reality.

This notion was particularly popular in the 1930s: eminent US journalist James Agee called the camera 'the central instrument of our time' (Stott, p.76), and influential stage designer Mordecai Gorelik believed 'the eye of the camera is an objective instrument' (Gorelik, p.327). Positioned as the observer to skilfully imitated realistic behaviours (or conventional TV and movie acting) the camera eye has given to the True Story the kind of 'I Was There!' gloss which first made the cinema newsreel, and then broadcast TV news, so popular. This culminated in the direct borrowing for True Stories of techniques deriving from the documentary. The 'I' behind the camera eye, which renders problematic all claims to objectivity, was for many years effaced from consideration, and even now is rarely questioned in news broadcasting.[2]

Only when news camerawork is interrogated closely does the univocal cultural 'I' behind-the-camera stand revealed. When a news broadcast
from one culture is placed alongside work from another, the one tends
to deconstruct the other, defamiliarising the 'known' version to the
extent that it can be more fully understood. For example, UK news
reporting of the activities of the Greenham Common women seemed
always to concentrate on the conditions *within* their peace camp. The
images shown were usually of mud and squalor, the camera lingering on
Third-World-style 'benders' made of sticks and polythene sheets. The
women, seen in close-up and mid-range shots, usually looked pinched
and cold, often they were muffled up against inclement weather. The
camp was denied its context, by being shown in and for itself. A point-of-
view shot might show the military base in the distance, or a Cruise missile
carrier driving out dramatically, but peace camp and base were the
subjects of quite different shot composition. Peace camp was 'human
interest'; military base 'information stock shot'.

By contrast, coverage by a Russian crew for Russian TV (seen in the UK
during 1986) put the camp firmly in a context of 'nearness to a military
base'. By going for a longer shot, and a wider field of focus, the Russians
showed their commentator talking against a background of the guarded
gates of a typical military site, with the peace camp off-centre in the
image, to the left of the screen. There was no *separation* of the human
interest from the strictly informative; the cultural background of the
Russian crew did not lead them, perhaps, to *make* such a separation. The
effect of the shot, even when one could not understand what the speaker
was saying, was astonishing; it *re-positioned* the peace camp, as it were,
making it no longer the incomprehensible habitat of a group of deviant
women in the approximate vicinity of a military base, but an appendage
clinging desperately (and bravely) to the coat tails of a highly-organised
military establishment. The ramshackle human scale of the peace camp
was asserted by placing it in its rightful situation, on the fringe of a power
which could crush it with ease.

Biased reporting or truth-telling? The Russian version of the particular 'truth' of Greenham Common would seem to have a great deal to
commend it, but this very contention would doubtless scandalise many
who will not entertain the thought that the British news reporting media
could be anything but even-handed. The answer is, of course, that they
mostly are – *according to the cultural lights by which they work*. That Russian
crews could have different, but comparable, lights (which in some senses
are clearer) is the sort of view which would inflame the Transatlantic

Right. But both crews, at any rate, were using cameras, microphones, the whole reproductive paraphenalia which once generated such confidence in its presumed power to replicate reality.

The movie documentary has been (apparently) aided and abetted in the quest for realism by the ever-increasing sophistication of the means of movie-making (in the sense of an image/sound-recording capability). This led Nicholas Garnham to conclude, in 1972, that 'the appearance of progress within this aesthetic has been largely technical, the search for the Holy Grail of a totally transparent technique'.[3] The 'Holy Grail' of Realism, although a chimera, has continued to hold out its promise, through cinéma vérité and 'fly-on-the-wall' techniques, via 'Steadycams' and mini-tape-recorders, and finally by means of the almost instantaneous response to events of the video-camera. The whole enterprise has had the effect of driving the True Story towards the ever-greater realism of the 'Real Story'.

Worship at the 'Temple of Facts' continues unabated. Although factuality itself is in crisis (and the regular controversies over TV documentary dramas are part evidence of this), the 'phantom objectivity' of camera/ microphone technology even yet haunts cinema, TV, and even theatrical representations of reality to the extent that the imaginary is still often accepted very readily as the real provided it conforms to the conventions of realism. The world of commercial screen entertainment is predicated upon such mystification. This is the force of Baudrillard's redefinition of the real; the single-minded hunt for an infallibly realistic mode has had the effect of inducing a kind of hypnosis in which cameras mediating events become the agents of those events' very construction in people's minds. It is not a case of an Eliotic human inability to 'bear very much reality', more that the range of 'realities' mediated do not tend to demand a very great deal of understanding. This is because, as in the case of The war game, there is inherent suspicion on the part of hegemonies about what civil populations might do if fully informed. Although this is masked behind a Podsnappery which presumes the right to protect that population, and which seeks to treat people as if they are unable to make up their minds (being too naive, or stupid, or both), what it reveals is the uncertainty at the heart of any hegemony's power, however strong that hegemony might appear to be.

The promotion of particular cultural modes acts as a kind of 'fail safe' securing that continuance of power which must be every hegemony's ultimate aim. Culture has thus become, 'a "Trojan Horse" for economic domination',[4] and this effectively means American domination. In the

UK a linkage between commerce and the arts is currently being forged via a concept of sponsorship which must inevitably suppress some ('un-sponsorable') activity and enslave much else to multinational capitalism. This is most dangerous where least criticised, most developed where mass mediated – in 'entertainment' cinema and television the camera eye's phantom objectivity still tries to persuade us to see and believe. For True Stories this remains their strongest selling point; they enable us to *be there* (sort of) as history is/was made. The controlling 'I' behind the camera eye is still mystified to the vast majority of consumers, who may quite readily accept an individual but not a corporate 'I'; a Richard Attenborough is preferred, in other words, to an Attenborough who is servant to (and outward spokesman for) organised capital.

Attenborough-style True Stories do not disrupt the camera's phantom objectivity; their lack of formal challenge is an index of their lack of political ambition. Films 'transgressive' of (or 'alternative' to) the conventional True Story form, however, not only nominate particular issues for discussion in a public forum by re-presenting them, they also increase political turbulence existing around such issues. Turbulence is manifest both in controversy, and in discussion of the 'ethics' of different modes of representation. Complications to the processes of production and consumption of 'entertainment' can ultimately disrupt hegemonic attempts to efface difficult issues, marking out an authentic cultural boundary for future reference (if not further challenge).

Hype-the-real America – the B-movie experience

As Baudrillard says, America is the place where Disneyland is not fantasy at all, but the reality of which all else is a pale reflection. Disneyland is 'a deterrence machine set up in order to rejuvenate in reverse the fiction of the real' – concealed is the far more sinister void which is Capitalist America itself. Baudrillard sees America as 'no longer real but of the order of the hyperreal and of simulation' (p.172). His categories of the 'hyperreal and simulation' point towards the present nexus of power in cultural production, much of which colludes in the project of making the impossible seem feasible. Hype-the-Real for commercial success – witness the taste for special effects films like the *Star wars* and *Indiana Jones* series (beginning in 1977 and 1981 respectively). True Stories, key inflectors of 'received history', are ultimately tied in to this promotion of the hyperreal.

Hyperreal America is the place where a B-movie actor can simulate the figure of a credible President (provided he sticks to the script and the special effects continue to function). This is such a truism that it is in danger of overlooking the fundamental truth that those fantasies and fictions which constitute 'the B-movie experience' are shapers of cultural experience; many people's inner lives are composed precisely of these things. Ronald Reagan, it is often forgotten, wasn't that bad at what he used to do; it is true that this didn't amount to very much, but it should be taken into account nonetheless. He was a reliable performer in a sphere of cultural production which has subsequently achieved cult status. Taken up by *avant-garde* European film-makers (such as Jean-Luc Godard) from the 1960s onwards, the humble B-movie has long been recognised as a cultural force. We cannot have it both ways: the scorning of Reagan as the B-movie President elides precisely those factors which have made him into such a force.

Where hyperreal America leads, the UK is sure to follow. The cultural production of the political leader can be mirrored in the UK, with its only superficially less obvious marketing of a Prime Minister. Margaret Thatcher may not be a movie actress, B-feature or otherwise, but she has run a gamut of more and more skilfully reproduced authoritarian female roles since she came to power in 1979. She is now making a fair fist of usurping the 'royal' style (witness her developing use of 'we' and 'our'). The conservative matriarch is (increasingly graciously) rampant in Margaret Thatcher's (increasingly skilled) impersonation. As with Reagan, the question of whether the time produced the person or the person the time would repay close attention, but suffice it to say that s/he who controls the re-presentation of events endows events themselves with meaning. In the politics of the hyperreal, the Image-maker Rules OK.

The making of a President from the arena of low-status cultural production could be seen as an acknowledgement that the B-movie as a genre was always more powerful than its 'A' companion precisely because it was watched in unguarded, uncritical, ways – accepted as second-rate, absorbed viscerally where the higher-profile 'main feature' was always scrutinised carefully. The 'just entertainment' argument will be familiar to anyone who has ever tried to argue a political case from an artistic example. 'Don't try to find a deep meaning,' one is frequently admonished, 'it's just entertainment.' This side-stepping manoeuvre has the effect of legitimating the concealed ideological thrust of cultural production – but it rarely seems that way to the person using the ploy. As the oppositional political case is put, it is blotted out by the most successful of all political arguments – the one that says it is 'not political' (even when it is). The power of the hegemony is at its greatest in those unconsidered areas of experience, where the knee-jerk reaction can be counted on with confidence. We are at our most vulnerable when relaxed, as any advertising agency will be happy to confirm.

Cinema and TV screens are the major mediators of this hyperreality, and their products must be subject to the most rigorous questioning if we are to resist the uninterrupted flow of capitalist meanings. In television, it must be remembered that, persuasive as it may be to argue from single texts, the world of the TV camera is always an intertextual world. Raymond Williams was among the earliest critics to point out that television's 'flow' of programmes ensures that it is necessary consciously to interrupt that flow in order to critique individual programmes.[5] Otherwise everything has a fatal tendency to *merge* – current affairs into news, into drama, into cartoons – until a relentless trivialisation occurs.

The flow is not quite so noticeable in film, but it is there nonetheless, especially now that film and TV are so often project-linked, and in that sense economically interdependent. Cinema 'needs TV's money invested in film production; TV needs cinema film as a reference point for its own production work, and also as fodder for broadcasting' (Ellis, p.1). Both cinema and television are increasingly dependent on large-scale multinational capital – the movie company Columbia, for example, was recently acquired by Coca-Cola. The highly-structured and integrated commercial/industrial arrangements that follow from this lead to an 'aesthetic conservatism' which then tends to prevail in such organisations, and which is comparable to the institutionalised conservatism of broadcast TV networks (Ellis, p.211). In the Disneyland view of the world which results, everything will turn out fine provided you keep your sense of humour; the hyperreal world will come right in the end.

'Bio-pic' True Stories

According to John Caughie, 'Drama tests, and occasionally extends, what is possible not only to say, but also and more perilously, to show'.[6] The financial stranglehold exerted on cultural production by capitalist organisation may ensure the mediation of the hegemony's messages, but only up to a point. As with any commodity, consumption is the point at which the commodity goes out of the producers' immediate control. Then, as Gramsci put it, '[m]ass adhesion or non-adhesion to an ideology is the real critical test of the rationality and historicity of modes of thinking'.[7] Thus there is turbulence about any piece of cultural production in which contentious social meanings condense, are challenged, negotiated, or re-interpreted. Norms and alternatives in True Story films demonstrate this, and offer examples of the 'testing and extending' nature of drama based on fact.

One need look no further than the work of Sir Richard Attenborough to give a preliminary account of True Story norms. All Attenborough's films have shown an interest in True Story material; from the 1969 *Oh what a lovely war*, through the 1977 *A bridge too far* (about the Allied defeat at Arnhem in World War Two), to *Cry Freedom* in 1988, the *documentary base* of each of his films is very easy to establish. As Eric Bentley has observed about documentary forms in general, the use of such material is aimed 'at surprising (and even appalling) audiences with the realisation, "Yes, and this actually happened!" '.[8] Attenborough's consistent use of True Stories seeks to capitalise (again the word is deliberately chosen) upon this *frisson* of recognition.

The selling-point of his *oeuvre* up to now has been the 'truth outside the artwork', his use of which is of a piece with his liberal politics. He is ready enough to stand up and be counted among those opposing injustices of all kinds, to commit himself at a fundamental level to a *content* which cannot be gainsaid because it is 'true'. But at the *formal* level, all his work is profoundly unadventurous, turning each True Story told into a sanitised *genre* movie. His version of *Lovely war* turned a stage play (which was challenging even when cleaned up for the West End)[9] into a screen musical for the aristocracy of the British acting profession; *A bridge too far* show-cased 'star-officers' in a movie-military firmament (we play Spot-the-Star, as we swallow the concealed ideological message that it is the officer class which does all the important things in wars as well as films).

His 1982 *Gandhi* had many of the hallmarks of the 'bio-pic' True Story. It stuck to a painstakingly chronological approach which valorises the individual story and treats history as background. The more we are drawn to 'attractive' individual True Stories, the less we are able to see those individuals as bearers of supra-individual messages. The order of priorities which in politics constructed Gandhi first as representative of his people, then as individual, is reversed in cultural production. The bio-pic almost always seeks the 'natural' dynamic of the life-story's chronology (although Clint Eastwood's 1988 *Bird* is an interesting exception to this rule). This dynamic enables Gandhi's 'just-like-us-ness' to be stressed, and from this follows a sense of personal elevation. The historical Gandhi's 'real' moral stature is conferred on us, merely by our taking-an-interest-in/empathising-with his screen imitator. A real person whose complex political significance would be all-important in any other arena is thereby turned into a 'screen hero', and people who would probably have opposed him bitterly in his own historical conjuncture are able to appropriate him (as well as feeling good about supporting him in a totally unthreatening situation).

The bio-pic narrative is organised on the common cultural ground of the 'ups and downs' of a universalised conception of 'life'. This 'bio-life' contains obligatory sections on formative experiences, education, love, marriage, and so on – spiced in Gandhi's case with such added ingredients as 'passive' resistance, imprisonment, and assassination. It is like *This is your life* with the gloves off – the emotional graph must always show some happiness, some tragedy. The whole thing must be reducible to the proposition that all lives great and small are an ineffable mixture of sunshine and shadow. There is not a great deal to choose, formally speaking, between *Gandhi* and *The Glenn Miller story* (1954); in fact, the inflated portentousness of the former makes the wartime band-leader's True Story quite attractive. All that *Gandhi* lacks is the linkage montage sequences of spinning newspapers, whose narrating headlines are set against racing locomotive wheels and images of hectic career activity in early versions of the bio-pic form.

It ain't half hot, Mum

GB 1973-81 42 approx. x 30m colour (VTR)
BBC (David Croft)
In World War II India, a platoon of British soldiers is busy organising a concert party. Efficiently nostalgic army farce with a preponderance of gay jokes. (*Halliwell's television companion*, p.408)

Set in an 'exotic' location (India), with plentiful (and cheap) extras, *Ghandi* may have made liberal concessions to the colonialist past on the surface, but it also made sure that the major role of the Indian statesman was played by an English actor (Ben Kingsley – who at least had the concessionary credentials of Indian ancestry). The sub-continent in the historical period 1940-1950 has proved a veritable gold mine for cultural production in the last twenty years. Even something as apparently distant from *Gandhi* as the BBC TV comedy series described above cashed in on Raj-nostalgia. The two pieces of cultural production are linked through their predatory attitude to a country, and a time, which they re-appropriate through their re-presentation. *It ain't half hot, Mum* was simply more vulgar in its appropriation, with a preponderance of blacked-up whites and a little theatrical 'camp' thrown in for good measure (always good for a laugh in 1970s comedy shows).

At the more august level at which a film like *Gandhi* works, we must ask why an Indian was not cast in the leading role. We might also, incidentally, inquire how many black Othellos the British theatrical profession (of which Attenborough is such a pillar) has sanctioned since Paul Robeson played the role in the 1930s. Ethnic minorities are as ghettoised in cultural production as they are in any highly-developed (and white-dominated) industry. In the movies, they are safe box-office in a film like *Guess who's coming to dinner?* (1967), or in 'blaxploitation' movies, like *Shaft* (1971). Like women's issues or gay issues, black issues will sell – but only if they are ghetto-ised, and blackness re-packaged as a 'feature'.

Gandhi re-colonises India for a cultural imperialist project in which Indians themselves (or their current ruling class) collude with British and American neo-colonialists in order to 'sell' an acceptable 'India' to predominantly white post-colonialist audiences. The film's producers were a characteristically modern multinational agglomeration of the US (Columbia Pictures), the UK (Goldcrest), and India (Indo-British/National Film Development Corporation of India). As well as aiming to please this multiplicity of masters, the film looked towards a multiplicity of 'international' audiences (with their racial and cultural differences erased). Elisions at the levels of history, ethnicity, and politics coalesce to ensure a 'universality' which is so bland you would think it must be noticed – on the contrary, *Gandhi* was an internationally-acclaimed 'success'.

Brecht's notion of a non-challenging 'culinary theatre' must be updated; *Ghandi* is part of a 'MacDonalds film industry', sold as *sameness* world-wide – just like a hamburger. Its casting reflects its corporate internationalism, including a veritable top ten of Great Brits (actors like Sirs Gielgud and Mills, to whom Americans are supposed to be partial), some Yank glamour (Candice Bergen), and a couple of obligatory token Indians (Saeed Jaffrey, Rohini Hattangady). To top it all off, there was an unknown actor (well, Royal Shakespeare veteran Ben Kingsley – unknown in the USA) who was ripe for discovery and valorisation, after being 'browned up' to impersonate the eponymous Indian statesman. Like a newly-clothed Emperor, Kingsley was taken up amid much inter-industry back-slapping. At the Academy Awards 'ceremony' (where American cultural imperialism celebrates its own survival and continuation, as any imperialist venture must) *Gandhi* was showered with Academy Awards – a sure sign that there was something profoundly mendacious at its heart.

There was the added attraction in *Gandhi* of a non-violence read as successful in a troubled, violent, present historical conjuncture where politics could less easily be separated from violence. Gandhi's 'goal was freedom . . . his strategy was peace . . . his weapon was his humanity', according to the film's publicity. In a present riven with 'terrorist' attempts to solve political problems with rather less peaceful weapons, which impinge more and more on 'ordinary' lives, this was immensely comforting. Northern Irish and Arab 'extremism' lurks behind this version of Gandhi's politics, like an uninvited fundamentalist ghost at the corporate celebration.

The bio-pic form is tried and tested enough to have survived virtually unscathed whilst others (the Western, for example) have encountered hard times as entertainment has gone international. Currently the resistance leaders of black nations (past and present) are a popular source of the bio-pic on TV as well as in the cinema. This is a sure sign that Western hegemonies are having trouble with the line that peaceful protest gets results, for even Black African leaders whose names are associated with un-Gandhian violence have been 'bio-pic-ed'. In 1987, for example, British television showed *Mandela*, in which Nelson Mandela of the ANC got the full treatment. The writer Ronald Harwood reveals his bio-pic priorities all too clearly:

I wanted . . . to balance Mandela's political activities with his private life. I was drawn to this shape because of the remarkable qualities of Winnie Mandela . . . The film, then, not only seeks to tell the story of the Mandelas' fight against apartheid, but also attempts to reveal something of the extraordinary bond between the man and the woman, a bond which sustained them through their struggle against a brutal and inhuman social system.[10]

Who played Mandela? The American actor Danny Glover – just as American Denzel Washington played Biko in *Cry freedom* and Briton Ben Kingsley played Gandhi. The reasons for this are primarily cultural and commercial, just as Mandela's politics must be 'balanced' (a revealing word in the present context) with a Love Story.

Donald Woods' effusive tribute to Attenborough, *Filming with Attenborough* has a section on the casting of the Biko role in *Cry freedom*.[11] Apparently, no black South African actor of 'the appropriate age and size and looks . . . showed enough acting skill at reading the scripted lines'. Assiduous searching in Africa discovered only actors who were 'below par' or those who had the 'wrong physical characteristics'. The 'only'

actor who 'looked to have what was sought' was the American Denzel
Washington. What was the magic ingredient which the director was
seeking? A 'kind of screen power', we are told, which Attenborough
'sensed'. This mystified explanation may suit Woods, but the immense
pressures on his ego which the whole process generated may be read off
his anxious valorisation of the Attenborough magic.

Soon this magic gets to work – Washington turns out to have a gap
tooth like Biko, puts on a bit of weight, listens to tapes of Biko's voice.
These peripherals are looked upon with wonder by Woods; his clin-
ching argument is that 'someone else who had known Biko' (but who is
not named) says, 'It's uncanny . . . It's as if he is him.' Woods, predictably,
ends up 'convinced no other actor could have bettered [Washington's]
performance as Biko'. Just as it is unwise to take egoists at their own
valuation, it is equally unwise to listen too closely to anyone deeply
involved in a film (or theatre) production, especially if it is telling their
very own True Story.

The process by which Washington and Glover came to play the parts of
key Black African political figures cannot be far distant from what Tom
Stoppard describes in the introduction to *Squaring the circle*, his 1984 True
Story (for US/UK TV) about the Polish trade union Solidarity:

> The first sign of ugliness concerned the matter of the narrator. Steve, or rather not
> Steve, nor Bruce, nor Dale, nor Chuck, nor Bob but in fact the dreaded advertisers,
> and not actually the advertisers but the dreaded public, felt that the narrator
> should be an American, a *famous* American, with whom the (American) public
> could identify.[12]

Such intricate, square-dancing manoeuvring is usually consigned so
firmly to the background of 'artistic' discussion that it disappears
completely; it is there nonetheless, assiduously protecting its interests.

A commercial alternative – strategic penetration or cultural assimilation?

An example of the negotiation of alternatives to the norm of True Story
film-making in the commercial cinema is the 1981 Warren Beatty/Trevor
Griffiths film *Reds*. This film was a major capitalist enterprise, costing its
parent studio (Paramount) anywhere between $35 million and $55
million (according to whose figures one believes). It had 'bankable'
international stars (Beatty and Diane Keaton), a challenging *political* subject (the story of American communist John Reed), and a socialist writer

(Griffiths) committed to the notion of finding the largest possible audience for his work. In commercial terms alone, this film on the subject of communism made the considerable achievement in Reaganite America of *not* being a huge disaster; it contained just enough radical content, mediated through just enough of a radical form, not to bomb out completely. This negative achievement is worth considering.

Trevor Griffiths's long-held notion of a socialist 'strategic penetration' of commercial cultural production is fraught with difficulty, as he himself has acknowledged. Fellow playwright David Edgar once pointed out that commercial television 'penetrates back' every twenty minutes with the pure capitalist doctrine of the advertisement.[13] The commercial movie is heavily dependent upon economic 'packages' which only have superficial connections with aesthetics. But if cultural production is indeed a site for the contestation of political meanings, it would be too simplistic to assume that there will be cut-and-dried 'victories' on either side. Capitalism quite obviously has the all-important economic upper hand, but the constant turbulence around contested ideas offers continual hope. In Eastern Europe turbulence has famously cohered around jokes (to the extent that some kinds of joking have been banned altogether by the Czech authorities). While it may be wishful thinking to see the present US and UK power élites as hanging on to power by their finger ends, it is certainly still possible to mount challenges to their orthodoxies, which may increase the level of turbulence. In the arts these challenges are often initially constituted at a formal level.

Mike Poole and John Wyver observe that 'the vast capitalisation costs of *Reds*, and hence its dependence on a recoupable market, meant that, inevitably, the logic of capital alone determined that its politics had also to be recuperable'.[14] This 'recoupable/recuperable' opposition is important because it ultimately drained the movie of much of its political potential. The picture was a very 1980s mix of production values allied to various branches of metropolitan New York 'lifestyle' politics. The strong love story element was played against a meticulously-observed (and expensive) period setting; a high premium was placed on modish, Method-acted repartee between the principals Beatty and Keaton. A designer-feminism reduced the historical Louise Bryant to an Annie-Hall-ish sparring-partner for Beatty's Woody-Allen-style Reed. (Allen's 1977 film *Annie Hall*, in which he and Keaton starred, set much of this agenda.)

As with African people in *Out of Africa* (1985), or workers in the nuclear energy industry in *Silkwood* (1983), or the generality of Jews in the

E

Holocaust in *Sophie's choice* (1982), the 'background' is important only insofar as it enables the movie to appeal at a 'serious' level to an audience still apparently hooked by the concept of the Individual as Essence. Thus the 1917 Russian Revolution section of *Reds* became a kind of 'Annie Hall Goes East', and the character 'Jack Reed' got a part to play in the events of the Revolution to which the historical Reed would not have aspired. In *Reds*, the Revolution became 'background', and as such it was 'saleable'.

But *Reds* did constitute a challenge to controlling American orthodoxies. Reed was, after all, an oppositional figure in American politics from a time when the USA still had a coherent socialist opposition (even a socialist Presidential candidate – Eugene Debs in 1908). Reed most famously wrote *Ten days that shook the world*, a 'reportage' account of the Russian Revolution of 1917. In addition, he was one of America's ruling class *malgré lui*; as well as being a symbol of a lost American socialist tradition, he was an acknowledged member of a twentieth-century literary élite which included Eugene O'Neill (impersonated in *Reds* by Jack Nicholson). For a Hollywood star like Warren Beatty even to want to make a movie about such a complexly-loaded subject was a remarkable gesture from an un-looked for source. But Beatty's status as society and Hollywood star (not to mention Diane Keaton's) fatally confused the mediation of political messages, which are there only in diffused and distorted states.

Reds had at least one unusual, formal, dimension which partially disrupted the idealised individualistic flow of the narrative. Intercut with the 'Adventures of Warren/Jack and Diane/Louise' were occasional inserts of 'talking head' interviews with real people, former associates and friends of John Reed and Louise Bryant. Beatty habitually referred to these interviewees as the 'old folk', and they appear from time to time in *Reds* to give a reminiscence about the period and/or the main protagonists. The idea of using these inserts stemmed from the narrator-figures of Griffiths's original screenplay, and Beatty's experimental interviews with these same people during research for the film. Far from providing the political contextualisation or overview which Griffiths intended (and which was a legacy of his political play-making), these inserts offered 'oral history at its most individualistic' (Poole and Wyver, p.128), a kaleidoscope of points-of-view. Modernist rather than post-modernist, this gave *Reds* a surface appearance of radical discontinuity, the 'talking heads' giving somewhat random factual glosses on the fictional 'acting-out'. 'Real' and 'pretend' were placed side-by-side in a way familiar in broadcast television documentary drama, but unfamiliar in the

Hollywood bio-pic.

Even more than a stage play, a commercial film is a site of struggle, that struggle intensified by the very presence of a higher degree of capitalisation. In *Reds* the struggle was for the extent to which a radical political story could be inserted into a major capitalist entertainment industry ultimately dependent for around 60% of its income on the American domestic market. Although the politics were mostly effaced in favour of an identificatory True Story, which would give Beatty and Keaton chances to jump through the hoops that stars are expected to jump through, turbulence is still evident at almost all levels of the film. Thus, the purely individualistic reading of history in the film was subverted at a minimal level by the talking heads' contributions. These not only relayed information, they also articulated substantive (if marginal) *gaps* in the continuity of such information. One example is Rebecca West's singing of 'The Internationale' for her (unseen) interviewer who, we must presume from West's reaction, does not know the communist anthem at all. The huge difference between two historical conjunctures can be read from this moment – the revolutionary song was, after all, the concluding act in most political meetings in Reed's period. It is an emblem of a lost continuity, something so alien to the present conjuncture that it has to be *explained*.

Griffiths had originally wished to use the Labour songs of the period extensively (the songs of Joe Hill, for example), Rebecca West's cracked-voiced rendition of 'The Internationale' is all that remains of that intention. The musical element of the film was carried almost entirely by 'a schmaltzy version of the popular hit "I Don't Want To Play In Your Yard" ' (Poole and Wyver, p. 134), which panders to the relatively recent Hollywood trend towards period-chic in background music. While this was most noticeable in the use of Scott Joplin's ragtime music in *The Sting* (1973), the best parallel would be the use of 'Raindrops Keep Falling On My Head' in *Butch Cassidy and the Sundance Kid* (1969). Both *Butch Cassidy* and *Reds* use a song to underpin a very modern concept of 'buddiness', the homoerotic aspect of Butch and Sundance's relationship kept firmly under 1960s wraps, the equals-ahead-of-their-time aspect of Reed and Bryant played for the winning trick it was. 'Raindrops' was period-pastiche (and actually a contemporary Bacharach/David composition), 'Your Yard' was authentic; the effect of the two songs as a sentimental narrative device was exactly the same.

To indicate his unhappiness with what was eventually released under the title *Reds*, Griffiths has always called his screenplay *Comrades*. He made this principled disassociation again in 1985, when he was screen writer for the commercial television co-production *The last place on Earth*. This story of the race for the South Pole between the Norwegian expedition of Roald Amundsen and the British expedition led by Captain R.F.Scott caused some controversy in the UK when first broadcast, because of its radical re-reading of the actions of a late-Imperial British Hero. Scott the Hero has been a major modern figure in ruling-class hagiography for over fifty years. It is not uncommon still to find his name used in state school house systems (along with figures like Dr Livingstone). Cast as antagonist to Scott's protagonist in the original Imperial fairy-tale is the Norwegian Amundsen, whose 'professional' expedition has always been derided because he used what are constructed as underhand means to reach the South Pole first (like eating dogs, which no True Brit would ever do).

Perhaps Griffiths's boldest stroke in this six-episode series (which he calls *Judgement over the dead*)[15] was to subvert one of the most famous death-speeches in British Imperial History. The badly frost-bitten Captain Oates (according to the journal written by Scott, and found with Scott's dead body) uttered the words: 'I am going outside. I may be some time', before walking into a blizzard and heroically sacrificing himself. Oates did this in the knowledge that, if he stayed, he would jeopardise what little chance of survival the rest of the expedition had. In the final episode of the TV series (provocatively titled 'Rejoice!', in a post-Falklands allusion to the sustaining British Myth of Self-Sacrifice) Griffiths changed this stiff-upper-lip line to 'Call of nature, Birdie' (Griffiths, p.279). His character Oates responds with these (conjectural) last words to Lt 'Birdie' Bowers's grief-stricken recognition of the sacrifice about to be made, and indicates in saying them a recognition of the 'easefulness' of death to someone whose life has become one of unendurable suffering. Subsequent controversy about this line overlooked the fact that, in context, the line was powerfully moving, with its many-layered pun on the word 'nature'. The line simultaneously reclaimed the historical Oates (privately very critical of Scott's leadership) from the pomposity of Scott's version of his dying words, debunked an Imperial myth, and said something profound about both exploration and death.

In his introduction to the published screenplay, Griffiths talks of the institutional pressures on the writer who aspires to work outside the theatre. He describes the theatre as a 'cottage industry', compared to the highly-industrialised processes of film and television:

the TV film, the cinema film, . . . will be deemed good or bad depending on how well it serves the interests of those who wish to make the film. And those interests, because of the higher capital involved, will not simply be another artist, a director, a star actor or whatever. They will be producers on behalf of capital. (Griffiths, p.xi)

Griffiths's annoyance is mirrored in Tom Stoppard's introduction to *Squaring the circle*. where he gives details of the almost Byzantine pecking order which obtains once higher capital is involved in a 'project package':

At the Pinewood end of the Metromedia chain of command there was Steve, who had to deal with Bruce, who had to deal with Dale, who had to deal with Chuck, who had to deal with Bob, and way beyond Bob, somewhere at the top of the mountain, there was the mysterious figure of Mr Kluge, remote as Buddha . . . (Stoppard, p.13)

Unlike Griffiths, Stoppard's irritation did not translate into the only independent action available to him – the changing of the name of his script.

The writer, on the testimony of two men who have some cultural power, has little control over the means of production in film and television, much less over the point of consumption. S/he is no more than a paid employee, a superior technician not expected to question major policy decisions (for which his/her agreement will not normally even be sought). The world of commerce and industry is not normally given to responding to individual attempts to deflect or alter its course, especially if that attempt is perceived as political. Artists can claim immunity from this iron law as much as they like, in reality they are in its grip – a grip only revealed when challenges are made to it. Rather more control, of course, can be exerted in areas of *alternative* cultural production; hegemonic restrictions will always operate more restrictively, as it were, in high profile activities, less restrictively in work which is already marginalised. Thus, although some compromising is evident in all spheres of cultural production, there is more room for radically creative manoeuvre in fringe theatre than in mainstream, in experimental cinema than in commercial movie-making.

Unfortunately, the resourcing continuum works in the opposite direction; the look of a cultural product cannot be ignored, and that look, at whatever level, has to be bought because it corresponds with audience expectation. The tune called by the American piper over the years has ultimately ensured that both the look of a film and its mode of production are quite precisely pre-determined. A low-budget movie has two basic choices: one is to 'attempt to reproduce the aesthetic of commercial films', costing perhaps forty times its budget; the other is to 'produce an aesthetic appropriate to its production costs', but looking inferior in comparison. In the first instance, failure is the likely result; in the second, the film 'will not be recognised as belonging to the cinema' (Ellis, pp.201-2).

True Stories are engaged in an on-going negotiation, then, between a resourcing which is adequate but likely to be determined politically at the point of production, and one which is without strings but likely to be inadequate. True Stories negotiate, and re-negotiate, their meanings not only within these economic boundaries (which obtain for all cultural production), but also within boundaries particular to the True Story, where there is a contest between views of reality, between, as it were, veracity and verisimilitude. This may convert into economic criteria, as when the 'look' of a particular period has to be bought (usually expensively) in order to 'convince' an audience; but the contest also exists at the level of the communicable-ness or otherwise of particular 'real' experiences, the level at which a 'truth-claim' will become convincing.

The Holocaust and the 'historians' quarrel'

Cultural production about the Third Reich's infamous 'Final Solution' straddles both boundaries: the slaughter of six million Jews during World War Two constitutes a True Story which has to be told somehow – to explain it, to understand it, to cope with its implications; and Holocaust True Stories, because they are especially difficult to tell, mark out the degrees of latitude available to cultural producers, degrees which are re-negotiated by the disruptive procedures of transgressive forms.

There has been a steady build-up in cultural production about the Holocaust in recent years. Material on the subject ranges from the straight documentary of Thames Television's 1975 *The Final Solution* (itself cashing in on a 'thirtieth anniversary' date) to the cinema fiction of Alan J.Pakula's 1982 adaption of William Styron's novel *Sophie's choice*. The former was a piece of 'serious' television journalism, in which the viewer is asked to trust the documentarian's lack of bias, access to information, etc; the latter was a film in which the romantic element (in which Polish Sophie appeared to be faced with a choice between two equally eligible young men in post-war America) was in important senses *authenticated* by her tragic concentration camp 'choice'.

Other notable contributions have been the 1978 US TV series *Holocaust* (where Meryl Streep first began to corner the acting market on tragic European-Jewish heroines), and the 1980 US TV *Playing for time*. This latter programme, seen in the UK partly as a result of the presence in the cast of the 'UK saleable' Vanessa Redgrave, told Fania Fenelon's True Story of a concentration camp orchestra of women, who had literally to play for their lives. In one of those cultural paradoxes which are sometimes unwittingly as instructive as the artworks that cause them, this programme was rather buried under controversy concerning Redgrave's support for the Palestinian Liberation Organisation.

Having raised the topic of the Holocaust in stage and film representations, it would be perfectly feasible to list many more examples, and to range further afield than the USA and the UK for them; but what I really want to establish is the fact of the subject's *continual* re-emergence in cultural production, a fact which I believe is to do with politics rather than art. In dealing with a subject like the Holocaust the arts could be seen to be exercising moral responsibility at the highest of levels. The slaughter of millions of European Jews by the Nazis has left an indelible mark upon twentieth-century history, and it is not surprising to find that there have been several attempts to find forms which can cope with such difficult content.

And yet there is a concomitant danger that this subject will be both trivialised and bowdlerised through representation. Arguably, one simply needs to know that Auschwitz existed, and to understand how and why it came into existence – to make it into the background of a romantic film is to trivialise it. Equally, to centre the Nazis' policy of racial murder exclusively on the Jews runs the risk of marginalising other groups who also suffered in the concentration camps – gypsies, Slavs, communists, the mentally-handicapped. These problems have been exemplified recently by the so-called 'historians' quarrel' in West Germany, in which anti-communist fervour is 'once more the handmaiden of conservative apologetics'.[16]

In 1986, a Frankfurt conference on the theme 'The Past That Won't Go Away' began an academic contoversy in Germany which has since spilled over into public life in the *Bundesrepublik*. At the eye of the storm is a revisionist interpretation of German history, with which the name of Ernst Nolte has been most often associated. Nolte's reading of Holocaust history has become controversial because of the continuing *political* relevance of all attempts to rationalise and explain Germany's Nazi past. Many Germans, and not just those on the left politically, have been very wary of any argument which seems to *excuse* the Holocaust; Nolte's argument may fall into this category.

He argues that the Holocaust was not a special case for which Germans should feel a special guilt, that it can be paralleled to earlier mass murders in the USSR. Stalin's Gulag Archipelago really *was* original, he says, Auschwitz a mere copy. His view is that, if the Nazis committed systematic race murder in the 1940s, Stalin's Russia had already committed systematic class murder in the 1930s. The former, he believes, was even a *consequence* of the latter. In other words, 'Red Menace' fears of the late 1920s fuelled middle-class support for Hitler, and those fears (being not entirely groundless) are therefore understandable and explicable. He even finds echoes of all this in recent history, arguing that the Cold War foreign policy which led to American atrocities in Vietnam was similarly motivated by a rational fear of communism.

Keyed in to this revision of history is, of course, the insidious notion of a present-day threat to European civilisation (for this, read bourgeois hegemony in Western Europe). In the new mythology of resistance to communism, West Germany is an important bastion for the 'free world'. Recognition of this led President Reagan to honour German war dead (including members of the SS) at Bitburg cemetery in May 1985. Nolte's explanation of why 'ordinary' Germans might have wanted to believe in Hitler is attractive to quite a spectrum of German centre and right opinion, especially those who see themselves as having expiated the Nazi past through the NATO present. The 1988 resignation of *Bundestag* Speaker, Philipp Jenninger, whose error was to allude to Nolte's thesis, shows how 'hot' an issue this still is.

Historians on the Left in Germany have rejected the Nolte thesis on the basis that a crucial *condoning* of responsibility is part of such an argument. The very bureaucratisation and industrialisation of policy which was the hallmark of the Final Solution, they believe, puts it into an altogether different category from any other atrocity, wartime or otherwise. For a start, the levels of overt and covert *participation* were spread further into the social fabric. Without minimising the brutality of Stalin's Russia, the left in West Germany continue to argue that the Holocaust must be seen as a *special* case, and that to make it historically relative is tantamount to beginning the dangerous process of condoning it.

Nolte's use of Vietnam as a comparison is provocative, but demonstrably inaccurate. The USA has to face the fact that acts of mass murder in places as diverse as Vietnam in the 1960s, Chile in the 1970s, and El Salvador in the 1980s are both product and by-product of its foreign policy. If its leaders came to understand that (if enough of its population could be persuaded to oppose policies which have these outcomes) then perhaps the policies would change. But there is a great deal of difference between this and a state which centres racial extermination as an instrument of home and foreign policy, then places the full weight of a state bureaucracy behind this ideological cornerstone.

The academic world is different from the world of the arts in degree rather than kind (as is evidenced by the suppression of both worlds which obtains in repressive regimes). Both communities have the function of circulating ideas and arguments, representing social and political life to the wider community of which they are part. They nominate, even promulgate, issues for a discussion which is, occasionally, very public. As part of a European 'past that won't go away', the Holocaust's continued re-presentation (in the academy, in theatre, and in film) is testimony to a continued cultural instability surrounding the meaning of this event (otherwise it would cease to be a subject about which meanings are made). The ways in which cultures attempt to make meanings about this subject tell us about the culture in which the meanings are being made, as well as about the Holocaust itself.

As surviving Holocaust victims have often enough said, the enormity of genocide on such a scale was/is numbing to the mind, a kind of protective barrier in the mind refuses knowledge. Just as the mind seems to slow at the moment of an accident, refusing to acknowledge that it is going to happen, concentration camp survivors' minds entered a different time-scale, one which was focused on minute-by-minute surviving. In Claude Lanzmann's 1985 film Shoah,[17] the single survivor of exterminations at Chelmno in Poland recalled,

> So when I came here, to Chelmno, I was already . . . I didn't care about anything. I thought: 'If I survive, I just want one thing: five loaves of bread.' To eat. That's all. That's what I thought. But I dreamed too that if I survive, I'll be the only one left in the world, not another soul. Just me. One. Only me left in the world, if I get out of here. (Lanzmann, p.103)

This 'selfishness of the organism' as it fights for basic survival is beyond the boundaries that constitute a 'social norm' (which is always about two people, not one – as Brecht once remarked). This is what makes the concentration camp experience, at a fundamental level, incommunicable. The available structures of feeling, and their capacity to cope with such matters, must be extended in treatments of this subject, each re-presentation seeking a rapprochement with its own historical conjuncture, as well as that of the Holocaust itself. Many film-makers, and theatre workers, have tried to approach the subject via radically different formal means, as each conventional approach to representation 'fails' to satisfy the continuing need to understand.

Painful reminders

If True Stories on radio, stage and screen are often merely reactive to situations (at least in part), the periodic return to questions about the Holocaust has been an indication of something beyond the merely reactive. The apparent inability really to finish with a subject, as it were, is an index of its power. True Stories about such subjects are far more than just reactive – they are 'painful reminders'. One of the earliest attempts to deal with the subject of the Holocaust was a film in the 'recording' documentary tradition called just that – A painful reminder.

Sidney (now Lord) Bernstein ordered the film to be made up from footage recorded by the Allied forces as they pushed into defeated Nazi Germany in the closing stages of World War Two. As well as compelling local Germans to walk through the camps so that they could see what had been done there, the occupying powers also decided that the footage showing the liberation of the concentration camps should be edited together and shown. The purpose of this was to impress upon the people of Germany the enormity of the crimes against humanity of which the Nazi leadership stood accused. In the end, it was decided that the conquered civil population was already so low in morale that the showing of the film would achieve nothing except to depress their morale still further, to a level which might prevent occupied Germany engaging in what was perceived as its primary task – the rebuilding of the shattered country, and in particular its economy.

When finally shown in 1985, the film became part of that 'anniversary game' by which television regularly beefs up its schedules. This is the game in which an historical anniversary is found which is deemed to have sufficiently wide appeal, then (if possible) film of the period is re-cycled. A painful reminder, an authentic 1940s recording tradition film, was transmitted to coincide with the fortieth anniversary of the end of the World War. Within its own conjuncture, the film's potential for 'reminding' was deemed less important than its capacity for disrupting economic rebuilding; outside its conjuncture, it became a curiosity, consumed as part of a re-packaging of contemporary history by a later generation. A better illustration of the economic forces which condition structures of feeling can scarcely be imagined.

Erwin Piscator was one of the earliest to recognise that there was a need in Germany to 'overcome the past'. Returning, unlike his country-man and former associate Brecht, to West rather than East Germany, Piscator perceived in Adenauer's West Germany of the Economic Mira-cle a disturbingly general 'desire to forget in matters of our recent history',[18] and the most important matter that Piscator saw being forgot-ten was the Holocaust. The single event which created sufficent tur-bulence for him to examine that 'recent history' was the 1961-2 trial in Jerusalem of Adolf Eichmann, one of the major organisational figures of the Final Solution – this put the problem back on the agenda for dis-cussion.

Of the two plays with which Piscator intervened in the debate over the Holocaust, Hochhuth's The representative and Weiss's The investigation (both 1965), only the latter was radically discontinuous. Weiss used an 'orato-rio' form in which counterpointed 'voices' were pre-eminent over stage action. While nine anonymous 'Witnesses' stand for the victims of the Holocaust, eighteen 'Defendants' are named (but significantly not characterised) in this play. In prefatory 'Remarks', Weiss argues (in a seminal phrase) that 'personal experiences and confrontations must be softened into anonymity' in order that understanding rather than emotion be emphasised for the audience. The aim is to understand 'a system which conferred guilt', rather than to find a group of scapegoats. The Holocaust is a subject which it is difficult to understand at the level of individual experience; it must be collectivised, as it were. This can only be done through a dialectical form through which the spectator is em-powered to create an autonomous point of view of the subject.[19]

Weiss's play was first presented in thirteen simultaneous productions on either side of the German Iron Curtain, and from that statistic alone its significance for both Germanies can be read. In the UK, it was given a 'public reading' at midnight (on the same day – 19 October 1965) by a group of RSC actors at the Aldwych Theatre in London. The reading was supervised by the RSC's charismatic director Peter Brook. Many things might be said of Brook, but a high degree of political commitment would rarely be claimed as one of his strengths, and his taking up of The investigation must be taken as both a positive and a negative statement about British theatre's ability to address the subject of the Holocaust. At the same time he was according the play cultural space as a result of his personal and institutional prestige, he was cutting its space down as a consequence of when and in what circumstances it was shown. He has

made no secret of his view that, after the first twenty minutes, one is likely
'to get bored' by it.[20] Historically, perhaps, the Holocaust was not a
subject as immediate to the national consciousness in the UK and the
USA as it was in Germany (and, of course, in Israel).

This has changed in recent years; the subject has gained greater centrality, in particular with TV's Holocaust series and the film Sophie's choice.
Whatever the merits of these pieces of cultural production, the 'law of
inverse proportions' seems to be operating just as firmly here as it did
with the subject of the nuclear deterrent. The law of inverse proportions
says that, the more difficult a subject, the more distanced its cultural
representations are from the set of historical events which constitute that
subject. It took the Holocaust forty-four years to become a subject for a
mass audience.

If these films are taken as modern markers for what is considered
appropriate to the subject of the Final Solution in popular dramatic
terms, there is also a film tradition which is comparable to Weiss/Pisca-
tor's theatrical one. In 1955, recording tradition newsreels compiled
from Allied and Nazi wartime footage were disrupted by Alain Resnais'
short film Nuit et brouillard ('Night and fog'). Here the juxtaposition of
cinéma vérité colour with newsreel black and white footage collision-mon-
taged past and present Auschwitz, enabling Resnais to present a convincing perspective on the camp ten years after its liberation. In the 'then'
(newsreel) sequences, mute people in a blighted landscape 'speak'
through suffering etched into their facial expressions; in the 'now' colour
sequences, there are, equally significantly, no people at all, merely an
empty landscape already greening over. Throughout the film, the voice
of the commentary is reflective, even poetical; it is not at all the informational voice of the 'normal' newsreel commentator. This was film of the
reporting tradition; like Weiss and Piscator's The investigation, it mediated a
frame through which to view otherwise mystified events.

Lanzmann's Shoah represents a continuation of the Resnais' tradition of
documentary film. The crucial difference is that, for Lanzmann, the
frame is the film itself rather than formal juxtapositions of any kind, 'poetic'
or otherwise. He speaks in his Introduction to the complete text of the
film of 'all the languages' existing in Shoah (p.vii). This plurality of language embraces both cinema language and spoken language. This latter
is a veritable Babel, and includes French, German, Polish, Hebrew and
Yiddish. In his travels through Europe, Lanzmann interviewed scores of
people, often through the intermediary of a translator. His film deliberately includes what he calls 'the crutches of the spoken language', since

Lanzmann believes that it is in their hesitations, repetitions, and evasions of questions that people's attitudes will most clearly reveal themselves. 'Nor,' says Lanzmann, 'have I purged my own questions.'

Instead of an unseen narrator who speaks for the viewing audience, or asks the questions s/he has prepared on their behalf, Lanzmann is both seen and heard in the film, as are his three translators. The 'problem' of the Holocaust is thus re-framed and re-focused dialectically, presenting the paradox of the communicative and un-communicative nature of all language. There is always a shifting proportion between what a language user reveals and conceals, and only when one *participates* in cultural production as a Brechtian-style 'active observer' is one in a position to gauge this proportion. Lanzmann is not afraid to slow the rhythm of his film almost to standstill in order to dwell on a particular face during wordless sequences.

For example, Henrik Gawkowski (the locomotive driver whose lined face appears on the cover of the printed text) is seen as he takes his train into Treblinka station. A board with the fateful name looms in the background while Gawkowski does what he has been doing routinely for over forty years. Later he is asked by Lanzmann why he looks so sad. 'Because I saw men marching to their death,' he says simply (p.37). He has told earlier how the Germans kept him and his fellow railway workers well-supplied with vodka, so that they would not pay too much attention to the screams of their human cargoes as they continued their necessary work. He is not a Gandhi-ish figure to whose level we are privilegedly elevated; he is an 'ordinary' man who, like most of us, has little or no access to that myth of individualised power which is cele-brated in the bio-pic. He carries his life story on his face, especially in unguarded silent moments – not in the conventionalised chronology of the bio-pic. He *knows* his lack of power, because he has *lived* it; it is expressed in the flick of his eyes towards and away from the figure of authority (in this case, Lanzmann's camera).

That other apparently-transparent language, the language of the cinema, is similarly contextualised in *Shoah*. Lanzmann frequently demonstrates the framed nature of his intervention into reality, in one memorable case re-staging it. His interview with Abraham Bomba rene-gotiates the 'rules' for documentary film-making by putting Bomba through a version of his camp trauma. This is done not by mocking-up a 'life-like' facsimile of the gas chamber in Treblinka where he cut the hair of those doomed to die within minutes, then having actors mime while he narrates in voice-over; nor is it done by showing the 'real' place where it all happened (in fact it no longer exists, apart from a Stonehenge-like memorial). It is done instead by filming Bomba working in a present-day barber shop (taken over for the purposes of the film, and thus, to an extent, a kind of fiction). As he works in the present, he answers Lanzmann's questions about his past. These turn upon the detailed minutiae of Bomba's previous 'work'. In all his questioning, Lanzmann quite frequently asks his interlocutors to give *precise* information, constantly drawing them back from generalised responses into ones of dispassionate detail.

Bomba is asked to imitate exactly how he cut the hair of the doomed women of Treblinka. 'How we did it – cut as fast as we could,' Bomba says in his heavily-accented English, as his hands begin to act upon muscular memory: 'We were quite a number of us professional barbers, and the way we did it, we just did this and this and we cut this like this here and this side and the hair was all finished. With big movements naturally, because we did not waste any time' (p.115). And even as he speaks, the job is done, and the pathos of his earlier contention that the calmness with which the barbers worked reassured the batches of women is established dialectically. He may try to comfort himself with the idea that the women believed 'they were getting a nice haircut', but he *knows* differently; and by the end of the sequence so do we.

Bomba survived because of the apparently-random fact that he could cut hair, and that skill was suddenly needed. Like Gawkowski, he survived by participating; he, of course, knows this only too well, and the culmulative effect of re-playing memories and re-exhibiting his skill (he had in fact retired by the time Lanzmann interviewed him) builds up until he is unable to continue speaking (p.117). 'I can't,' he says, 'It's too horrible. Please.' The off-screen film-maker insists, 'We have to do it. You know it.' Why this should be so is never explained, although the text's dedicatory quotation from Isiah 56:5 ('I will give them an everlasting name') was probably crucial to Lanzmann's project, if not Bomba's. Although Bomba has to all intents and purposes broken down, and a lengthy pause ensues as he tries to control his feelings, he *continues with his work* – eloquent testimony to the nature of the 'real' experience, and as near as anyone is ever likely to get to that reality, without having to live it.

The pause which ensues is lengthy in terms of what might be acceptable in other kinds of True Story. The time in which someone can be shown breaking down under the pressure of remembered experience could probably be quantified – a brief pause in *Holocaust*, say, could be matched to a longer one in *Sophie's choice*, before comparing both to this harrowing moment from Shoah. The time spent on such a moment will depend upon the total time-frame of the piece to some extent, and (in a dramatic piece) on the skill of the performers involved. Such moments must be set within the economic paramenters of the project being undertaken, too; if you are selling yourself, you cannot afford to be unattractive beyond a certain point because it will put people off.

This point is an obvious one, but its corollary is not as often accepted; this is that the very range of significations on offer gives us clues as to the ways in which society is *prepared* to understand itself. This, ultimately, has more to do with the receiving audience and the film-makers' expectations of them than with any considerations of 'real life' emotions. Shoah is important because it deliberately transgresses norms. In offering an alternative to ways of mediating a piece of twentieth-century experience it would be difficult to ignore, it makes the ground rules under which other pieces of cultural production operate all the clearer *by violating them*. Generalising out from Bomba's pause, the nine-hour duration of the complete Shoah makes a dialectical statement too – about the length appropriate for a 'commercial' movie (*Sophie's choice* runs at just over two and a half hours).

The 'uncommercial' length of Shoah, in other words, is transgressive, and it can only articulate its transgressiveness through uncommerciality. Shoah shares this feature with certain other examples of alternatives to controlling myths. Marcel Orphuls's *The sorrow and the pity*, for example, was four and a half hours long, and in 1988 he produced *Hotel Terminus*, a film about Klaus Barbie, the Nazi ruler of occupied Lyons (of similar form and length). In 1987 *The war game*'s Peter Watkins produced a new anti-nuclear film, *The journey*. This runs at *fourteen and a half hours* (but could be used, says its maker, in 'modular' form as well as seen in its entirety).

The use both Orphuls and Lanzmann make of oral history techniques is also fundamentally transgressive of filmic norms. Verbatim interview material has been used in cultural production before; it was part of Charles Parker's BBC Radio Ballads in the 1950s and 1960s, and it formed a staple of the 'New Journalism' of (for example) Studs Terkel in the USA. Such material has been brought into modern stage production via the Verbatim Play on both sides of the Atlantic.[21] In *Reds*, verbatim material even found its way into a commercial movie. But the *process* by which such material is obtained is normally elided in the released *product* to the extent that it is invisible, the potential messiness of the 'crutches of language' being erased. *Reds* emphasised this by allowing the 'old folks' only very short interventions before returning to the naturalisticallydriven main narrative. It also gave them a de-contextualised setting (a featureless, black background). *Shoah*, instead, not only underlines filmed context, it also allows us to witness something of the film's method of construction, too (or part of it – it is worth remembering that the film's nine hours represents *one-fortieth* of what Lanzmann actually shot).

By refusing identification devices, *Shoah* draws the spectator in, reconstituting him/her as a participant in the manner envisaged by Brecht and Piscator. In the absence of a central, univocal, figure or figures (factual or fictional) attention is focused instead on 'speaking survivors', whether they are speaking in a literal or a metaphorical sense. Nowhere is this more evident than when another kind of 'survivor' – an economic one – 'speaks'. This occurs during the examination of the use of gas vans at Chelmno (see pp.100-5). By a simple mechanism, the vans' exhaust gases were re-routed to asphyxiate their human cargoes; provided they were driven at the correct speed, the vans could thus deliver dead bodies to the ovens or burial pits, and become simultaneously transport and industrial plant. A Polish man ('Mr Falborski') gives a brief testimony at the site of the ovens, followed by Chelmno survivor, Simon Srebnik, whose job it was to unload the bodies from the vans.

The film then cuts to the interior of a car, driving through an industrial landscape. It could be any one of hundreds of modern industrial areas of Europe or America (but is probably the Ruhr). It is difficult to connect it with the previous rurality of the ovens' site, against which Falborski and Srebnik have spoken. The connection lies precisely in that concept of industrialisation which was the distinguishing feature of the Final Solution. Lanzmann reads an authentic primary source document as the car speeds through the industrial landscape; he gives its date – 5 June 1942. The document is a memo about the vehicles used to gas Jews, though this fact is distanced by the blandness of the official-ese in which it is couched. It begins: 'Since December 1941, ninety-seven thousand have been processed by the three vehicles in service, with no major incidents' (p.103). Before there is time to register the enormity, and yet the ordinariness, of this, before one can even question what a mind which so casually writes off 'ninety-seven thousand' (without according them their title of 'people') would construct as a 'major incident', the document gives a list of suggestions for 'technical changes' to the vehicles. These include a 'sealed drain in the middle of the floor . . . so that fluid liquids can drain off during the operation'.

The people whose bodily-functions are masked in this discourse are described as 'pieces', 'merchandise', and 'the load'; when being gassed (or rather 'processed') they display 'a natural tendency to rush to the rear doors'. This is ingeniously built into the writer's suggested modifications to the balance of the death-vehicles. Lanzmann's camera-operator has been dwelling all the while on the view through the back window of the car. A large lorry is following, and it is brought sharply into focus as Lanzmann concludes his reading of the memo. As he reads of the ten new vehicles ordered from the motor manufacturer – Saurer – we see from the close-up that the modern truck following Lanzmann's car is made by the very same company.

It is rare for the film True Story to include an item like this 1942 memo, because such things are usually constructed as 'unentertaining' by their very nature (being pieces of 'boring' official discourse). It is rarer still for the industrial drive towards efficiency (usually deemed as 'natural') to be connected so directly with the Holocaust, and with an industrial production not even interrupted by the unnatural suffering of its concentration camp slaves. Shoah makes such a connection clear time and time again (as when, on p.62, the former SS man Suchomel describes Auschwitz as 'a factory' and Treblinka as 'a primitive but efficient production line of death'). Shoah can include such things precisely because it is a transgressive form.

Transgressive forms not only examine the extent of what is formally possible in cultural production, they also establish political parameters of difference in the wider system of social significations of which films and plays are part. This can be seen most precisely in relation to particular cruxes in contemporary experience; such subjects are often touched most closely by True Stories.

True Stories/Real Stories – demystifying the document

In *True Stories* I stay away from loaded subjects – sex, violence, and political intrigue – because as soon as you get on those subjects, everybody has preconceived ideas about them. I deal with stuff that's too dumb for people to have bothered to formulate opinions on. (David Byrne)[1]

Introduction – 'Some pretty weird stuff'

Talking Heads' David Byrne made his movie *True stories* (and also released a record, and book-of-the-film) in 1986. His deliberate use of a seventy-year old sensationalist magazine title (borrowed for this book, with the addition of the all-important interrogative) made his film intertextual with American journalism's (and the American media's) ever-increasing galaxy of the weird and the strange. Like the 'True Stories That Shook The World' discussed in Chapter 2, sensationalist journalism is in business to beggar belief (and hence its perennial attraction). Sometimes it does this by exploring the borderline between what can be readily believed and that which seems (initially at any rate) downright crazy. The modern publications which Byrne ransacked all portray 'real characters' in 'real events', but they are of Baudrillard's order of the hyperreal. His film is a jokey and bizarre 'reality testing' of True Story truth-claims, a kind of post-modern True Story.

Byrne's 'dumb stuff' ('Laziest Woman in the World', 'Loving Couple Hasn't Spoken for 31 Years', 'Man Advertises on TV for Wife') is difficult to rationalise, and yet it claims 'true/real-ness' by virtue of being constructed as 'factual' through the discourse of 'journalism'. The published screenplay solemnly documents the newspaper and magazine articles which inspired the film, and which justify Byrne's view (expressed in the 1980 song 'Crosseyed and painless') that 'facts are nothing on the face of things' – they can be seen merely as phenomenological flotsam and jetsam, or as things which become more significant the more you consider them. In common with Baudrillard, Byrne seems to believe that modern America is surface.

Sources which might be constructed as 'reputable' (such as *The New York times* and *Newsweek*) jostle with publications like *Weekly world news, Conspiracies unlimited* and *Current events and Bible prophecy newsletter*. These sources form part of a print-continuum stretching all the way from 'objective' journalism to paranoia and born-again fundamentalism. Just like the UK's own *Sunday sport*, the product of the weirder, sensationalist, kind of journalism is habitually dismissed because, as Byrne says, it's 'too dumb' to bother with. However, its very popularity demands that the nature of its truth-claims be recognised and assessed. The range of sources, and the way the narrative of the film is driven visually, throws the 'true' of Byrne's title into question and doubt in a quirky subversion of both journalistic and movie concepts of 'true/real'. Film-making, he says, is just like any kind of story-telling, it's 'a trick to get you to keep paying attention' (p.9). If the 'documents' that he uses in themselves partially demystify the Document, the film itself demystifies the Documentary.

Byrne himself is the film's stetson-hatted narrator, giving his views on such neglected aspects of American life as shopping malls and metal buildings. He often addresses his audience from behind the wheel of a red sports car, or while walking through the streets of his archetypal Small Town. Engaging the camera in conversation, or lecturing in voice-over, he is for all the world like an authentic television 'talking head' in any 'real' documentary programme, the 'intelligent outsider' discovering and explaining what he finds around him. It appears to be the classic omniscient documentary stance, except that the things he finds are so strange and he reports them in such a deadpan manner. Who, you want constantly to ask, is he kidding?

The section on shopping malls is supported by an article from *Texas monthly*, which quotes a businessman as saying, 'What you're trying to create here is almost a university . . . You're trying to create an alumnus instead of a consumer. If you don't create an alumni association, then those consumers will be here today and gone tomorrow' (p.71). Revealed in such 'dumb' overstatements is the colossal hubris of the quintessential Free Market nation of the commercial 'go-getter'. Byrne's film is an intertextual 'documentary' on post-modern consumerism, animated by the kind of 'naive' viewpoint which has dominated a great deal of modern art in America; it is difficult to locate any critical judgement of the subjects by the author, they are taken at face value with a sense of distanced wonder. On Talking Heads records, and especially in

live performance, Byrne's singing persona has habitually been that of an
apparently 'ordinary' middle-American, revealed by the songs (like the
archetypally alienated 'Once in a Lifetime') to be just barely hanging on
to sanity. Those familiar with the psychotic 'nerd' of the records will see
him also in the film's narrator. Thus True stories is intertextual with art,
journalism, film, television and rock music.

The friendly-but-strange narrator/outsider occasionally disrupts the
informational spectacle by providing information so manifestly in excess
of immediate requirements it makes for a distanciation of which even
Brecht might have approved. Ending a link from the red sports car, for
example, he suddenly looks at the camera and remarks, 'This isn't a hired
car, you know. It's privately owned.' On one occasion, the visual frame is
broken by Brechtian-style spoken stage directions. Outside a shopping
mall, the narrator explains that here people can 'comparison shop'; the
sequence continues:

MARGIE (off-screen): Everybody could hardly wait until the mall opened.
NARRATOR: Said Margie Ortiz.
MARGIE (enters frame): I go there just about every weekend. So do two of the other
gals at work.
NARRATOR: That's exactly what I'm talking about, See, I told ya. (p.68)

The film is a constant disruption of apparently-accepted cultural
boundaries.

In cultural production, societies transform some of their most contentious problems into plays and films. True Stories are particularly engaged
in these transformations because they address issues with apparently
unassailable truth-claims. Byrne's film generates its quirky amusement
from a mis-match which depends upon an awareness of common
'serious' modes of constructing the true/real, which it then subverts. In
other words, the film demystifies those 'documentary' accounts of the
'real' world which shape our knowledge and understanding of that
world.

The Sunday sport-ish Woman Who Won't Get Out of Bed and the Man
who Advertises for a Wife are 'documents' inhabiting a borderline
between individuality and eccentricity; they mark the outer reaches of
the American project of Expressing Individuality which, in its most
extreme manifestations, is mad. America is the country which recognises,
almost as an act of faith, that pre-eminence of individualism which is the
quintessence of capitalism. Its 'real characters' are surely an indication of
the fact that, as Byrne himself points out, 'Empires in retreat get into
some pretty weird stuff' (p.14).

Starring Roger Rabbit – the American heritage industry

The kinds of things constructed as popular give clues as to a society's general orientation and the current state of some of its most treasured concepts. For example, one of the most expensive popular films of 1988 was *Who framed Roger Rabbit*. Like much successful Disney cartoon production of the past, the film features an anthropomorphised cartoon animal (spearhead for an invasion of the market in the form of cuddly-toy, T-shirt and other branded goods spin-offs). Not only does the eponymous rabbit follow in the famous footsteps of cartoon ancestors Mickey Mouse and Donald Duck in carving out a new consumer empire, he also interacts with human performers – he is, in fact, the 'star' of the film. Interaction between human and cartoon performers is not new in itself, of course, the mixing of live and cartoon performances in films make up a sort of sub-genre (a list might include, for example, the execrable *Mary Poppins* of 1964). What could be claimed as new is Roger Rabbit's *pre-eminence* over the film's human actors.

If stars are, as Richard Dyer claims, a means of articulating crisis in 'the sense of freedom, creativity, continuity, optimism and enterprise that founded the concept of the person in bourgeois society',[2] then a cartoon star who relegates humans into positions of secondary importance problematises the current cultural status of the individual. This is especially the case in a culture in which 'individuality' has become a kind of cult. This seems to be part of the point David Byrne makes in the *True stories* movie – when does individuality shade into the eccentricity of madness, when does fact shade into a fiction only tolerated for its oddity (hence its value as 'entertainment')? Read the sensationalist press on both sides of the Atlantic, and you will see that there is no boundary, merely an apparently seamless continuum of manufactured meanings, all with their own axe to grind, all apparently tending towards that diversity in contemporary America which Jean Baudrillard calls hyperreal.

The producers of *Roger Rabbit* clearly always intended their cartoon figure to be pre-eminent. The English actor Bob Hoskins plays the gum-shoe who is the major human foil to the cartoon characters in the film. Hoskins's performance may be a skilled and engaging one, but as a star he isn't in Roger Rabbit's class. It would probably be fair to say that the production was geared to a concept of 'Roger Rabbit' from the outset, in the knowledge that his 'reality' would be relatively easy both to establish and to popularise in the Land of the Hyperreal. Spielberg's 1982 E.T. falls into a similar category, of course. Received professional theatrical wisdom has long held that the human adult performer will always come off second best when sharing stage or screen with children or animals; following *Roger Rabbit* and E.T., the list would seem to be urgently in need of an update – cartoon characters and Special Effects Cuddlies should also be avoided.

True Stories may seem to be worlds away from these films, but they epitomise that smiling, sentimental, familial face of Reagan's Hyperreal America which loads all cultural production with its meanings (and against which any oppositional meaning has to fight). Spielberg's productions are the epitome of this; his E.T. is suffused with values that elsewhere surface in right-wing pronouncements about Country, Home and Family. *Roger Rabbit* is infected with a 'Smile, Darn Ya, Smile!', cracker-barrel optimism imbricated into a cultural imperialism which once showed (in an advertisement) children of all nations of the world rejoicing in the consumption of Coca-Cola. As we move into the 1990s, President Bush's much-hyped extended family indicates that we should expect more of the same.

The sophistication of this means of production should not be underestimated. Like much modern cultural production, *Roger Rabbit* is postmodern in the way it pastiches not only the 'Toon' world of Sylvester, Tweety Pie *et al*, but also films of the 1930s. Publicity material for the film proclaimed that 'fun and laughter lie in wait for all the family, but serious-minded movie fans will find much to appreciate as well: the film pays tribute to the golden age of Hollywood . . . with a plot reminiscent of a Humphrey Bogart black and white thriller'. Intertextuality of this kind has become vital in post-modern cultural production, which serves a public grown increasingly sophisticated in its knowledge of, and ability to handle, the complex codes of audio-visual presentation and representation. It is revealing that the publicists for *Roger Rabbit* made their appeal *both* to 'all the family' *and* to 'serious-minded movie fans'.

'Official' media in Western cultures have to collude in post-modern times in making the viewer think – but not too much. High-selling popularity is more likely to result from this strategy than from one in which the public is treated as an ass. But the intertextuality of *Roger Rabbit* (added to the more and more dangerous special effects being used in order to sustain a state of awed stupefaction), gives a clue to the enormous efforts necessary to hold the whole operation together. While bereft of any (obvious) politics, movie intertextuality of this kind is the American Heritage industry. The celebration of a 'golden' Hollywood past assiduously re-makes not only that 'Hollywood past', but also a political past which was partly mediated by Hollywood in the first place. It does this in its continual exclusion of troublesome subjects, like politics.

If one is a 'serious' movie buff, to what, exactly, does one see 'tribute' paid in *Roger Rabbit*? The Bogart, 'Sam Spade', film has enjoyed critical and popular acclaim during the past twenty years, but is partly celebrated for its idealised version of Depression America. Current predilection for between-the-wars America (Coppola's 1984 *The Cotton Club* is a good recent example as, of course, is *Reds*) is as much an icon of hyperreality as the Disney cartoon. The mythology of the 'Speakeasy' animates every-thing from fashion to an advertisement for alcohol-free lager (the 'Barbi-can' ad). Through such means the past is reappropriated on behalf of the hegemony of the present, its disruptive political elements purged. In the early 1930s, there was a strong *socialist* movement in the USA which is persistently occluded in favoured Hollywood 'classics' of the period, just as the *poverty of* the period is elided into a carefully-tailored fashionable 'look'. This cultural activity denies oppositional politics for a *second* time, and by effacing this history helps to ensure the continuity of a hegemoni-cally-constructed 'America'. The past 'America' of the movie industry is not unlike the past 'Great Britain' of the UK heritage industry – both constructs tend to convey the message that, if it existed, opposition to the hegemony has now served its purpose.

Cultural production can be a kind of safety-valve which protects hege-monies from revolutionary change (by diverting some of the potential energy of oppositional forces), or a barometer of pressures within a culture which gives more or less precise information (about the meanings a culture can and cannot take). 'Official culture' True Stories are an excellent means of judging which aspects of its history (remote and recent) a society needs to acculturate (or bring within present parameters of cultural understanding). Those parts of a national history which are 'difficult', which 'will not go away' (like German experience of the Holocaust, or British experience of colonial and post-colonial periods), need constant attention if they are to be prevented from disrupting and subverting. Cultural treatments of the Vietnam experience exemplify this.

Vietnam – the American past that wouldn't go away

Partly because of its pre-eminence in the motion picture industry, and partly as a result of its emerging status as the chief military and economic power of the western world, US mediations of war (ancient and modern) have always been particularly interesting. It is only necessary to compare two Second World War documentary films about bomber crews, one from the UK, the other from the USA, to make the point about transatlantic cultural relativities. Harry Watt's 1941 *Target for tonight* and William Wyler's 1943 *Memphis Belle* treat similar subjects (heavy bomber raids over Germany), they were made for similar purposes ('information' and/or morale-boosting propaganda) by government-backed agencies (the Crown Film Unit and the War Activities Commission), they even run for similar lengths (43 and 48 minutes), and both have subsequently been much cannibalised for bombing raid 'stock-shots'.

There the similarities end. Watt's black and white film adopts a Grier-sonian documentary approach, in which characters are not as important as information which will (the reader may remember) help constitute a responsible citizen fully cognisant of war efforts being made on his/her behalf. Like many non-American film-makers, film economics would have condemned Watt to mine this rich, but marginal, seam regardless of his intentions because, like most non-Americans, he lacked immediate access to a more extensive means of production. Wyler's film by contrast is in Glorious Technicolor, and the characters aboard the Flying Fortress 'Memphis Belle' are delineated via a kind of shorthand Hollywood adventure film narrative which depends upon 'action film' cutting and 'dramatic' camera angles. The directorial notions behind the film have been forged in a movie industry. The word that springs to mind for the Wyler film is 'professional' – it is 'mini-movie', not 'documentary-short' and its visual and aural values are assured by the superior camera and microphone technology to which its director had access.

Harry Watt is still virtually unheard of (to anyone not interested in that specialised field, the documentary film); Wyler, however, is a famous Hollywood director with 'classic' films to his credit such as *The big country* (1958) and *Ben-Hur* (1959). Even when making a less than feature length war propaganda/information film, Wyler inflects his task with the working processes of which he has experience. When Hollywood went to war, its directors went too, John Ford, John Huston and Frank Capra as well as Wyler; all of them made their war-meanings within the parameters of their pre-war working experience. Since the war, understanding of the nature of warfare has been inflected by Hollywood war movies from the 1949 *Sands of Iwo Jima*, to the 1962 *The longest day*, and beyond. The

mid-1960s was the high-water mark of the celebratory war movie. There-
after, the escalating conflict in Vietnam made the genre more problematical.

Proponents of a '1968 watershed' tend to argue that that year (which
began with the Tet offensive in Vietnam) signalled the beginning of the
end for America's military adventure in south-east Asia, but it is worth
recalling that the process of 'escalation' had been going on at least since
the Gulf of Tonkin incident in 1964. Protest against the war was a feature
of American civil life from 1965, when demonstrations in the USA and in
Europe followed the build-up of US military activity. Forms of protest,
from the beginning, took on a theatrical aspect (in November 1965, for
example, protesters symbolically 'invaded' the Pentagon). Draft card
burning was an inherently theatrical gesture, and on one occasion
became the subject of a documentary play (Daniel Berrigan's 1970 *The trial
of the Catonsville Nine*). America's students were the focus for activism, and
Vietnam became a major unifying issue for opposition politics.

The year 1966 provided what was to become a major media image of
the Vietnam War. From April of that year, South Vietnamese students and
Buddhist monks intensified their campaign for a return to civilian rule (in
a South Vietnam now 'governed' by a military establishment sustained
almost totally by the USA). This culminated in acts of self-immolation by
Buddhist monks on the streets of Saigon. This piece of 'real theatre' was
assiduously recorded by newsreel cameras; in the West, it became one of
the controlling contemporary images of the conflict. (Another image
which controlled understanding of the war was the film/still photograph
of a little Vietnamese girl running along a highway to escape the fire that
had eradicated her village, her naked body scarred by the horrific effects
of napalm – so deeply was this one felt that the grown-up little girl was
sought out twenty years later for a TV documentary on Vietnam.)

The image of people burning, by choice or random stroke of technology, was a central feature in the Royal Shakespeare Theatre Company's
1966 production *US*. Put together from a combination of research
and improvisation by a collective of writers and performers, *US* is a kind
of template upon which can be superimposed many characteristic 1960s
attitudes. *US* had a transatlantic cultural 'mirror' in Megan Terry's *Viet
rock*, produced by Joseph Chaikin's Open Theatre at New York's Café La
Mama. Pre-dating *US* by nearly five months, this production, too, was
based upon research and improvisation; it, too, used contemporary
cultural markers such as rock music (Chaikin was later involved in the
rehearsals for *US*). *Viet rock* was positioned in a far more alternative

context vis-à-vis US culture, but the similarities between the two plays are nonetheless marked. Both explored a confrontational Theatre of Cruelty style for which the ultimate source was Artaud (and behind him psychological interest in rituals of sacrifice and suffering). Although there was a coterminous interest in Brecht (Brechtian *mannerisms* were much sought after in both the UK and US theatres of the 1960s) the exhibitionist tendencies of Artaudianism proved more in tune with the times.

As with *Oh what a lovely war*, the collectivity of such pieces has posed problems for criticism, but once again charismatic directors were constructed as 'onlie true begetters'. There was, however, a vital difference between the historical conjunctures within which Littlewood, and Brook/Chaikin worked. Littlewood's roots were in the highly politicised 1930s; Chaikin's and Brook's were in the mystical, 'do-your-own-thing' 1960s, where the figure of the Guru lurks. Like the Beatles (and almost everyone else), theatre was in search of a guru (or a chemical substance, or a method) which would afford a dazzling light by which reality could be transformed and understood. The published script of US includes two accounts of the rehearsal process of the play (by Peter Brook's 'assistants' Michael Kustow and Albert Hunt). These show very clearly the extent of Brook's shamanistic control, and his portentous and gnomic utterances are much quoted. For example, after the first night (13 October 1966) he is quoted as saying to the cast, 'The experiment we have been making since the start is, what is the relationship between theatre and everyday life?' (p.150). It must be assumed that this was heard in reverential silence, as many of Brook's pronouncements seem to have been.

Brook has suffered from being British theatre's Only Authentic Guru, and as a result his often brilliant ideas have rarely been subjected to systematic political analysis. He has tried earnestly to escape from the potentially stultifying role of wise man by seeking an ever-wider international cultural base. But, significantly, the British theatre establishment can accept Brook's 'brilliance', while it has consistently rejected the more politically orientated qualities of a Joan Littlewood or a John McGrath. Brook is a (relatively) comfortable figure in his brilliance, since it is directed at the opaque and the ineffable rather than the specific and the local. Charles Marowitz pointed this out at the time US was first performed, arguing that if the theatre's purpose had once been to ask questions, it now had a responsibility to indulge in a real risk strategy – the supplying of *answers*, because, 'we are not disputing esthetic [sic] theories, but a theme for which *real* American soldiers, and real Vietnamese people are really dying'.[3]

Today, US looks chock-full of images, and examples, of a Pop, 'Happenings', culture (what Marowitz calls 'arty-farty tactics'). It loses all sight of Vietnam by its second act, Andy Warhol and John Cage becoming as important to the show's project as Ho Chi Minh and President Thieu. Looking back, Albert Hunt felt 'that we spent far too much time agonising over the liberal conscience'. This was most manifest in the way the company 'raced through Vietnamese history, slipped over land reform, said almost nothing about the NLF' (Brook *et al*, p.95).

America, too, was in search of its gurus, theatrical and otherwise. Polish theatre director Jerzy Grotowski became very much 'flavour of the month' on both sides of the Atlantic, and both the RSC and Open Theatre collaborated with him. Grotowski's highly-wrought improvisational style stems from Roman Catholic roots, tortured through the post-war Polish experience of a hard-faced communism inimical to the very concept of the 'freely-choosing' individual. Grotowski's work characteristically sought a kind of epiphany which, in his own culture, is expressive of that tragic collision.[4] His methodology has much in common with such things as 'encounter group' psychology and transcendental meditation, which are themselves icons of the Sixties (perhaps this was why privileged Western artists wanted to 'buy in' to his vision of the crucified individual). Grotowski influenced not only Brook, but also some of the best American alternative directors (including Chaikin himself, and Living Theatre's Julian Beck).

A process so concentrated on the ineffable was sometimes in danger of being mystified out of all proportion to the significance of its ultimate product. Michael Kustow describes the RCS's ten days rehearsal with Grotowski as 'difficult to describe, because it took place on such a private, naked level, because it was in every sense a workshop, a consulting-room, a confessional, a temple, a refuge, a place of reflection, but reflection conducted not only with the mind, but with every fibre and muscle of the body' (Brook *et al*, p.132). Clearly, it is always difficult to talk about profound experience, but this quasi-religious air is redolent of a kind of 1960s intensity which was not just found in the theatre.

Shifting a structure of feeling

Joan Littlewood would sometimes tell over-cerebral performers that there were, in her view, two kinds of actor – 'those who think with their whole bodies, and heads on sticks.' In the 1960s, however, it seemed sometimes that the head had been abandoned altogether, in favour of an

often bogus spirituality which sometimes had the effect of effacing
thought completely. It was not as if there was no politics around in the
theatre at the time; it was simply that politics was not always constructed
as being as important as self-discovery. A Brechtian-style play on Vietnam
was available in the 1960s (in the form of Peter Weiss's 1967 *Discourse on
Vietnam*); but the politically-confrontational style of Weiss was not
favoured by the British and American theatrical establishments.

The tenor of mainstream cultural production can be indicated by
reference to two events. In 1966, in record charts on both sides of the
Atlantic, a pop song called 'Ballad of the Green Berets' achieved a large
measure of success. It was sung by a former member of that élite corps,
who was significantly given his rank on the record label – *Staff Sergeant
Barry Sadler*. This True Story song was authenticated by Sadler's
experience (and declared rank). It positioned the military individual
where he (the gender-specific pronoun is deliberate) had always been –
centre stage, suffering and dying for a noble cause. In 1968, John Wayne's
movie *The Green Berets* was released. Memorably described by Penelope
Gilliat as 'best handled at a distance and with a pair of tongs' (Halliwell,
1988, p.429), this film presented the American Establishment's case for
the Vietnam War. It was a case not dissimilar to the one accorded to film
versions of the Hitler War, with the added anti-communist ingredient
which had re-inflected war movies quite successfully in the 1950s. But
the oppositional cultural activity already in place by 1968 showed that
shifts in attitudes were taking place, especially amongst the young. By
failing to recognise this, Wayne's 'obsolete' movie revealed itself as a
cultural dinosaur.

The mediation of Vietnam is illustrative of two important cultural facts:
that all 'fiction' treatments of True Stories normally have a built-in time
lag, and that the mainstream is normally well behind the alternative in
keeping up with shifts of attitude. If news cameras are, as it were, first to
the scene of the Real Story, and documentary film-makers are second,
the makers of True Stories tend to lag much further behind. Whereas the
'provisional' treatments of True Stories possible within alternative styles
allow a speedy, direct response to a shift in attitude, the laborious
processes of 'big money' cultural production are not as quick. When they
try for a quick response, they run the risk of missing the point
completely.

This manifestly happened to *The Green Berets*, where the film's gung-ho
attitude achieved a spectacular mis-match with some of the new feelings
in American society. A growing attitude of suspicion and opposition

rendered other attitudes inappropriate. Wayne's film was vying with other mediations which had already begun to make his treatment suspect. In 1965 CBS screened a despatch from correspondent Morley Safer (showing a Vietnamese village being fired by American troops) which alarmed and shocked the viewing public; news coming back to mainland America in increasing amounts from about this time depicted the inevitable confusion of a 'front-less' war, in which the enemy were clearly refusing previously understood rules of engagement. Whereas in film coverage of the more consensual Hitler war there had been time to 'shape' a movie to fit the desired mood, here the more confused and frightening mediation, made it less easy to construct a univocal view.

Documentary directors such as Emile de Antonio ensured that dissenting accounts showed people struggling in a lethal world of total chaos which ultimately unhinged the sense of *rightness* which *The Green Berets* tried to foster. It became impossible, as Tom Harrisson once observed, to separate the collapse of South Vietnam from 'a whole saga of ecology, sociology, economy, politics, money and corruption'.[5] De Antonio's 1969 *In the Year of the Pig*, a documentary account of the Tet Offensive, was part of a cultural production which built on the inevitable intertextuality between the TV news report and the documentary film. The 'structure of feeling' about Vietnam which was constructed via such mediations did not support the orthodoxy favoured by the American establishment, it supported the view that the war was a bloody failure. Ultimately, the USA could not sustain its neo-colonial adventure and was forced into progressive withdrawal; culturally-determined representations of historical reality and that historical reality itself were more in harmony with each other, but there was nothing to celebrate in this. When the last combat troops left South Vietnam in 1973 (followed closely by North Vietnamese final victory in 1975) there seemed nowhere for American mediations of Vietnam to go.

The American public not only had to accept a military failure (to which it was not accustomed), it also had to accept a catalogue of atrocity which began with Safer's report in 1965 and culminated in the 'Pinkville massacre'. At My Lai (a small rural village in South Vietnam – called 'Pinkville' on US campaign maps) on 16 March 1968, US troops not only destroyed a settlement and massacred its inhabitants irrespective of age and sex, they also (metaphorically) deconstructed a whole policy of 'pacification'. When this information was revealed (and it took until November 1969 before it was revealed) it was no longer a matter of the rightness or wrongness of a war; a revelation had been made of a decline in morale and morals, in the very 'American Way of Life' which they had been trying to bring to/force upon the Vietnamese, which demonstrated the wide gulf between officially sanctioned accounts of the war and the manifest reality of how it was being fought on the ground. That such a thing could be revealed speaks volumes for the nature of American democracy; but the fact that it was happening also spoke volumes. The existing structure of feeling about Vietnam had been shifted to a point where organised capital (the movie industry) could no longer make *immediate* use of it. It was almost ten years before Vietnam could be reflected in some kind of tranquillity, or overtly mediated in commercial films.

Vietnam fictions – ideological reflections in tranquillity

With some distance in time, it became possible to reflect Vietnam in some kind of tranquillity. As Vietnam news-vet Michael Herr wrote in his 1977 *Dispatches*, it was 'already a long time ago, I can remember the feelings but I can't still have them'.[6] Michael Cimino's *The deer hunter* (1978) was the first Vietnam film to receive widespread attention and recognition, and it was several years more before *First blood* (1982) could begin the project of re-appropriating the myth of American superiority. In the years before, other kinds of cultural production subsumed the Vietnam experience through the distancing mechanism of allegory (like the late 1960s/early 1970s representations of the Decline of the Heroic West evident in Sam Peckinpah's 1969 *The wild bunch*, for example). One might even seek a covert mediation of My Lai in the 1970 Dustin Hoffman vehicle *Little Big Man*, with its 'confessional' account of the massacre of Red Indians at Wounded Knee in 1890.[7] But the historical process by which *direct* treatment of the subject of Vietnam made its way back on the cultural agenda is worth considering.

In 1979, when the USSR invaded Afghanistan, a huge sigh of relief was almost audible in the USA. Here was the other 'Great Power' of the post-war binary divide making a Vietnam-sized mistake to balance out their own. The pressure of accumulated guilt about Vietnam began to be released at this nodal point in the late 1970s. This coincided almost exactly with the release of *The deer hunter* and the first publication of Herr's influential book. Herr's influence is evident in the fact that he has been involved as screenwriter in two Vietnam films, Coppola's 1979 *Apocalypse now* and Kubrick's 1987 *Full metal jacket*. *Dispatches* was one of the first attempts to articulate what it was like to *have been there*, one of the controlling aims of the True Story. The mournful tone of Cimino's elegy for lost American innocence has been followed up in subsequent movies by a continued effort to position the experience of the Vets as a 'growing up', on both micro-personal and macro-national levels.

America in the 1980s has been engaged in a widespread cultural re-reading not only of Vietnam, but also of its wider post-war past. This 1950s/1960s 'growing up period' (for the all important 40-50 age group, many of whom are now part of the power élite's lower echelons) has been the focus for many recent films which have reviewed the USA of the 1950s and 1960s. This territory is now colonised by TV advertisements for jeans, chewing gum, and Coca-Cola as well as movies. The Vietnam experience could not be left out of this re-reading, because everyone between the ages of 18 and 28 in the USA in the 1960s *had* to have a formative attitude to Vietnam, however weakly held. Vietnam has become part of this retrospective cultural tourism which confers credibility even upon those who did not go there, provided they hold an authenticated 'attitude'.

'Attitudes to Vietnam' are constructed culturally via one of two 'real' experiences – serving or not-serving. If you served, you didn't necessarily fight; you could have stayed in the USA for the duration of your service, or been in Europe, or in a relatively quiet base area. If you didn't serve, it might well be because you were a conscientious 'peacenik' objector (burning your draft card, invading the Pentagon, going into exile, deserting), or it might equally be because you were 'unfit' for some reason (real or invented); it might even be that (Quayle-like) you could shunt yourself into a more comfortable siding. But only 'serving/fighting' and 'not serving/protesting' positions are fully articulated, other positions becoming evident only in absence. The articulation of the 'protest position' has become attenuated in the 1980s as the war has acquired retrospective validity (it was even attacked in John Irvin's 1987 *Hamburger Hill*). 'Serving/fighting' has finally been positioned centre stage (or, at any rate, screen) in the 1980s; it has finally been constructed as *valuable* in the current historical conjuncture in a way which was not possible twenty years ago.

Following the opening in 1983 of the black marble Memorial Wall in Washington D.C., which rises and falls with the number of dead per year of the conflict, the Vietnam Vet has acquired a status he must have thought would be denied him for ever. Now the Vet's experience is nationally recognised by a memorial, and a Vice-Presidential candidate can be challenged because he did *not* go to Vietnam. The Vet has been culturally valorised following official reinstatement, he even travels to the USSR of *perestroika* in order to counsel the Russians' own newly-constructed Vets, the *Afghantsi*. The Vet has his new anthem, too; instead of Barry Sadler's noble narrative ballad of muscle-bound inarticulacy, there is Bruce Springsteen's 1984 'Born in the USA'. The stadium-rock *braggadocio* of the chorus of this song (the verses are broadly oppositional) has unfortunately been hi-jacked by right-wing versions of a born-again national pride most infamously evident in Sylvester Stallone's *Rambo* movies.

First blood reconstructed the Vietnam Vet as a misunderstood and mixed-up hero (film makers now cannot ignore the often-quoted statistic that more Vietnam Vets have died through self-slaughter since the conflict than died in it). Audiences reportedly stood and cheered Rambo's exploits, as being gloriously credible. But if such films appear to present few problems of interpretation, so nakedly are right-wing values being proclaimed in them, they demand reassessment of the view that American tastes have changed to a significant extent. Stallone zapping the Cong (or the Russians in Afghanistan in the most recent manifestation of the genre) seems little different in kind from Red Indian slaughter in Westerns, or John Wayne wading into Germans or Japs (or even Mexicans in his 1960 *The Alamo*).

Rather than celebrating a version of history, the Rambo films wilfully *deny* a history, then *re-invent* it in a preferred image. They do this in order to construct a nationalistic triumphalism that was never possible in the Vietnam experience itself. The films reappropriate the manifest failure of the Vietnam adventure, constructing it into a heavily-personalised 'success'. The element of failure has been shifted into a failure of nerve on the part of the (then) American leadership, or into 'misunderstandings' about the nature of military power. In the children's TV show *The A-Team* (from 1983), violent military skills are constructed as *dangerous but necessary*; the series sometimes seems to be an up-date on the famous Great War question to conscientious objectors, 'What would you do if you saw a German soldier about to violate your sister?' The Rambo-style movie reasserts the *necessity* of male violence, stridently proclaiming not only that might is right, but also that might is the only guarantee of right. All this is complicit with Reagan/Thatcher's view that Western 'strength' has brought about Soviet willingness to negotiate over nuclear weapons, human rights, and so on.

The 1980s right-ward political swing in the West has seen Thatcher elected in the UK, Helmut Kohl elected in West Germany, and first

Reagan then Bush become President in the USA. It has pushed several 'pasts that won't go away' back on to political and cultural agendas. In all three countries a more confident right has sought to re-appropriate versions of nationalism which many on the left had confidently assumed were dead. These monsters were sleeping and not dead, it would appear, and the Right in the West are assiduously revising history in their favour. The question of South Africa (in UK cultural production) has been a site for the contestation of post-colonial meanings in which apparently 'liberal', mainstream mediations can cloak more right-wing ideology than their makers would believe (to judge from their published effusions), and the 'historians' quarrel' in West Germany is a similar indication of a contest for re-interpretation of the Nazi past. In the USA, re-inflections of the Vietnam experience have occupied a central cultural arena in roughly the same period.

The key problem with mediations of Vietnam has been the need to please two very contrasting constituencies. On the one hand, Vietnam Veterans (treated as virtual pariahs for many years) now demand that their essential suffering be depicted accurately; on the other, those who had opposed the war in the 1960s have demanded that its essential *wrongness*, asserted then, should not be fudged now. For the Vets, the bitter memory of the years in which America forgot them, or tried to pretend that they didn't exist, could only be assuaged by some kind of *recognition* of their doomed sacrifice; for the 'peaceniks', who felt that they had 'won' the argument about the war in the 1960s, there could be no *limitations* placed upon that victory, for limitations would dilute the earlier message of 'My Country Right, But Not Wrong'. In the 1980s, this apparently unresolvable dilemma became achievable as the war went back on the cultural and political map.

In 1980 Vetco, an American alternative theatre company, was formed by a group of Vietnam veterans. The company's production of *Tracers* (which came to the UK in 1985) is an important manifestation of the changing times because it works with a verbatim testimony hitherto effaced from the cultural account, except in books like Michael Herr's. The initial activity of Vetco was concerned at least as much with *therapy* as it was with cultural production. Much post-1960s alternative arts on both sides of the Atlantic has, like Vetco's, been similarly process (not product) orientated. Meeting to help each other come to terms with what was at best a harrowing experience, at worst the depths of PTS (Post Traumatic Stress Syndrome, into which category what used to be known as shell-shock would now fall), the group talked, experimented,

F

improvised, and ended by creating Tracers. This was a very typical piece of
alternative theatre, with the trademarks discussed already – rapid trans-
formations of time, scene and character, direct address of the audience,
effective dialectical use of music, minimum props and setting, and so on.
Most important of all, its therapeutic component, unlike that of US, was
related to something concrete. The play has been performed by a
number of different casts, all veterans, all participating in what the
originator of the group, John DiFusco, has called 'a cleansing and a
purging' of their experience.[8]

Oliver Stone's 1987 Platoon is an important example of the attempt to
cleanse and purge America itself of its Vietnam experience via a commercial movie. Authenticated (especially in pre-publicity) by Stone's real life
experience as a soldier in Vietnam, Platoon invokes a new kind of hero.
Unlike the Vice-President Quayles of America, Stone actually went to
Vietnam, even though he didn't have to. Coming from a social class
which was able to avoid serving if it wished to 'pull strings', he chose to go.
Stone (the new hero who chose service instead of the avoidance of
service) exercised a choice denied to countless working-class blacks and
whites, of course, but this is rarely mentioned. For almost fifteen years
the experience which resulted from his choice was an albatross, just as it
had been for the members of Vetco and for the lost legions of Vietnam
Vets; in the 1980s, it was transformed into the proverbial golden egg-lay-
ing goose on a scale undreamed of by the alternative theatre 'therapists'
of Vetco.

Movie (and play) makers often reveal themselves most clearly in their
published introductions, those places where there is an almost formal
compulsion both to justify and to express satisfaction. The published
screenplay of Platoon is preceded by Stone's queasily-titled essay 'One
From The Heart'.[9] Like Donald Woods's approval of the 'rightness' of
Denzel Washington as Steve Biko, Stone's account celebrates the way
Charlie Sheen (playing Chris – or the young Stone) 'becomes' an authentic Vietnam Vet. The director finds 'an eerie sense of mental bonding'
between himself and Sheen, and says, 'Over the weeks, he's become
tougher, sharper, a jungle vet who can hump sixty pounds and walk right
up on a deer in the bush without being heard' (Stone, p.7). Trained by
'real' Marines, the heroic 'grunts' whom Stone so admires, the unit live in
approximately 'real conditions', in a geographical approximation of
Vietnam (the Philippines). 'Reality' is thus assured even down to 'a spirit
of cameraderie – of gruntdom' which Stone finds emerging amongst the
cast, and which he duly finds reflecting the cameraderie of Vietnam.

Platoon more than justifies Stone's apologia for approximate realism, especially in its climactic 'firefight' sequence. This was the sort of assault on the senses which not only has a powerful effect on the viewer, it was also judged favourably by veterans themselves. The film went a long way towards satisfying the True Vet's call for accurate depiction of his experience. Its direct treatment both of brutality against civilians and of the terrifying confusion of an unwinnable war also satisfied the opposi-tional camp.

But for a film setting out its stall so resolutely within the parameters of an authenticated realism, *Platoon* is an amazingly *literary* film, and therein its shortcomings are revealed. It is inflected with the values of a macho literary (as well as a macho cinematic) tradition. Stone's introduction makes great play with this literariness; he compares his characters Barnes and Elias with Achilles and Hector, his younger self with Conrad's Lord Jim and Melville's Ishmael. But most revealing of all is the hint of Hemi-ngway. This is present in the way he defines his Vietnam experience in terms of growing up – a movement from youthfully gauche 'East Coast social product' to 'a more visceral manhood, where I finally felt the war not in my head, but in my gut and my soul' (pp.9-10). Could it be that we are in the presence of a Literary Rambo?

The hero Chris is poised between two powerful fields of influence in the film; both, significantly, are Sergeants. Sergeant Elias (Willem Dafoe) is a force for 'good', intervening when the 'bad' Sergeant Barnes (Tom Berenger) perpetrates atrocities which hover on the edges of My Lai hideousness. Having stood by, frozen into inaction, as Barnes shoots the wife of a village chief, Chris is energised by Elias's intervention (which prevents further immediate slaughter). When next confronted by an American atrocity (the rape of a twelve-year-old Vietnamese girl by members of the platoon), Chris himself intervenes, incoherent with rage, but making 'a conscious decision to do something' (as Stone's stage direction says, pp.72-3). Elias, who has wrought this change in Chris/ Stone, is a dope-smoking good angel; his eventual death is caused by Barnes (Stone's textual stage direction calls it a 'crime against nature', and he directs the very birds of the jungle to cry out against it – p.95). Barnes, someone says in the course of the film, quite simply 'comes from Hell' (p.76).

The hero, then, is very specifically an American 'Mankind' in a modern version of a medieval morality play, with the Devil and God fighting for possession of his immortal soul; this is made explicit in Chris's final voice over. 'Chris' is a figure in this presentational drama too. He not only 'stands for' Stone, he also embodies certain American qualities, which the film-maker wishes to extrapolate from his personal experience, and which clearly found sufficient echoes in servers and non-servers to make the film a huge success. Chris/Stone is/was neither good nor bad; like all the youthful servicemen of Vietnam, he is/was waiting for his life to be shaped. He is forced to conclude, 'There are times since I have felt like the child born of those two fathers . . . ' (p.129).

America in Vietnam, according to Stone's self-consciously literary analysis, was both Elias and Barnes, kindness and cruelty, bravery and atrocity; America now, however, should know its responsibility, as Chris clearly does when he says 'those of us who did make it have an obligation to build again. To teach others what we know and to try with what's left of our lives to find a goodness and meaning to this life . . . ' (p.129). In the closing moments, as stirring music surges, images from the film are replayed, culminating in a very 1960s image – Elias with his dope, smiling beatifically. The Vietnam Vet has been successfully rehabilitated as that most American of archetypes, the freely-choosing Prodigal, who only went away to Find Himself and who can now Come Home.

The absent text

Textual gaps say a great deal about hidden political agendas in cultural production. That which is excluded, for whatever 'good' reason, is as legitimate material for interrogation as that which is included. This 'absent text' must be scrutinised for its ideology, which will sometimes be at variance with the declared position taken by the makers of True Stories. Although the trauma of Vietnam is now the stuff of commercial movie making, the positioning of the central figures in Vietnam movies is crucial.

All recent films position 'ordinary American soldiers' centrally, with an NCO figure frequently antagonist to a young white American protagonist (as in both Platoon and Stanley Kubrick's 1987 Full metal jacket). The system which has created Sergeants Barnes and Elias (and Kubrick's Sergeant Gerheim) is never examined, even as background. Women's experience (except as passive 'servicers' of the servicemen) is persistently elided, and the Vietnamese themselves are as resolutely excluded and de-centred as ever. With the American political establishment of the day (apart from Nixon, a perennial easy mark since Watergate), all this forms the 'absent text'.

The only 1960s play which dealt fully with contextual topics was Peter

Weiss's *Vietnam discourse*. Albert Hunt, a man with impeccable Documentary Theatre credentials, recorded his disquiet at the fact that US gave such subjects short shrift, but other cultural producers seem not to have minded. Topics ignored or elided both before and since (but included by Weiss) include pre-colonial Vietnamese history, the French colonialist background to the conflict, the Viet Minh and the Viet Cong, and the progressively more compromised American political and military interventions. This history, too, is part of the absent text of the new wave of films and plays dealing with Vietnam; they are no different from earlier work, in fact they are slightly worse.

The Vietnamese are not presented much at all (unless they are females being courted or raped). The similarities with the de-centring of black history in cultural production about South Africa, and the exclusion of Jews (and all the other 'condemned' groupings) from German discussion of the Holocaust parallels this American exclusion of any centred version of Vietnamese history or experience. At an individual level, a psychological trauma may tend to blot out whatever capacity one might have for alterity or reciprocity: so it seems to have been with the generalised American experience of Vietnam, as figured in its cultural production.

The only really useful analysis of such cultural production as the Vietnam movies must come from those alternatives to traditional critical practice which have become important over the past fifteen or twenty years. I am referring to the challenging discourses of Marxism, feminism, and post-structural mixes which often include psychoanalysis. A feminist might well read Stone's work in terms of a *machismo* which has simply translated from a formative experience (his military background) to a summative experience (in the equally male-dominated world of the American movie). This male-dominated world is simply churning out 'male weepies', films in which men are permitted to cry and to hold each other by a War Movie rubric. The celebration of 'gruntdom' reveals a *problematised* concept of masculinity only just held in place by the deeds of derring-do with which war films inevitably deal (and which they inevitably sanction). It is almost as if there were no political context whatever to the Vietnam War; it was simply a matter, as Hemingway is supposed to have said, of morality being whatever you felt good after doing.

David Puttnam – a True Story maker's True Story

Andrew Yule's recent book on David Puttnam reveals what kind of explosive mixture of wealth, sexuality and power is in the background in a movie industry dominated, like war, by the Macho Ethic[10]. Puttnam, the Golden Entrepreneur of British Cinema, was so successful that he seemed for a time destined to become a *bona fide* Hollywood Mogul (until sacked by Columbia). Puttnam made his name with the Falklands-antici-pating 1981 *Chariots of fire*, a thinly-veiled piece of patriotic integration propaganda telling a 1924 True Story. This was followed in 1984 by a film called *The killing fields*, dealing with the mass genocide perpetrated by Pol Pot's Khmer Rouge régime in Cambodia/Kampuchea between 1975 and 1979 (when around half the country's population died in a combination of civil war, famine and the slaughter of those 'killing fields' where former citizens of Phnom Penh were brutally 're-educated'). Foregroun-ded in this movie were the personal stories of an American journalist, Sidney Schanberg, and his Cambodian interpreter, Dith Pran.

Makers of True Stories, whether they are located at the documentary or the 'based on fact' ends of the spectrum, always look for extra-textual legitimation of their product. *The killing fields* is an especially interesting example of the lengths to which this search may go. I have argued that there will always be a diminution of the contextual background to any film which is determined on foregrounding personal relationships through a social realistic style, but *The killing fields* sought authentication at the level of individual performer. The film was not only authenticated by Schanberg's 'real' account of events (in his book, *The death and life of Dith Pran*), it also featured a 'real Cambodian' as Dith Pran, in the person of Haing S.Ngor, an ex-gynaecologist from Pnom Penh.

Like Dith Pran, the 'real character' he was playing, Ngor had had his own 'real experience' at the hands of the Khmer Rouge, and it closely paralleled Pran's; it *authenticated* both performance and movie. The co-ordinates of Kristeva's Real and True (see Chapter 1) criss-crossed wildly in the pre-publicity for this movie, but always at the micro level of the individual, never at the macro level of the politics which ultimately shaped *both* lives. The addition of this concept of the 'human-being-as-document' represents a significant shift in Hollywood's valorisation of the Experienced Individual. Another example of this was in Kubrick's *Full metal jacket* where the brutal (and brutalising) Marine drill instructor Sergeant Gerheim (who trains the young recruits to be killers) was played by Lee Ermey. The character Gerheim was authenticated not just by Ermey's playing, but by the fact that he *really was* (or had been) a Marine drill instructor.

Reflections of the conflict in south-east Asia have called forth an 'I Was

There' realism which, in its concentration on the individual experience, loses sight of any effort to situate that conflict in its previous (or indeed in the present) historical conjuncture. Something of this absent political text is revealed in Yule's account of Puttnam. Redolent of a world-wielding *machismo* seemingly inevitable at such heady levels of money and power, Puttnam's words are often inscribed with assumptions not greatly different from Michael Herr's freely-cursing 'grunts' – that most important matters can be described in terms of bodily functions. Thus he 'feels in his balls' that Roland Joffe is the right director for his movie, although he suspects Joffe of being 'one of those hairy-arsed realists' (especially after an early accident on set which practically incinerates his star, Sam Waterston – he goes 'fucking berserk' at this). Film or war, it seems, the discourse of Men will be marked by its scatological and sexual reference – sex-power/money-power, it's ultimately all a matter of who screws whom. Most revealingly of all, he believes that the $10 million budget means that you shouldn't 'bugger off and make a personal statement' (Yule, p.225). His loyalty to capital, in other words, situates him in the movie market place; that this powerfully inflects his True Story *The killing fields* is recognised by Yule, who asks whether the film is not reduced 'to the level of a melodrama reprehensibly using a tragic backdrop to trade up' (pp.240-1) as a result.

This is precisely what happens in all True Stories using historical 'backdrops' to authenticate personalised foregrounds, and it seems currently to be the going rate for putting any political subject on the mainstream cultural agenda. This is Puttnam's world: he may admire a film like *The Battle of Algiers* (Gillo Pontecorvo's classic 1965 'reconstruction' of 1950s French colonial defeat and disgrace in Algeria) but he knows that it lacks 'a central relationship with which you could identify' (p.241), and which the film-maker can easily sell. For a *commercial* movie, as all good professionals know, this is a *sine qua non*. Unfortunately, the 'human interest' of the foregrounded personal True Story is by now imbricated into the kind of continuous history which forecloses political debate and ensures that the hegemony's version of events remains largely unchallenged.

Continuous history – (Un)true Stories?

While the True Story may seem initially just a variant of the History Play (the oldest dramatic True Story of all), it is very different. The History Play has been present in some form or other since antiquity; it usually told audiences stories they already knew – myths and legends, parables which honoured ancestors, celebrated origins, and warned against human overreaching. The sense of a past to compare with the sense of a present (the sense of history) has gone hand-in-hand with an apparent compulsion to *dramatise* 'history', and all dramatists working with history have used 'documents', in the widest sense, to make plays. The 'documentary' end of the present spectrum, however, has offered a new range of opportunities, which hold out some hope for the forcing into the light of matters hegemonies would much prefer to keep dark.

The term 'documentary drama' was introduced into critical terminology in the present century in order to make distinctions between plays taking a markedly different approach from the historical dramas with which people were more or less familiar. I have argued that this 'approach' was conditioned largely by new modes of access to 'reality', by the technology of the camera and the microphone (or rather by the assumptions made about these instruments). The promise inherent in the term 'documentary drama' is the promise of 'factuality', of 'documentariness'; the notion that culturally produced information (in itself, and of itself) will provide the key to understanding. Like a series of Chinese boxes, absolutes open up one on another – 'fact' and 'real' on to 'natural' and 'true'. The equation seems so often to be that factuality plus verisimilitude equals veracity. Thus the True Story is twentieth-century culture's attempt to posit an Absolute Drama which is both real and true, and thus unassailable.

The value of True Stories, almost irrespective of their inflection, is the way they inevitably problematise such absolutes. The makers of True Stories may set great store by the authenticity of their 'sources' (items which exist outside the drama, but upon which it depends); but the important matter is the use they make of them. If there is a distinction to be drawn between the different ways a documentary and an historical dramatist will work with their sources, it is that while the latter tends to use source material at one remove, writing *from* a sense of history which is fully-formed and continuous, the latter may well work with the assumption that the historical record can be altered, or added to. If the historical dramatist is mostly willing to take a unitary view of history's unproblematical 'continuum', it is possible for the documentary dramatist to write *towards* a sense of history; s/he has the chance of transforming history, through the use of documents overlooked or previously ignored.

The crucial distinction is whether the True Story comes from the 'recording' or 'reporting' tradition. Writers, and the directors who venture into this field, work within the defining parameters of the True Story, and these are not fixed at all but subject to much ideological slippage in an on-going cultural 'debate'. Therefore it is ultimately not so much *what* documents are used as the fact that they are used *at all* which is important culturally. The generality of True Story espouses the notion of a 'continuous history' which is at the root of our faith and interest in the form. Some 'documentary dramatists' write from this 'fully-formed' sense of history, too – uninterested in reclaiming or re-inflecting history, content to work within the same old continuum. Whether 'historical' (like Robert Bolt's 1960/1966 play/film *A man for all seasons* and Peter Shaffer's 1980/1984 *Amadeus*), or 'documentary' (like Ian Curteis's 1979 tele-plays *Churchill and the generals* and *Suez 1956*, and his as yet unproduced *Falklands play*), cultural production which takes official lines sutures discontinuities with the purpose of effacing difference. When discontinuity and difference are presented (usually in 'alternative' cultural settings), they are routinely labelled 'tendentious' or 'biased' – which is tantamount to being 'untrue', of course.

In Michel Foucault's view, 'continuous history' is 'the indispensable correlative of the founding function of the subject', and History itself 'is that which transforms documents into monuments'.[11] His critique of the discourse of written 'history' turns on the description of a process which deliberately elides the manifest discontinuities of history, converting them into a seamless continuum. This is of benefit only to one social grouping – those in power. It was this kind of 'unruptured narrative', purged of all that might disrupt its hold on power, which the Marxist critic Walter Benjamin wished to 'blast open' in the 1930s, in order to reveal it as a fundamentally class-based project.[12]

One way of blasting history open is to view it as a kind of *fiction*, or rather as a *discourse*; it then ceases to be idealised and unitary, and yields its meanings to cultural analysis just as any discursive practice does. This enables us to challenge all ruling-class history in radical ways, and offers an opportunity both to re-read individual True Stories and to reclaim marginalised and radical forms of the True Story. Hayden White has argued that the historical text, so far from being a repository of (or even evidence of) a search for 'objective' truth, is in fact, 'a verbal structure in the form of a narrative prose discourse that purports to be a model, or icon, of past structures and processes in the interest of *explaining what they were by representing them*'. The much-vaunted 'historical consciousness' (from which so many True Stories come) is, he says, 'little more than a theoretical basis for the ideological position from which Western civili-sation views its relationship not only to cultures and civilisations preced-ing it but also to those contemporary with it in time and contiguous with it in space' (White, p.2).

True Stories, then, appeal to a history which can itself be seen as a form of enabling fiction. For this reason, authenticating source material might be called, after White, 'a historio-dramatic discourse' – one which makes use of sources as a means to a dramatic end. If a True Story makes radical use of documents (as in *Oh what a lovely war*), a history is sought which resists the notion of the continuum, and advances instead Foucault's notion of a 'discontinuous' history. Discontinuousness is shifted, in Foucault's phrase, 'from the obstacle to the work itself . . . into the discourse of the historian' (Foucault, p.9). The greater foregrounding of challenging source material sometimes places the dramatist in a different relation to that material from the writer of the history play. In his Captain Scott tele-play, for example, Trevor Griffiths thrust discontinuous facts about one of their heroes into the faces of the UK Establishment, and this was not liked; *The last place on Earth* was not suppressed, but it produced signs of the turbulence which exists (or can be made to exist) around crucial meanings in a society.

Turbulence is not a fixed absolute, it is culturally relative: hence, while the UK and the USA could easily accommodate *Cry freedom's* account of the Biko Affair, P.W.Botha's South Africa baulked. The South African government found it expedient to ban what I have elsewhere charac-terised as a piece of cultural tourism – so *Cry freedom* in South Africa served the purpose of challenging (and, by challenging, identifying) a precise historical reality which the South African government usually denies. The banning was arguably the most useful achievement of the film, it positioned South African government politics (they don't just efface the black experience, they do the same to oppositional whites). Within whatever cultural relativity obtains, the True Story can work in two ways: it can make a contribution towards the formation (or re-formation) of historical knowledge in the minds of its audience; or it can problematise (or de-form) the very concept 'historical knowledge'. It does the latter by calling documents themselves into question. True Stories not only present a version of history, and in that sense reflect it; they also re-circulate a discontinuousness which inflects History.

But a hegemony will always attempt to have its cake and eat it – 'writing' the history it prefers, and simultaneously claiming to 'find' it in 'real life'. One index for this process is the cultural production of True

Stories on film and television, continuing unabated as we move towards the twenty-first century. The preferred formal appearance of the filmed True Story is what marks the 'documentary realist' style of twentieth-century cultural production out from the older 'history play'. Cultural materialist analysis of True Stories will recover the history they seek to elide; textual *gaps* in particular will reveal concealed ideological construction.

Blasting open the continuum

The tendency of True Stories in mainstream manifestations is first to open up debate, then to close it down in a ritual of self-congratulation in which entertainment industry and audience alike pat themselves on the back. But spaces can be re-opened through a combination of critical method and radical 'alternative' practice. Through such means, dominant modes of representation can be challenged, and oppositional versions of historical reality can be mediated which will both position culturally determined (and favoured) representations of that reality and substitute alternatives. This is the legitimate business of cultural study and commentary, to reveal that iconic hegemony which, by being favoured, becomes servant to the politics of a dominant class.

Special attention must be paid to the differing values and activities of what I have called the 'mainstream' and the oppositional 'alternative' in cultural production because they carry the seeds of both the formal and the political debates. Steve Gooch notes (in his 1984 *All together now*), that the valorisation of particular modes of production for ideological purposes is not the sole preserve of one political system. He concludes that there is a *samizdat* culture in the West as well as in Eastern Europe, in which the various projects of the hegemony are demystified and revealed as strategies of power.[13] Resistance to power is important in any system (except an impossible to imagine Utopian one) because, on the whole, those wielding power cannot be expected to do other than seek to perpetuate that power.

Gooch also believes that any 'official' cultural production is governed by two constant factors, which ultimately ensure that a *samizdat* (or unofficial) culture will parallel the officially sanctioned one: 'first, . . . you cannot prevent people saying what's on their mind simply by closing the principal channels of communication to them; second, . . . artists in any society will inevitably work either through or around the channels that are available' (Gooch, p.33). The 'principal channels of communication' will clearly not be available to everyone; those to whom they are unavailable will, as Gooch says, 'work around' them. I am aware that I have tended to categorise mainstream and alternative activities quite crudely, the former being, on the whole, compromised, the latter gallantly standing out against the forces of the hegemony. This view at least has the function of inserting an initial scepticism into one's reception of official culture.

Fundamentally, I believe that it is to artists of the mainstream of any area of cultural production (be it theatre, film, radio or television) that we should look in order to read the 'signs of the times' within an historical conjuncture. That they should do more is an unreasonable expectation given the morass of compromised undertakings necessary to get 'official' plays and films even to the starting blocks. I also believe that it is to artists of the opposition to any mainstream (regardless of what forms they use, and regardless of which political system they work in) that we should look in order to try to discover in which direction times may be about to shift, or to read the extent of political *exclusion* within a society. The Czech leader of 1968, Alexander Dubcek (victim of a brutal hegemony if ever there was one), said in a recent interview, 'I am equally interested in *samizdat* reading. It tells me what is not allowed to be published in our country'.[14] In *samizdat* True Stories, facts in themselves are demystified, shown to be mere servants to an overarching ideology, because they are placed in contexts from which it is difficult for the hegemony either to recuperate them for, or to incorporate them in, its ideology.

I have taken issue with naturalist/social realist True Stories only because of their present dominance in anglophone cultures, and because I believe that the individualistic structures of feeling 'naturalised' by such modes partially account for the gaps in most True Story texts. In other cultures, at other times, these dramatic conventions have permitted a level of disruption which I have ascribed to the formal techniques of Epic Theatre. The cautionary tale of the 1957 reception of Beckett's *Waiting for Godot* at San Quentin penitentiary (where inmates found it all too real) lies in ambush for anyone trying to suggest any failsafe dramatic methodology.[15] I have offered the model of the oppositional theatrical practices of Brecht and Piscator because these have represented one way of blasting open the historical continuum that continues to dominate the True Story. Such practices have extended and enriched our culture, even when forced to operate from the margins. In the present conjuncture, it may be necessary to look for models in the Third World, in order to discover what Documentary Theatre as a 'guerrilla' technique can still do. Augusto Boal's recent work in South America is a case in point.[16]

But I should like to offer one further brief illustrative example from the world of film to show that a disruptive space is equally possible there, too – provided there is political commitment on the part of the artist in control. Leslie Halliwell's *Film guide* (from whose 6th edition I have sometimes quoted in this book) is a good place to start the discussion of Derek Jarman's 1986 *Caravaggio*. Halliwell is a very open recorder of middle-class prejudice; especially in matters of politics and sexuality, his cryptic comments on films (and on broadcast television, in the *Television companion*) are standard for the kind of critical discourse which constructs itself as 'normal'. To take an example, he can quite unproblematically throw a term like 'propaganda' around, with an assumption of a common understanding. This is a *ruling-class* assumption; the term almost always describes (as it does in Halliwell's case) any clearly stated political position with which one disagrees. You can search the 1986 edition of the *Television companion* in vain for an entry on the much-praised, and highly political, 1974 BBC television version of John McGrath's 1973 stage play *The Cheviot, the stag and the black, black oil*: it does not appear. But an entry on McGrath himself (which calls him a 'director and film-maker of ardent left-wing views') briefly dismisses *The Cheviot* as a 'tendentious' piece 'alleging capitalist exploitation of Scotland' (Halliwell, 1986, p.494). Ian Curteis, perpetrator of the thus-far unproduced *Falklands play* (a piece of very direct right-wing propaganda), is not described, however, as a 'writer of ardent right-wing views', nor are his already transmitted True Stories described as 'tendentious' – they are neutralised as 'biographical reconstructions', with their political programme the absent Halliwellian text (p.180).

Halliwell's terse comment on Jarman's 1986 *Caravaggio* is worth pondering; he calls it, 'A classic for the gay crowd; something of a mystery for anyone else' (p.168). In this sentence, an unproblematical antithesis is set up between a 'gay crowd' and 'anyone else'. There may be lots of the former group, but they're constructed as a self-defining (and presumably self-evident) minority; on the other hand, the category 'anyone else' is used to denote a much larger group. The behaviour of this minority grouping (which can articulate its social position well enough to recognise a movie 'classic') is demonstrably odd and non-normal, since Halliwell states it is likely to be the case that what they find 'classical', the larger social group will find 'a mystery'. The sub-text seems to be that you will like the film if you are gay (and odd); but it will baffle you if you are not-gay (and normal). If there is one thing 'normal' middle-class (male) film critics like Halliwell cannot take, it is the political gay film-maker. There are other groups in their demonology (feminists, for example, who are usually described as 'strident'), but the gay is particularly disliked. A political gay film-maker is, of course, precisely what Jarman is.

Caravaggio is a remarkable movie in which homosexuality then (sixteenth century) and now (1980s) is brought into collision with notions of the historical and the aesthetic. Jarman demonstrates not only how 'art' was/is ruthlessly commodified as a means of controlling its potential for subversion, but also how sexuality itself has been/is 'policed' by hegemonies in their preferred icons of representation. The significance of the quite considerable mainstream cultural traffic in True Stories is the continuing belief that discourses of factuality will offer insight into current affairs, recent and past history; in a kind of 'magic realistic' discourse, Jarman suspends the narrative dynamic of the realist film in favour of a series of set-pieces which meticulously reconstruct Caravaggio paintings. The 'characters', meanwhile, dress and speak in demotic styles which openly 'declare' slippages usually elided by the historicist approach. Their dress and language openly proclaim the 'then' and 'now' dialectically, by juxtaposing them.

In a Smiths' song ('Bigmouth Strikes Again' – 1985), singer Morrissey collapses the martyr's flames of the fifteenth-century and the aural technology of the twentieth, saying he knows 'how Joan of Arc felt' when the fire engulfed her 'and her Walkman started to melt'. As with Jarman, anachronism is used to disclose the culturally determined nature of representations of historical reality. The implicit acknowledgement of Joan of Arc's 'non-Walkman' consciousness in the humour of the line positions not only his own present 'martyrdom', but also the preposterousness of understanding 'her' in 'our' terms. In most historical films, Jarman's project of revelation would have been foreclosed through a full-blown reconstruction of sixteenth-century Italy which collapsed 'then' into 'now' as if we could step back in time just like that. We would be forced to 'read' any stray modernity through gaps in the text. By declaring the gaps, Jarman challenges his audience to meet him within a defined debate about history, art and sexuality. Jarman's True Story carefully positions himself as maker, his subject Caravaggio, and his audience in a radical re-thinking of the process of representation.

Remarkably, Jarman made his film for £475,000, a tiny fraction of the likely cost of a major Hollywood movie. Had a major studio decided to do a film on the same subject, location filming in Italy would have been *de rigueur*; Jarman made his film in a derelict warehouse in London's dockland. Costumes and props would have been a major financial undertaking; in a 1986 newspaper interview, Jarman castigated that view of the past which makes it 'a kind of neurotic archaeological construction' in the present.[17] The strangeness of deliberate historical collisions like the ones in *Caravaggio* gives a *perspective* on history rather than a flattened tourist view.

Jarman is able to do these things because he *makes use of his marginality*, turning it from a 'weakness' into a potential political strength. In Jarman's hands, marginality is a weapon rather than a curse. Most artists accept the mainstream's terms right from the outset, knowingly or not, and try to fight their way into the mainstream from the marginal cold (unaware of or not caring about the Faust-like deal which has to be struck on qualification for the mainstream). A gay artist like Jarman knows better: he is not necessarily *content* with this state of affairs, but uses it to define the nature of his oppositional project. He is an example of the effectiveness of the alternative/marginal in its continued, and continual, confrontation of entrenched power.

Conclusion – informational imperialism

It is conceivable that the nation-states will one day fight for control of information, just as they battled in the past for control of territory, and afterwards for control of access to and exploitation of raw materials and cheap labour. (Jean-François Lyotard)[18]

The power of 'nation-states' in post-modern times is increasingly vested in *sanctioned mediations* (the various ways they present themselves to themselves, and to each other). Those 'documents' which hegemonies are prepared to disclose have become part of the construction of what did or did not happen in a certain place at a certain time, what was and was not said there; they too become a site of contestation of meaning (witness the Clive Ponting and Oliver North affairs). Lyotard's vision of future 'Information Wars', in which the document is more dangerous than ever, places True Stories in a crucial position, for they often dispute the very boundaries between what is commonly constructed as 'fact', and what is more readily accepted as 'fiction'. To paraphrase Brecht, the need for 'a kind of resistance' in the consumer of True Stories, and his/her 'mobilization and redrafting as a producer' is greater now than ever. The form this 'resistance' should take is ultimately shaped by politics and not by taste. This being so, the time has come for me openly to declare what political 'shape' I believe such resistance should take.

In my Introduction, I quoted John McGrath's remarks on the class nature of British society. Resistance to a society organised in such a manifestly unfair way must be linked to a positive alternative in which the class basis of society is fully recognised, and in which the system which shores up and perpetuates a class society is opposed. The ultimate aim of opposition must be the re-making of society in a truly democratic (which is to say a socialist) image. The interrogation of cultural production which addresses a past or present 'problem' through a True Story must thus seek the gaps, or elisions, in the text with the purpose of disclosing whose interests are served by these gaps.

'Alternative' treatments of the same problem should also be actively sought, for they are still likely to be less compromised. Here, in the local and the specific, our control, our most *immediate* social leverage, resides – whether we are makers or consumers of cultural products. Western societies are swinging further and further to a Right growing accustomed to fashioning a historical and factual mirror which reflects only its 'best side'; it becomes a matter of crucial importance to dispute these reflections. In the UK, the government has become highly adept at manipulating, massaging and generally playing around with statistics and facts; True Stories, especially those making direct use of documents, can form part of an active opposition to this malign trend. Indeed, G.F.Newman (himself the writer of a considerable number of TV True Stories, like the 1983 *The nation's health*) even believes that 'this type of contemporary drama has moved into the vacuum of political opposition' in the 1980s.[19]

The truly subversive structures of feeling are always available, but are mainly at 'street level'. Whenever they rise above street level, they may be recuperated and incorporated. But incorporation has its price (the incorporation of the European theatre techniques of companies like Theatre Workshop precipitated an alternative methodology which continues to nag away at cosy orthodoxies to this day). Whenever an alternative form (whether it is in the theatre, in film, in rock music, or whatever) has to be brought in from the margins, it is a sure sign that subversion has worked to some extent. It is not, however, a sign that subversion can cease (for that which *cannot* be incorporated is sometimes the raw material for future subversion).

It is never sufficient for a subject to be 'put on the agenda' by a True Story (as the apartheid regime in South Africa has been via films like *Cry freedom*). Our understanding of such films must push past their stated liberal politics (all that can reasonably be expected from cultural production so deeply mortgaged to capital interests) to disclose their ideological complicity with Western hegemonies which keep the apartheid regime in place. The demystification of officially sanctioned cultural products will be assisted by a parallel attention to what Black Africa is telling us through its own cultural production. In this particular debate, Black Africa offers the major oppositional alternative, and whether they like it or not whites can only *assist* in a project outside their *direct* experience – some things cannot be totally colonised.

As with any document, the True Story does not come to us cleansed of context, but rich in political and historical meanings which are usually unspoken. These meanings must be 'read' if we wish to make the effort to recover them from the elisions and lacunae present in official discourse. We are additionally aided by a set of 'other' cultural practices which, although marginalised, give us access to a context hidden because it does not fit the hegemony's scheme of things. These practices most notably reverse the priorities of mainstream work by bringing the 'background' to events into clearer focus. If some creators of True Stories fight shy of supplying a 'frame' through which this kind of reading may be attempted, if they seek shelter behind the privileged discourse's smoke screen of 'real/trueness', modern critical practice can supply both context and frame.

I am advocating not only a scepticism in relation to mainstream cultural production, but a committed resistance to any attempt to displace problems simply by raising them: take the information offered in the mainstream True Story, then *look behind* that information for its hidden deep structure. In such a 'guerrilla' critical practice, the marginal and alternative will always provide one means of identifying and deconstructing an iconic hegemony always at the service of the *status quo*. Rightly regarded, a melding of the discourses of factuality and fictionality in documentary drama ultimately subverts *both* discourses; where else can the search for Magic Authenticity go after Haing S.Ngor and Lee Ermey?

Participation in the 'debate' about True Stories is not an exercise in rhetoric and oratory (like the public school game which underlies our much-vaunted 'parliamentary democracy'), it is *political* – a way of resisting what Hans Magnus Enzensberger has called 'the mind industry'. This exists 'to sell the existing order, to perpetuate the prevailing pattern of man's domination by man, no matter who runs the society, and by what means'.[20] To resist and oppose the Mind Industry, the Persuasion People, is part of the task of denying the existing order's assumed *right* to call tunes, to define what 'the facts' are. This is particularly important at a time when Conservatism in the UK is busy doing its own kind of revolutionary re-distribution of wealth and resources (re-distributing resources formerly held communally into the individual possession of the already-rich and the greed-excused new rich).

The widespread appeal to the 'truth' of factuality is ultimately one further manifestation of the crisis of understanding into which capitalist societies in the twentieth century have been plunged. The dominant order's truth-claims can and must be challenged by, and on behalf of, those whose own truth is persistently occluded, deleted and consigned to the margins (such groups include working people, the ethnic minorities, and women of all classes; trade unionists, one-parent families, and gays and lesbians; True Stories on the 'other' side of the North/South divide, nationally and internationally, need also to be told). If these stories are not told, the amount of 'useable information' (G.F.Newman's phrase) circulating in society will be drastically reduced. In True Stories, 'true' is only ever an honorific term, and the question must constantly be asked, 'Whose truth?' – and, 'By whom, and for what purposes, is it being told?'.

Notes

For full references, see *Texts cited*

Introduction – The promise of fact

1 Jacques Ellul, *Propaganda*, p.xv.
2 Stuart Hood, *On television*, p.1.
3 Beyond the theatrical and cinematic True Story, there is the documentary novel (Thomas Kenneally's 1982 *Schindler's ark* being one well-known example) – even the 'doc-rock' song and the documentary comic. Bob Marley's 1976 'War', for example, has a lyric composed entirely of a 1968 Haile Selassie speech; several 'Documentary Comic Books' (like the 1978 *Nuclear power for beginners*) were published in the late 1970s, and the first 'documentary comic', *Brought to light* (about covert US intelligence operations) appeared in 1989.
4 Court cases are a popular source of the 'reconstruction' (in, for example, the 1987 BBC TV *Trial of Klaus Barbie*). BBC TV's 1986 *Inquest* series investigated the mysterious deaths of Mozart, Marlowe, and others using a court format (and a mixture of real barristers and actors). Most bizarre of all was Channel 4's 1986 reconstruction of the Lee Harvey Oswald trial-which-never-happened (filmed in front of a 'real' Texan judge and jury, using eminent American counsels).
5 Andrew Goodwin and Paul Kerr, eds., *BFI dossier 19*, p.1.
6 Raymond Williams, *Television*, p.72.
7 John McGrath, *A good night out*, p.20.

Chapter 1 – The twentieth-century myth of facts

1 Robert David MacDonald, 'Preface' to Rolf Hochhuth's play *The representative*, p.ix.
2 See Charles Wood, *Tumbledown* (Penguin, 1987), and Ian Curteis, *The Falklands play* (Hutchinson, 1987).
3 Herbert Lindenberger, *Historical drama*, p.x.
4 Colin MacCabe, *Theoretical essays*, p.34.
5 See Gerald Mast and Marshall Cohen, eds., *Film theory and criticism*, p.367.
6 See Forsyth Hardy, ed., *Grierson on documentary*, p.37. The phrase 'the creative interpretation of actuality' comes from John Grierson's 1933 essay 'The documentary producer', p.8.
7 E.Mendelson, ed., *The English Auden*, p.291.
8 Dan Isaac, 'Theatre of fact', p.10.
9 Hayden White, *Metahistory*, p.6 – his emphasis.
10 See Jim Allen, *Perdition*, pp.72-152.
11 Peter Weiss, 'The material and the models', p.41.
12 Raymond Williams, *Drama from Ibsen to Brecht*, p.9.
13 See Alan Bullock and Oliver Stallybrass, eds., *The Fontana dictionary of modern thought*, p.411.
14 John Ellis, *Visible fictions*, p.38. Ellis acknowledges Roland Barthes as the source of this idea.
15 Raymond Williams, *Marxism and literature*, p.163.
16 John Willett, ed., *Brecht on theatre*, p.196.

17 See *World theatre*, 17 (1968), p.399. The whole edition was a memorial tribute to Piscator which, among other things, demonstrated the world-wide spread of Documentary Theatre techniques in the 1960s.
18 George Szanto, *Theater and propaganda*, p.21.
19 Williams (1974), p.73.
20 Bertolt Brecht, *The Messingkauf dialogues*, p.25.
21 Williams (1977), p.116.
22 For Gramsci himself on 'hegemony', see *A Gramsci reader* (especially editor David Forgacs's gloss, pp.422-24). See also Williams, 1977 (pp.108-112). 'Ideology' is discussed in Janet Wolff's *The social production of art* (pp.49ff), in Bill Nichols's *Ideology and the image* (pp.1-2), and in Williams (pp.55ff).
23 Elizabeth Wilson, 'All in the family', p.7.
24 Williams (1977), p.199.
25 Louis Althusser, *For Marx*, p.143.
26 Hilda S.Rollman-Branch, 'Psychical reality and the theatre of fact', p.57.
27 See Toril Moi, ed., *The Kristeva reader*, p.217.

Chapter 2 – The clash of facts and entertainment

 1 Daniel Boorstin, *The image*, p.8.
 2 Walter Benjamin, *Illuminations*, p.252.
 3 See William Stott, *Documentary expression and thirties America*, p.129.
 4 See S.L.Mayer's *Hitler's wartime picture magazine* (Bison Books, 1978).
 5 For Vertov's description of *kino-pravda*, see Luda and Jean Schnitzer, and Marcel Martin, eds., *Cinema in revolution*, pp.78ff.
 6 Elizabeth Sussex, *The rise and fall of the British documentary*, p.194.
 7 Don Macpherson, ed., *Traditions of independence: British cinema in the thirties*, p.5.
 8 Terry Eagleton, 'Afterword', in Graham Holderness, ed., *The Shakespeare myth*, p.206.
 9 See Eric Barnouw, *Documentary: a history of the non-fiction film*, pp.26-7.
10 Terry Eagleton, *Walter Benjamin*, p.59.
11 See Marie Seton, *Sergei M.Eisenstein*, p.62. See Edward Braun's *Meyerhold on theatre* (pp.318ff) for Meyerhold's ideas on 'linkage' and 'collision' montage.
12 Erwin Piscator, *The political theatre* (ed., Hugh Rorrison), pp.93-4.
13 John Willett, *The theatre of Bertolt Brecht*, p.168 and p.110.
14 John Willett (1984), p.71.
15 See Lisa Appignanesi's *Cabaret* for further details.
16 McGrath (p.30-1). For McGrath's account of revolutionary theatre see pp.36ff. The notion of 'complex seeing' is, of course, Brecht's (see Willett, 1984, p.44).
17 Willett, (1984), p.32.
18 Paddy Scannell, 'The stuff of radio', p.5.
19 Colin McArthur, *Television and history*, pp.22-23.
20 Karen Malpede Taylor, *People's theatre in Amerika*, p.147.
21 See John O'Connor and Lorraine Brown, *The Federal Theatre Project*, pp.33-34.
22 For detail on workers' theatre movements between the wars, Richard Stourac and Kathleen McCreery's *Theatre as a weapon* is excellent (see also David Bradby and John McCormick's *People's theatre*).
23 See Arthur Goldman, 'The life and death of the Living Newspaper Unit', p.69.
24 See Pierre De Rohan, *Federal Theatre plays*, p.viii.
25 Mordecai Gorelik, *New theatres for old*, pp.435-6.
26 Malcolm Goldstein, *The political stage*, pp.277-8.
27 Arthur Arent, 'The techniques of the Living Newspaper', p.57.
28 See Nikolai A.Gorchakov, *The theatre in Soviet Russia*, pp.377-378.

Chapter 3 – The broken tradition

1 Ronald Bryden, The observer, 14 December 1969.
2 Roswitha Mueller, 'Montage in Brechtian theatre', p.486.
3 This term has been made difficult by a combination of translation problems, relative lack of exposure to Brecht's work in anglophone cultures, and wilful misunderstanding. The words 'estrangement', 'defamiliarisation', or 'distanciation' are better than 'alienation'. Elizabeth Wright's Postmodern Brecht defines the technique interestingly, calling it 'a series of social, political, and ideological interruptions that remind us that representations are not given but produced' (p.19 – my emphasis).
4 See Kenneth Tynan, Tynan right and left, p.320.
5 See Chapter Ten of Howard Goorney's The Theatre Workshop story – 'Foreign tours: not without honour save at home', pp.142-157.
6 The edition of Oh what a lovely war used is the 1981 Methuen reprint.
7 See Paul Radinow, ed., The Foucault reader, p.101.
8 See Raphael Samuel, Ewan MacColl and Stuart Cosgrove, Theatres of the Left, p.254.
9 Tony Jackson, ed., Learning through theatre and Christine Redington, Can theatre teach? are useful on TIE documentary work. See George Rowell and Jackson's The repertory theatre movement for details of the Local Documentary.
10 The phrase 'broken tradition' is Stourac and McCreery's (p.xiii).
11 From my interview with Cheeseman (Stoke-on-Trent, 27 March 1985).
12 Peter Cheeseman et al, The Knotty, p.xi.
13 Dan Garrett, 'Documentary in the provinces', p.2.
14 The first of Jellicoe's community plays was The reckoning, at Lyme Regis in 1978; the most recent was David Edgar's Entertaining strangers – Dorchester 1985 (see Jellicoe's book Community plays).
15 See John Bull, New British political dramatists. He suggests that the 1960s 'went out with more than a suspicion of a whimper' (p.10), and that subsequent political drama was the product of despair, not hope.
16 David Edgar, whom I interviewed in September 1985, is one important 'alternative' playwright of the 1970s who acknowledges that he 'learned about workers' theatre later', after becoming a practitioner.
17 See Eric Bentley, ed., The storm over 'The deputy', p.12.
18 See Jack D.Zipes, 'Documentary drama in Germany: mending the circuits', p.57.
19 Bentley (1964), p.14.
20 The writer was American journalist T.F.Driver (see Bentley, 1964, p.33).
21 See interview with Hochhuth in Martin Esslin's Reflections, p.134.
22 For details, see Theodore Shank, American alternative theatre.
23 Donald Freed's Inquest was published in the USA in 1970.
24 See The guardian, 1 April 1989.
25 Foster's plays (notably the 1967 Tom Paine) are worthy of revival, but are probably too radically discontinuous for modern audiences.

Chapter 4 – Re-producing realism

1 Robert Pirsig, Zen and the art of motorcycle maintenance, p.4.
2 See Martin Banham, 'Jeremy Sandford', p.197. Lucie-Smith was writing in the New statesman, 28 October 1971.
3 Terry Lovell, Pictures of reality, p.58.
4 Jeremy Sandford, Cathy come home, p.140. Des Wilson, founder of 'Shelter', pointed out in I know it was the place's fault (1970) that the problems raised by Cathy actually got worse in the four years after the play's transmission (see Banham, p.211).
5 John Fiske and John Hartley, Reading television, p.64.

6 Goodwin and Kerr, p.17.
7 See David Edgar, 'On drama documentary'. Edgar believes 'the factual basis' of documentary drama is what gives it 'credibility' (p.17).
8 See Ibsen plays: Two (ed., Michael Mayer), p.23.
9 The diary of Rita Patel was written by Carole Boyer, directed by Michael Jackley. John Naughton, of The observer, described it as a Cathy for the 1980s. Like Cathy, it concluded with statistics (in this case of 'racial incidents' in the Metropolitan Police area of London).
10 See Michael Tracey, 'Censored: the War Game story', p.40. Tracey convincingly demonstrates the high level at which 'refusal' of The war game's thesis took place.
11 From Leslie Woodhead's 'Guardian Lecture' at the BFI, 19 May 1981.
12 Quotations from The war game are taken directly from the film itself.
13 John Pilger, 'Losing freedom in the fog', The guardian, 10 December 1988.
14 Quoted in his Guardian Lecture by Leslie Woodhead.
15 All Road cast and production team quotations are taken from the BBC TV programme 'Open Air', 8 October 1987.
16 Jim Cartwright, Road, p.5.
17 Clarke used this technology again in Elephant (BBC TV, 25 January, 1989). This 'play' showed continuous sequences of sectarian murder in Northern Ireland; bereft of character, plot, dialogue or explanation, the 'attraction' of this play lay entirely in the sense of immediacy generated by the Steadycam.
18 See The daily telegraph, 20 September 1988.
19 See The mail on Sunday, 4 December 1988. The hapless editor, Stewart Steven, fell foul of the police; his treatment caused him to realise 'how thin is the social fabric which makes this country work'.

Chapter 5 – The camera eye's phantom objectivity

1 Jean Baudrillard, Selected writings (ed., Mark Poster) p.45-6 – Baudrillard's emphasis. This chapter's notion of 'phantom objectivity' originates from the work of Georg Lukács, who saw the process of 'reification' working towards a naturalisation of the dominant social formation; the end result of reification was the construction of the controlling class's preferred views as 'objective' (see R.Livingstone, ed., Georg Lukács: essays on realism, p.5)
2 For a strenuous critique of TV news, however, see the work of the Glasgow Media Group (e.g. the Bad news series – published by Routledge and Kegan Paul from 1976).
3 Nicholas Garnham, 'TV documentary and ideology', p.111 – my emphasis.
4 Peter Golding and Graham Murdock, 'Ideology and the mass media: the question of determination', p.222.
5 Williams (1974), p.86.
6 John Caughie, 'Progressive television and documentary drama', p.328.
7 See Forgacs, ed., p.341.
8 Eric Bentley, Theatre of war (Methuen, 1972), p.369.
9 Lovely war was altered in some important respects when it transferred to the West End. Among other things, the Act Two War Profiteers scene was toned down considerably, and the ending was made more 'upbeat'. See D.Paget, 'Oh what a lovely war and the broken tradition of Documentary Theatre', (PhD thesis, Manchester University, 1988).
10 Ronald Harwood, Mandela, p.ix.
11 Donald Woods, Filming with Attenborough, pp.34-6.
12 Tom Stoppard, Squaring the circle, p.13.
13 See David Edgar, 'Ten years of political theatre 1968-1978', pp.28-33. For Griffiths's notion of 'strategic penetration', see The leveller, November 1976.
14 Mike Poole and John Wyver, Power plays, p.126.
15 Judgement over the dead was published a year later, in 1986.
16 Geoff Eley, 'Nazism, politics and the image of the past: thoughts on the West German

Historikerstreit', p.177.

17 'Script' published as Shoah: an oral history of the Holocaust, introduction by Claude Lanzmann.

18 Bentley, ed. (1964), p.12.

19 Peter Weiss, The investigation, p.10.

20 See Albert Hunt's 'Narrative one', in Peter Brook et al, US, p.25.

21 See Derek Paget 'Verbatim theatre: oral history and documentary techniques', pp.317-336.

Chapter 6 – True Stories/Real Stories

1 David Byrne, True stories, p.9.

2 Richard Dyer, Stars, pp.182-3.

3 Charles Marowitz, Confessions of a counterfeit critic, p.120.

4 See Jerzy Grotowski, Towards a poor theatre (E.Barba, ed.), and Jennifer Kumiega's The theatre of Grotowski for details of Grotowski's theatrical career and ideas.

5 Tom Harrisson, Living through the Blitz, p.290.

6 Michael Herr, Dispatches, p.30.

7 This incident also inspired Arthur Kopit's 1969 play Indians.

8 Vetco stands for 'Vietnam Veterans Ensemble Theatre Company'. See The guardian, 5 August 1985.

9 Oliver Stone, Platoon/Salvador: the screenplays, pp.5-12.

10 Yule's book is called Enigma: David Puttnam – the story so far.

11 Michel Foucault, The archaeology of knowledge, p.12 and p.7.

12 See Benjamin, pp.264ff.

13 Steve Gooch, All together now, p.33.

14 From Dubcek's interview with the Italian Communist Party newspaper L'Unità, in Bratislava in October 1987. Reprinted as 'The wound can be healed' in The guardian, 11 January 1988.

15 See M.Esslin, The theatre of the absurd, pp.19-21.

16 Boal's theory (and its implications for the practice of his various revolutionary theatre groups in Brazil) is to be found in the inspiring Theatre of the oppressed. Boal argues convincingly why all revolutionary theatre must be provisional: 'The bourgeoisie already knows what the world is like . . . and is able to present images of this complete, finished world. The bourgeoisie presents the spectacle. On the other hand, the proletariat and the oppressed classes do not know yet what their world will be like; consequently their theatre will be the rehearsal, not the finished spectacle' (p.142).

17 See the interview with Jarman in The guardian, 17 April 1986.

18 Jean-François Lyotard, The post-modern condition, p.5.

19 G.F.Newman, 'The friction over faction', The guardian, 15 May 1989.

20 Hans Magnus Enzensberger, Raids and reconstructions, p.14.

Texts cited

Allen, Jim, *Perdition* (Ithaca Press, 1987).

Althusser, Louis, *For Marx* (Penguin, 1969).

Arent, Arthur, 'The techniques of the Living Newspaper', *Theatre quarterly* 1, no. 4 (1971), pp.57-59.

Aubrey, Crispin, ed., *Nukespeak: the media and the bomb* (Comedia, 1982).

Banham, Martin, 'Jeremy Sandford' in Brandt, ed., 1981, pp.194-216.

Barnouw, Eric, *Documentary: a history of the non-fiction film* (Oxford University Press, 1975).

Barratt, M., Corrigan, P., Kuhn, A., and Wolff, J., eds., *Ideology and cultural production* (Croom Helm, 1979).

Baudrillard, Jean (ed., Poster, M.), *Selected writings* (Polity Press, 1988).

Benjamin, Walter, *Illuminations* (Collins, 1973).

Bennett, T., Boyd-Bowman, S., Mercer, C., and Woollacott, J., eds., *Popular television and film* (BFI/Open University, 1981).

Bentley, Eric, ed., *The storm over 'The deputy'* (Grove Press, 1964).

—— *Theatre of war* (Methuen, 1972).

Boal, Augusto, *Theatre of the oppressed* (Pluto Press, 1979).

Boorstin, Daniel, *The image, or what happened to the American dream* (Weidenfeld and Nicolson, 1961).

Bradby, David, and McCormick, John, *People's theatre* (Croom Helm, 1978).

Brandt, George W., ed., *British television drama* (Cambridge University Press, 1981).

Braun, Edward, *Meyerhold on theatre* (Methuen, 1969).

Brecht, Bertolt, *The Messingkauf dialogues* (Methuen, 1985).

Brook, Peter *et al*, *US* (Calder and Boyars, 1968).

Brustein, Robert, *Seasons of discontent* (Cape, 1966).

Bull, John, *New British political dramatists* (Macmillan, 1984).

Bullock, Alan, and Stallybrass, Oliver, eds., *The Fontana dictionary of modern thought* (Fontana, 1977).

Byrne, David, *True stories* (Methuen, 1986).

Carr, E.H., *What is history?* (Penguin, 1985).

Cartwright, Jim, *Road* (Methuen, 1986).

Caughie, John, 'Progressive television and documentary drama' in Bennett *et al*, eds., 1981, pp.327-52.

Cheeseman, Peter *et al*, *The Knotty* (Methuen, 1970).

Corner, John, ed., *Documentary and the mass media* (Edward Arnold, 1986).

Craig, Sandy, ed., *Dreams and deconstructions: alternative theatre in Britain* (Amber Lane, 1980).

Curteis, Ian, *The Falklands play* (Hutchinson, 1987).

De Rohan, P., ed., *Federal Theatre plays* (Da Capo, 1973).

Dyer, Richard, *Stars* (BFI, 1986).

Eagleton, Terry, *Walter Benjamin, or towards a revolutionary criticism* (New Left Books, 1981).

—— 'Afterword' in Holderness, ed., 1988, pp.203-8.

Edgar, David, 'Ten years of political theatre 1968-1978', *Theatre quarterly* 8, no. 32 (1979), pp.28-33.

—— 'On drama documentary' in Pike, 1982, pp.14-29.

—— *Entertaining strangers* (Methuen, 1986).

Eley, Geoff, 'Nazism, politics and the image of the past: thoughts on the West German *Historikerstreit*', *Past and present* 121 (November 1988), pp.171-208.

Ellis, John, *Visible fictions: cinema, television, video* (Routledge and Kegan Paul, 1985).

Ellul, Jacques, *Propaganda: the formation of man's attitudes,* (Alfred A.Knopf, 1971).

Enzensberger, Hans Magnus, *Raids and reconstructions: essays on politics crime and culture* (Pluto Press, 1976).

Esslin, Martin, *The theatre of the absurd* (Penguin, 1968).

—— *Reflections: essays on modern theatre* (Doubleday, 1969).

Fisk, John, and Hartley, John, *Reading television* (Methuen, 1978).

Flanagan, Hallie, *Arena* (Duell, Sloan & Pearce, 1940).

Forgacs, David, ed., *A Gramsci reader: selected writings 1916-1935* (Lawrence and Wishart, 1988).

Foucault, Michel, *The archaeology of knowledge* (Tavistock, 1972).

Freed, Donald, *Inquest* (Hill and Wang, 1970).

Garnham, Nicholas, 'TV documentary and ideology', *Screen* 13, no. 2 (1972), pp.109-115.

Garrett, Dan, 'Documentary in the provinces', *New theatre magazine* 12, no. 3 (1973), pp.2-4.

Golding, Peter, and Murdock, Graham, 'Ideology and the mass media: the question of determination' in Barratt *et al*, eds., 1979, pp.198-224.

Goldman, Arthur, 'The life and death of the Living Newspaper Unit', *Theatre quarterly* 3, no. 9 (1973), pp.69-83.

Goldstein, Malcolm, *The political stage* (Oxford University Press, 1974).

Gooch, Steve, *All together now* (Methuen, 1984).

Goodwin, Andrew, and Kerr, Paul, eds., *BFI dossier 19: Drama-documentary* (BFI, 1983).

Goorney, Howard, *The Theatre Workshop story* (Methuen, 1981).

Gorchakov, Nikolai A., *The theatre in Soviet Russia* (Columbia University Press, 1972).

Gorelik, Mordecai, *New theatres for old* (Dobson, 1947).

Grierson, John, 'The documentary producer', *Cinema quarterly* 2, no. 1 (1933), pp.7-9.

Griffiths, Trevor, *Judgement over the dead* (Verso, 1986).

Grotowski, Jerzy, *Towards a poor theatre* (Methuen, 1969).

Hainaux, René, ed., 'Piscator and the Documentary Theatre', *World Theatre* no. 17 (1968).

Halliwell, Leslie, *Television companion* (Paladin, 1987).

—— *Film guide* (Paladin, 1988).

Hardy, Forsyth, ed., *Grierson on documentary* (Collins, 1946).

Harrisson, Tom, *Living through the Blitz* (Collins, 1976).

Harwood, Ronald, *Mandela* (TVS/Boxtree, 1987).

Herr, Michael, *Dispatches* (Picador, 1978).

Hochhuth, Rolf, *The representative* (Methuen, 1963).

Holderness, Graham, ed., *The Shakespeare myth* (Manchester University Press, 1988).

Hood, Stuart, *On television* (Pluto Press, 1983).

Hurren, Kenneth, *Theatre inside out* (W.H.Allen, 1977).

Isaac, Dan, 'Theatre of fact', *Drama review* 15, No. 3a (1971), pp.109-135.

Itzin, Catherine, *Stages in the revolution* (Methuen, 1980).

Jackson, Tony, ed., *Learning through theatre* (Manchester University Press, 1980).

Jellicoe, Ann, *Community plays: how to put them on* (Methuen, 1987).

Kumiega, Jennifer, *The theatre of Grotowski* (Methuen, 1985).

Lanzmann, Claude, *Shoah: an oral history of the Holocaust* (Pantheon, 1985).

Lindenberger, Herbert, *Historical drama: the relation of literature and reality* (Chicago University Press, 1975).

Lovell, Terry, *Pictures of reality: aesthetics, politics and pleasure* (BFI, 1980).

Lukács, Georg (ed. Livingstone, R.), *Essays on realism* (Lawrence and Wishart, 1980).

Lyotard, Jean-François, *The post-modern condition: a report on knowledge* (Manchester University Press, 1984).

McArthur, Colin, *Television and history: TV monograph 8* (BFI, 1980).

MacCabe, Colin, Theoretical essays: film, linguistics, literature (Manchester University Press, 1985).

McGrath, John, A Good Night Out (Methuen, 1981).

Macpherson, Don, ed., Traditions of independence: British cinema in the thirties (BFI, 1980).

Marowitz, Charles, Confessions of a counterfeit critic (Methuen, 1973).

Marowitz, C. and Leonard, H., 'Two views of The representative', Plays and players 11, no. 3 (1963), pp.39-40.

Mast, Gerald, and Cohen, Marshall, eds., Film theory and criticism (Oxford University Press, 1971).

Masterman, Len, ed., Television mythologies: stars, shows and signs (Comedia/MK Media Press, 1984).

Mendelson, Edward, ed., The English Auden (Faber, 1977).

Moi, Toril., ed., The Kristeva reader (Basil Blackwell, 1986).

Mueller, Roswitha, 'Montage in Brechtian theatre', Theatre journal 39, no. 4 (1987), pp.473-486.

Nichols, Bill, Ideology and the image (Indiana University Press/BFI, 1981).

O'Connor, John, and Brown, Lorraine, The Federal Theatre Project (Methuen, 1980).

Paget, Derek, 'Oh what a lovely war and the broken tradition of Documentary Theatre', (PhD thesis, Manchester University, 1988).

—— 'Verbatim theatre: oral history and the documentary method', New theatre quarterly 3, no. 12 (1987), pp.317-336.

Pike, Frank, ed., Ah! mischief: the writer and television (Faber, 1982).

Pirsig, Robert, Zen and the art of motorcycle maintenance (Corgi Books, 1981).

Piscator, Erwin (ed. Rorrison, H.), The political theatre (Methuen, 1980).

Poole, Mike, and Wyver, John, Power plays: Trevor Griffiths in television (BFI, 1984).

Radinow, Paul, ed., The Foucault reader (Penguin, 1984).

Redington, Christine, Can theatre teach? (Pergamon, 1983).

Rollman-Branch, Hilda S., 'Psychical reality and the theatre of fact', American imago 26, no. 1 (1969), pp.56-70.

Rowell, George, and Jackson, Anthony, The repertory movement: a history of regional theatre in Britain (Cambridge University Press, 1984).

Samuel, Raphael, MacColl, Ewan, and Cosgrove, Stuart, Theatres of the left 1880-1935 (Routledge and Kegan Paul, 1985).

Sandford, Jeremy, Cathy come home (Marion Boyars, 1976).

Scannell, Paddy, 'The stuff of radio: developments in radio features and documentaries before the war' in Corner, ed., 1986, pp.1-26.

Schnitzer, Luda and Jean, and Martin, Marcel, eds., Cinema in revolution (Da Capo, 1985).

Seton, Marie, Sergei M.Eisenstein: a biography (Bodley Head, 1952).

Shank, Theodore, American alternative theatre (Macmillan, 1982).

Stone, Oliver (and Boyle, Richard), Platoon/Salvador: the screenplays (Ebury Press, 1987).

Stoppard, Tom, Squaring the circle (Faber, 1984).

Stott, William, Documentary expression and thirties America (Oxford University Press, 1973).

Stourac, Richard, and McCreery, Kathleen, Theatre as a weapon: workers' theatre in the Soviet Union, Germany & Britain 1917-34 (Routledge and Kegan Paul, 1986).

Sussex, Elizabeth, The rise and fall of the British documentary (California University Press, 1975).

Szanto, George, Theater and propaganda (Texas University Press, 1978).

Taylor. John Russell, Anger and after (Methuen, 1969).

Taylor, Karen Malpede, People's theatre in Amerika (Drama Book Specialists, 1972).

Theatre Workshop and Chilton, Charles, Oh what a lovely war (Methuen, 1981).

Tracey, Michael, 'Censored: the War Game story' in Aubrey, ed., 1982, pp.38-54.

Tynan, Kenneth, Tynan right and left (Longman, 1967).

Wandor, Micheline, Understudies (Methuen, 1981).

Weiss, Peter, The investigation (Marion Boyars, 1966).

—— 'The material and the models: notes towards a definition of documentary theatre', Theatre quarterly 1, no. 1 (1971), pp.41-43.

White, Hayden, *Metahistory: the historical imagination in nineteenth century Europe* (Johns Hopkins University Press, 1973).

Willett, John, *The theatre of Bertolt Brecht* (Methuen, 1977).

—— *The theatre of Erwin Piscator* (Methuen, 1978).

—— *Brecht on theatre* (Methuen, 1984).

Williams, Raymond, *Television: technology and cultural form* (Fontana, 1974).

—— *Marxism and literature* (Oxford University Press, 1977).

—— *Culture* (Fontana, 1980).

—— *Drama from Ibsen to Brecht* (Penguin, 1981).

Wilson, Elizabeth, 'All in the family: Russell Grant on breakfast TV', in Masterman, ed., 1984, pp.7-9.

Wolff, Janet, *The social production of art* (Macmillan, 1981).

Wood, Charles, *Tumbledown* (Penguin, 1987).

Woodhead, Leslie, 'Dramatised documentary', *Guardian* Lecture – British Film Institute, 19 May 1981 (unpublished).

Woods, Donald, *Asking for trouble* (Penguin, 1987).

—— *Biko* (Penguin, 1987).

—— *Filming with Attenborough* (Penguin, 1987).

Wright, Elizabeth, *Postmodern Brecht: a re-presentation* (Routledge and Kegan Paul, 1989).

Yule, Andrew, *Enigma: David Puttnam – the story so far* (Mainstream Books, 1988).

Zipes, Jack D., 'Documentary drama in Germany: mending the circuits', *The Germanic review* 42, no. 1 (1967), pp.49-62.

Index